The Mask of Oyá

A Healer's Journey into the Empowering Realm of
Ancestors and Spirits.

Flor Fernández Barrios

The Mask of Oyá

by Flor Fernández Barrios

The Mask of Oyá

A Healer's Journey into the Empowering Realm of
Ancestors and Spirits.

Flor Fernández Barrios

Table of Contents

Acknowledgements

I am indebted to my teachers Don Tomas and my Grandmother Patricia for the teachings and wisdom they shared with me. I acknowledge also my clients for their incredible willingness to journey into the realms of the unknown. Their courage to face the mystery has been a great source of inspiration.

My aunt Herlinda Scorza, whose faith in spirit was undefeated even at the moment of her final breath, inspired me greatly.

Thanks to Keri Shaw, Santera priestess, your presence in my life has been a constant reminder of the commitment and the love for the Orishas. Thanks for sharing the journey with me.

I am grateful to my mother Felicia Barrios and to my father Antonio Fernandez for instilling in me great respect for my culture and my language.

My endless gratitude goes to Carole Glickfeld, my mentor and keen-eyed and open hearted friend. Carole, your words of advice and support held me through many moments of doubts and fear. Thanks for believing in this book

Thanks, Helga Kahr, for all your legal advice as well as your creative input in the design of the cover. Your help has been invaluable. Thanks also to Vincent Plourde for his imaging work on the cover design.

To my godbrother Antonio Contreras for his creative vision and the original painting of Oya whose image appears on the book cover. I am thankful to Pete Allen, editor and publisher, for embracing this book with such kindness of heart and openness of spirit.

Finally, I'll like to give thanks to my Madrinas Maria Concordia and Rosa Parilla for their spiritual guidance and support.

Glossary of terms:

Within the text are a number of terms that may be unfamiliar to the reader. Some are specific to Santeria religion, some are Spanish terms and some particular to Cuban Spanish. While many are defined on their first occurrence within the text, in the interest of saving the reader from trying to remember definitions, these terms have been collected and defined here

Agallas: courage
Asesinos: murderers
Babalúe-Ayé: one of the most respected orishas. In santería he is syncretized with Saint Lazarus
Bembé: party to celebrate the orishas
Pollas: a young pretty woman
Botánica: stores where Santería items are sold
Brujería: witchcraft
Cabeza loca: scatterbrains
Campesinos: farmers
Caracoles: seashell divination
Carajo!: oh hell
Changó: Afro-Cuban deity of fire, thunder, and lightning
Chico/a: pal, young fellow/girl
Comparsas: dance parades
Coño: all-purpose Cuban curse word; may be used in a variety of ways from situations where it simply means "wow" to others to where it has strong profanity such as "cunt" or "twat"
Cosas buenas: good things
Criollo: Creole, native-born Cuban of European descent
Curandera/o: Folk healer
Escombros: rubbish
Esperanza: hope
Espíritos protectores: guardian spirits
Fantasma: ghost
Fondillo: buttocks
Fuerzas poderosas: powerful forces

Güero: blonde hair man
Guerreros: soldiers, warriors
Hijo de puta: son of a bitch
Iki: spirits
Iko: winds
J'meen: shamans
Lana: money
La muerte: death
Mala: energía bad energy
Mierda: shit
Mija: term of affection for one's daughter
Milpa: space of land for growing beans, corn, squash and herbs.
Mugrosos dirty, filthy
Oh Virgencita: little virgen
Oloddumare: creator or God among the Yoruba
Orisha: Yoruba deity
Oyá: deity of the winds, owner of the cemetery, gatekeeper
between life and death.
Padrino: godfather
Palillo: toothpick
Rateros: thieves
Santera/o: priestess and priest of Santería
Se encabrono: became angry
Susto: fright
Tabaqueros: cigar makers
Vago: lazy
Viejas: term used by Mexican men to refer to women
Welferistas: someone who abuses the government assistance

To the memory of my Grandparents: Petra Alvarez, Jose M. Barrios, Patricia Hernandez and Victor Fernandez. To the memory of my Aunts and Uncles Ana, Emerenciana, Herlinda, Antonio, Jose Manuel, Osvaldo, Tomas and Victor. And finally to the memory of my adopted Grandmother, Hazel "Tilly" Buckner.

To all of my ancestors...

ONE

The Mask of Oyá

I N THE YEARS following my arrival in America, I was less than proud to be Cuban. I call that time the dark phase of my development, when I would have gladly have exchanged my dark hazel eyes for a pair of blue ones. As a fifteen-year-old, I was plagued by a desire to turn my black hair into blonde. Dyeing my hair would not have disguised my origins because, unlike many of my Hispanic friends who were lucky enough to have a fair complexion, I had skin that was brown. The innocent but intrusive inquiry, "Where are you from?" made me feel separate and different from the rest of the White world.

I detested being the only Latina in my biology class at Morningside High in Inglewood, California, surrounded by Anglo-Saxon teens wearing cool clothes. I was sure their bell-bottomed pants came from expensive stores; mine were from K-mart. Tired of my constant rejections of her creative and a lá moda pieces, my poor mother had given up sewing clothes for me. While the garments she made were as good, if not better, than those sold at the boutiques in town, they were one more reminder of the financial and class limitations that made me different from other teenagers I knew in high school.

My height had never been an issue in my life, but now I was a midget among the giant Americans. Mr. Long, the biology teacher, an ex-football player, six feet tall with wide shoulders, never missed an opportunity to remind me how short I was. Not only was my stature a source of annoyance to him, but the size of my brain as well. After I received two consecutive As on the weekly exams, Mr. Long called me into his office. Bluntly, he accused me of cheating. At first, I thought it was a joke, but with a serious face, Mr. Long told me he did not believe it was possible for me to get As, given that I spoke so little English. I was furious!

For the rest of the semester, Mr. Long sat by my side on examination days. On every single occasion I proved his suspicions wrong with my outstanding performance. At the end, the report card he handed me became a trophy of my triumph, but deep inside, his prejudice left some scars. From then on, I walked into my classes armed against the racism of the teachers. My challenge was to become invisible among the Whites. That way, I thought, they would leave me alone to do my work in peace.

My invisibility, of course, was only the product of my imagination. The reality was that no matter how hard I tried to disguise my ethnicity, my heavy accent was stubborn and defiant. Even when I pronounced words in the proper way, my intonation of the phrases, sweet as molasses, gave away my Cuban identity. I learned to joke about my accent. I ignored the candid corrections of my mispronunciations. I moved inside the cocoon of my denial and I kept Cuba behind the Communist curtain so to speak.

Then, in 1980, when I was twenty-five and working on a doctorate degree in psychology, the unexpected occurred. Grandmother Patricia, the curandera whom I wrote about in *Blessed by Thunder*, announced her impending visit to the United States. Of course, I was excited about seeing her again. I loved my grandmother. I was her favorite grandchild! But news of her visit threw me into a maelstrom of anxiety.

I was torn between my memories of the woman I had left in Cuba and the reality of my present life. Back home, my grandmother was an authority, a well-respected healer, someone I had loved and admired. In my mind, the images of Grandmother in her healing room, surrounded by candles and the statues of her favorite saints, were like old pictures that hung on the walls of my past. But where in the context of my acquired American culture was there space for the old woman's traditions? I wasn't sure I knew how to relate to her without revealing my feelings and fears about what I believed were superstitious rituals.

Acquainted with the material in my science books, I found the reappearance of Grandmother Patricia and her spirits a big threat. For years I had managed to keep her in the basement of my consciousness, not an easy task. Grandmother Patricia was stubborn and she had a personal investment in my future career. In her curandera tradition, I was the one who had been chosen at birth by the spirits to carry on the flaming torch of her healing practice. When I left Cuba in 1970, my grandmother's dream and my early apprenticeship came to a halt.

Ten years in exile, away from her and from my homeland, was more than enough to create a deep wedge between us. At the forced labor camps in Cuba, I poured out my anger and sadness about a lost childhood. My voice had found a way in the poetry that I wrote late at night. A woman now, I had been changed by my experiences in this country. The process of assimilation began that second when I stepped onto the soil of this land of freedom. For a young woman, who originated in a small town under the oppressive dictatorship of Fidel Castro, being able to express thoughts and opinions freed the rebellious adolescent within. I was no longer my grandmother's little Negrita, as she used to call me.

In America, I could speak without having to worry about getting thrown in jail. I could do anything I wanted to do, go places, buy books, learn new technology. I was thrilled when I took my first driving lesson and more so when I drove my own car. That became a symbol of my own personal freedom, not just from Castro but from the repressive Cuban culture. I did not want to be part of a tradition where women are expected to give up their personal dreams for the good of the family. I knew Grandmother Patricia was not going to be happy about this. Even though she had worked as a curandera, family always came first. She was a proud homemaker whose house was spotless. The kitchen was a sanctuary because, to her, a nurturing meal was more than well put-together recipes. Food preparation required the proper state of mind: One must feel relaxed and in good spirits.

As a woman, Grandmother had strong ideas, as most Cubans do, about proper appearance. Before she went out, she dressed in clean clothes, neatly combed her hair, and powdered her face. For her, the right presentation was key to success and respect. But also, besides the superficial, was her profound belief in the spiritual world. When I was a child, she used to tell me: "Negrita, death happens not when the body dies but when the spirit leaves. Some people are dead and they don't even know it. They walk around like empty shells."

As a curandera, Grandmother knew about the deep communion between humans and the realm of spirits. She relied on this connection to bring forth the healing forces of the universe and the ancient wisdom of the ancestors. Her allies were many—the medicinal herbs from her garden, the spirits who lived in the quiet corners, the saints to whom she lighted candles every day. She had absolute trust in the messages given to her via her dreams. Intuition, rather than intellect, was the navigational skill she depended upon. She lived a simple existence, tending to her home, her garden and those who came for healing.

In contrast to my grandmother, I rejected the notion of becoming a housewife. I did not want to be like the women in my family. To me, they were old-fashioned! In the book of my life, they were past history. I was more interested in having a career, being successful and traveling around the world. As for Grandmother's dream of my becoming a curandera, I did not picture myself as a practitioner of folk medicine. I had joined the Americans in their belief that all those spirits and herbs were useless. In my new way of looking at health and healing, modern medicine was the answer.

When Grandmother finally arrived in Los Angeles, I was disheartened by her fragile and aged appearance. Skinny and wrinkled, she was a shadow of the woman I had left in Cuba. Only her dark brown eyes sparkled with the light of her wisdom. But as days went by, I soon discovered the spirited old Patricia of my childhood. She took charge of my parents' household. She ordered everyone around as she used to do in Cuba. Again, the old woman became the strong matriarch.

The scrutinizing gaze of Grandmother Patricia was sharp. She did not miss details when it came to family conflicts. From the moment of her arrival, Grandmother was quick to notice the gap that now separated us and made us feel like strangers, even when we were in the same room. She could easily read into our emotions, but she always waited for the right moment to bring up her observations.

"Teresa," Grandmother said, and I knew she was upset anytime she called me by my middle name. "What's happened to you? I don't recognize you."

All of a sudden, the sunny California morning turned dark. For days I had avoided this moment, but my astute abuela had waited patiently for the right time when we would be alone. And there we were, seated across from each other in my mother's kitchen. The penetrating eyes of Grandmother were fixed on me as she waited for me to say something. I shriveled inside.

"Grandmother, I'm the same person but older."

"No, Teresa! I'm not talking about age." Grandmother knew I was evading her. "You're not my Negrita. You know this old woman can see beyond your looks. There is darkness in your soul. You are ashamed of your family and of yourself!" Grandmother hit the table with her fist. "What is wrong with you?"

Grandmother got up from her chair and poured herself some coffee from the pot, brewing on top of the stove. She did not offer me any, but I was too afraid to say anything. She came back to the table. As I watched her sip the coffee, I waited for the next round of questions. In all honesty, I didn't have answers.

"Maybe you have changed so much that you don't even know yourself," she continued. "That shame is no good. It's killing your spirit. Let me tell you, Teresa, those Americans are not better than you, and no matter what you do, you'll never be one of them."

"I'm proud of being Cuban!" I said in my defense.

"Don't lie, Negrita. I have been watching you. I'm not a dumb old woman. I've seen how embarrassed you look when we are out in public. The other day you asked your father not to talk so loud. Well, Cubans are boisterous! But that's only minor. Like the Americans, you are a liberated woman who lives in her own apartment, who eats those jamburguesas and frozen meals. You're too busy to cook. You don't even bother to iron your clothes. Is that the American look? Well, I feel sorry for you."

I knew it was a waste of time to explain to Grandmother how in this country, women don't have time to live life the way women do in Cuba. In the past, I'd had that same battle with my mother, who had managed to keep her house immaculate, cook three meals a day and work a forty-hour job in a factory. It had been fruitless for me to argue with my mother and now it was so with my grandmother. Out of respect for her age, I let her lecture me. Deep inside, I was disturbed at the loss of our connection. As a child, I had seen Grandmother Patricia as an authority I trusted and admired. But now, all I could see in front of me was an antiquated woman. And that made me very sad.

Apart from giving what I used to call her neurotic lectures, Grandmother worked hard on reopening the link to our hearts. As a skillful storyteller, she took me back to the world of my childhood, to the richness of the moments, not forgotten, but simply buried in the dark soil of my psyche. Patiently, she brought back the little Negrita in me, the playful child, still innocent and curious about life, who enjoyed listening to Patricia for hours.

Once more, Grandmother reminded me of the night of my birth. The roar of thunder announced my entrance into this world. With tears in her eyes, Grandmother told me how the lights went out, leaving the small town's hospital in total darkness. The doctor did not think I would survive, but she knew I would, because thunder was a powerful omen and a sign that I was to become her apprentice in the curanderismo tradition.

What happened to us? I was supposed to follow in a tradition of women healers. But when I left Cuba, the link to the chain appeared to have been severed. But was it? The question itself became a challenge for me to dig into the darkness of my soul. This was the beginning of a journey I had not anticipated. The presence of Grandmother with her pertinent questions swept me into confusion. Over and over, she asked, "What has become of you? Why are you so changed?" At first, I was annoyed with her insistent reminder of alterations I couldn't see. Then, after a while, I found myself wondering about her words. Who was I before? In what ways was I different from the person Grandmother knew?

Where to begin? How does one confront the vast and complicated essence of a concept such as destiny? If I was indeed meant to be her successor, I would think the great choreographer of our lives would have managed to at least keep us together in the same place. But no, we were oceans apart. I was no longer the girl to whom Grandmother used to talk about herbs, the girl she had allowed to participate as a witness and as a helper in her healing practices. I had been changed into a young woman with a vision of the world that was turning White and American.

Occasionally, when nostalgia visited me, I would daydream about my grandparents' farm. I could see myself galloping on the back of my horse Almendro. I could hear the voice of Carmen, my Afro-Cuban nanny, calling me from the kitchen, "Niña, come and help me peel these plantains." I had images of my Grandmother Petra and me picking guavas for marmalade. I heard the raspy voice of Graciela as she told stories to all of us children in the neighborhood. Cabaiguán, the town where I grew up, was a vague picture that became brighter as I recalled the warm nights of the summer. Cuba became a tiny point on the map of my life. It was too painful to think about all my losses, about all those left behind, and therefore I learned to keep Cuba inside a compartment in my heart.

I was aware to some degree of my choice to stay on the margins, detached from the pain and grief I felt every time I thought of Cuba. Instead, I learned to keep my attention on the future. Education became the key to freedom. I became a recluse behind the pages of my science books and a prisoner of my own denial. I chose the path of least resistance where I lived, pretending to ignore those parts of myself that constantly threatened to come to the surface—the girl who left Cuba and who wanted so desperately to find a new home amid the American melting pot.

Grandmother Patricia made me aware of a deeper connection I had forgotten. She was the old ceiba tree deeply rooted in the traditions and spirit that many generations have followed with passion, wisdom and humility. Every day, Grandmother observed and listened to signs and messages from spirits unseen to others, but not to her. Her daily existence was colored with supernatural and mystical appearances of guides who communicated to her the proper daily preparations of food, about prayers and even energies affecting the house and family. I came to realize how much my grandmother's life was a constant meditation that required alertness and intuitive skills.

To the old lady, everything had meaning, from the army of ants in the backyard to the single leaf that fell on her shoulder. "That leaf is the touch of God," she might say. She held the leaf in her hand, searching for a weather prediction: "This winter is going to be a mild one." Surprised, I waited for her to say more, but her words were always to the point. She never said more than was needed.

During her visit to Los Angeles, Grandmother became the personification of the deity Oyá, the one who represents the wind that blows, not just across the surface of the earth, but through the psyche, disrupting stagnation and resistance to change and growth. Grandmother became the archetype of the spiritual winds that linked the realm of the ancestors with Earth. She became my connection to the elders in my family and to the source of ancient wisdom.

One evening before Grandmother's return to Cuba, she sat at the kitchen table at my parents' home. She lit her little cigar. I sat across from her and waited with anticipation for more stories of my childhood. Instead, Grandmother surprised me with a different kind of tale.

"Negrita, last night, I had a dream."

"Yes, Grandmother," I said with apprehension.

"Oyá spoke to me about you."

"Yes," I repeated as I tried to remember what I knew about this *orisha* [spirit].

"Don't you know about Oyá? She is the messenger between the ancestors and us. In my dream, she told me that you had forgotten about your ancestors. That's bad, Negrita! We must remember and honor those who have gone before us. Otherwise, we become lost souls."

Grandmother's eyes were like sparks from a flaming fire. I could tell that it was not only Oyá who was mad at me. I braced myself.

"Let me tell you, Negrita, you don't want to anger Oyá. She is unpredictable. She brings chaos as she walks. She is the heart of hurricanes and tornadoes. And when she comes, you can bet she'll teach us about humbleness and death." Grandmother looked at me, making sure I was paying attention. "Death and wind are mysteries. Both are invisible *fuerzas poderosas* [powerful forces] one must respect. When Oyá comes to pay us a visit, she doesn't waste any time. She has a lot to do. One of her jobs is to stand at the doorway between life and death. From there, Oyá midwifes the souls of the dead into the invisible place of the ancestors."

Grandmother paused to relight her little cigar and to order

me to make some Cuban coffee. Grandmother, as a good Cuban, drank sweet cafecitos throughout the day and night, even right before she went to bed. I was always amazed by how she didn't lose sleep.

"Negrita, let me tell you a tale I heard from my friend Chucha."

"Who is Chucha?"

"She is my Santera friend and a daughter of Oyá."

"I don't remember her. Did I meet her when I was a child?"

"No. That's not important. Listen. Oyá is like a boat that travels back and forth from the land of the ancestors and the Earth. When Oyá visits this world, she first comes to the forest. There she becomes a deer. Then she changes into a woman, so that she can go to the market and sell her multicolored cloth. During one of Oyá's trips to the market she was spotted by Changó, the deity of thunder and lightning. Changó fell in love with Oyá at first sight. He tried hard to get her attention, but Oyá ignored him and went about her business selling cloth. When she was done, she left the market and headed back to the forest.

"Changó, who by this time was unable to keep his eyes away from the beautiful woman, followed her into the forest. Changó was surprised when he saw Oyá put on the skin of deer and change into an animal. Filled with curiosity, Changó returned to the forest a few days later. From his hiding place, he saw how Oyá changed herself back into a woman. Changó waited until Oyá left for the market and he stole her deerskin. Later that day when Oyá returned to her home in the forest, she found her deer dress was gone. Oyá was mad and she was worried, because without her deerskin, she couldn't stay in the wild. So when Changó came around again, she agreed to become his wife.

"Of course, Oyá's problems didn't end there. Changó had two other wives: Oshún and Oba, who immediately disliked her. They were jealous and wanted to make Oyá leave the house. They called Oyá a rude and savage beast. Unhappy, Oyá searched for her deerskin until she found it inside Changó's bag. Without wasting any time, Oyá took it and ran to the forest.

"When Changó returned home that day, he was so stricken with sadness that he went looking for Oyá. In the forest, he found a deer with two strong horns. The deer stared at Changó with defiance, ready for battle. Changó lifted his bow and arrow. He was ready to kill the animal when he recognized the deer, and instead of letting go of the killer arrow, he kneeled down and offered the deer a plate of bean cakes. Oyá was so moved by Changó's kindness that she removed the horns from her head and gave them to Changó. From that moment on, any time Changó was lonely for Oyá, he used the horns to call her spirit."

Grandmother finished her coffee, and reaching out to me, took my hand into hers. Grandmother had strong hands with long fingers. I studied the sunspots of the skin—a galaxy of brown spots that extended up her thin arms.

"Negrita, you must remember this story. Think about it after I've gone back to Cuba." Grandmother's face was solemn.

"Sure, Grandmother, I will, but why? Why Oyá?"

"I see in your eyes that the time away from your home and from us has changed you into an Oyá without her deerskin. Oyá without her deerskin was lost in the forest of the world, and so are you. You need to touch inside your heart and find your own deerskin. But don't let this old woman tell you what to do. I know what you're thinking—why in the world would you need a deerskin in this city of concrete?"

"No, Grandmother, I—"

"Negrita, listen to me. There is great wisdom in this tale. When Changó and Oyá join hands inside our hearts, one is blessed with their strength and their courage. Changó has been by your side from that moment when you were born. He has been your companion. As a warrior orisha, Changó has guided you through difficult times. Like a good and protective father, Changó has guarded your spirit and taught you how to use his sword and his ax.

"Both Changó and Oyá are your allies. When called to be the

warrior, Changó becomes the spirit of lightning. But without Oyá, Changó's power would die, because his thunderbolt is spawned by the wind of Oyá. They need each other." The old woman paused and her brown eyes filled with tears.

"Negrita," she said tenderly, "I always knew your life was not going to be an easy one."

"Why, Grandmother?"

"The life of a curandera is full of challenges. We face a great deal of testing from our helpers in the spirit world. They want to make sure we are strong. Most healers are loners in their walk on this earth."

"Are you a loner?" I asked.

"Yes I am. But—I am not alone," she said firmly. I detected a tinge of sadness in her words. Then Grandmother quickly changed the subject, leaving me to figure out the rest at a later time. "Both Changó and Oyá will continue walking with you. During the next phase of your life, as you mature into a woman, Oyá will be your teacher." Grandmother gazed into my eyes, as if she were in search of my soul. "Be careful with her, Negrita! Her rage and dark sense of humor are deadly as a tornado. When she comes, she sweeps everything away."

The words of my grandmother echoed deep inside my heart. How could I trust that I would be prepared for such a meeting with the dark and mysterious orisha? As if she had read my fears, the old woman said, "Don't worry, Negrita. Whatever situation brings her to you, she always appears in a swirl of confusion and darkness, so that she won't be seen. There is no way to prepare for such a moment. You just trust that behind her dark cloth there is a promise for good to happen."

A few hours before Grandmother Patricia returned to Cuba, we sat at the kitchen table in my parents' home. This time, she spoke to me about the "place of no return," where the souls of the dead go, from which they may be called back spiritually to bless the living. She said, "Negrita, when I'm gone to that place, you won't be alone. I'll be there in the company of your Grandfather Victor, and of my own parents and grandparents and their parents. We will be watching you. So, mi niña, if you ever need our help just call on us."

Grandmother's last words created other questions. Aware of how little time we had to be together, I hurried to ask: "Where is this place of no return?"

"Some say that it is an island that Oyá hides behind her dark cloth. Oyá is the only one who knows the secret ways to move back and forth between life and death. She keeps that place invisible to us living creatures."

"Would I be able to see you when you're gone? Would Oyá let you talk to me?"

Grandmother bobbed her head. Then she moved closer and hugged me. She held me in her arms. For a moment I became the little girl who used to sit on her lap. I could feel this was a good-bye hug. Grandmother was not just returning home to Cuba. Soon, she would be going home to the place of no return. I wrapped my arms around her fragile body. I wanted to protect my beloved abuelita from the grip of the fierce deity Oyá.

The concept of Oyá and her black cloth stayed with me long after Grandmother Patricia returned to Cuba. Like Oyá, the old lady disappeared behind the cloth that protected my cherished island of Cuba. Even though I never saw her again, the essence of her teachings tore to shreds the fabric of my social, emotional, psychological, and spiritual realities.

Since my arrival in the United States, I had lived in denial of the spirit world. I had rejected my early childhood memories of the spiritual practices of my Grandmother Patricia and of the Afro-Cuban traditions my nanny Carmen shared with me. To me, their beliefs were superstitions. In order to succeed, I became comfortable in a structure that negated the supernatural. I had focused on education and social conformity, obliterating intuition and the metaphysical domains from my life. I became adept at surviving in a patriarchal world that insisted on materialistic success. I gained the skills that allowed me to move through the bureaucratic maze of the educational system, where getting good grades was just one hoop among the many one had to jump through. For that part of my journey, Changó, as my grandmother said, had been an excellent guide, teaching me about the linear pathways of male dominance, where logic and intellect reign above all. I became a well-armed warrior, ready to shoot my arrows in self-defense.

Grandmother, as usual, had been able to see into my future. She knew that I would become restless with the limitations of patriarchy and its linear structure. She wanted to remind me of the female counterpart of the warrior, Oyá, the one who, with her fierceness, carries the mystery and transformational forces of the wind, combined with the intuition of a wild and primal energy. Oyá is a businesswoman at the market and is a deer in the forest.

Grandmother knew that it was important to leave me a tale that would help me find my place in this world. The mythology of Oyá was the perfect gift. Like Oyá, I was a ferryboat constantly crossing back and forth between two cultures. Oyá, as a creature of many colors, embraces the essence of transformation. Not death herself, Oyá uses her dark cloth to protect the spirit of the one who has just died. Protected by the darkness of her cloth, Oyá sneaks away, taking with her the soul of the dead. Oyá is not life, but she carries those who come back from the ancestral land. Dressed in Oyá's multicolored mask, they enter this world through the red cloth or stream leading into the womb of a new mother.

Grandmother had foreseen my need for information I could use in my work. Oyá and Changó would teach me and guide me in her absence. Oyá would ease the flow of souls into and out of my office when, years later, I became a therapist. The old curandera had the common sense to see across the boundaries of cultures. In her trip to Los Angeles, she had prepared me with spiritual tools to bring forth the same healing energy she had called upon in her practice in Cuba. The context was different, but what I learned after many years of reflection was that there was no need for altars and for candles. Inside the modern ambience of my office space lived the world of Oyá with her invisible winds of transformation.

The process of healing is a journey that requires a willingness to cross the threshold of death. Old patterns of behaviors, ill aspects of the self, unhealthy relationships and attitudes must die to give place to the birth of the new and healthy. The role of therapists is similar to that of Oyá. We are constantly navigating the waters of the unconscious in search of connections. From the shadows of the past, ancestors become alive and speak their wisdom.

The dark cloth of Oyá allows the therapist to move in and out of the client's subconscious unnoticed. Any trace of fear on the client's part could heighten resistance and increase defenses against change. Hiding behind the death mask, the therapist works her way into the underworld of the mind in search of the lost soul. Like Oyá, the therapist must swirl through narrow labyrinths and sweep the dusty corners of the psyche. Finally, the anticipated moment arrives and the new self is pulled from inside the birth canal. Dressed in the vibrant color of life, the client opens his eyes to a world of unlimited possibilities and growth.

TWO

Voices of the Spirits

G RANDMOTHER PATRICIA returned to Cuba, but left behind a wake of turmoil. It was as if the unpredictable and swirling nature of Oyá had taken up residence in my life. I was restless and confused about my path. My interest in clinical psychology dwindled as I encountered its great emphasis on pathology. The academic curriculum was plagued with labels and categories of dysfunction. I was disturbed by the hopeless view it held of the human capacity to heal.

As I advanced in the doctorate program at the Professional School of Psychology in Los Angeles, I found myself deeply concerned by a mechanistic view of behavior and how it was affecting my own feelings and thoughts. Suddenly, I was walking around thinking of friends and family members in the context of their problems rather than their ability to survive trauma and enjoy life. The classroom atmosphere was one of paranoia where we were careful not to reveal our inner fears and struggles; otherwise, we felt, a label would be stamped on the front page of our academic files.

Each semester, we were mandated to participate in a weekend of group therapy. My first encounter with group dynamics was not very enlightening. The leader of the group, I'll him Dr. Blackwell, was a middle-aged man, with a doctorate in

25

psychoanalysis and an aura of mystery. Mostly, he was feared by all of us because of his incessant need to penetrate our psyches. Every word said in class was analyzed and taken apart in a search for abnormalities. A typical Freudian, he viewed sex as being at the root of all our problems.

Before the first weekend of the marathon group, I prepared myself for two days of emotional workouts where we would spill out all our childhood traumas. Already exhausted from a week of work and class assignments, we arrived at the designated room. Against one of the white walls was a large table where we placed our contributions of food. I was impressed with the diversity and the abundance—fruits, cakes, vegetables; chips and dips; an assortment of rice, potatoes, and bean recipes; juices and bottled water. If anything, I was reassured that after the door was closed for the day we were not going to go hungry.

Dr. Blackwell spelled out the rules of the game. We were only allowed to leave the room to take care of "bodily necessities" but we were free to roam around the space, if needed, to stretch our legs. Well, I thought to myself, this was beginning to feel like the camps in Cuba. All the restrictions were supposed to break through our defense mechanisms. Then, with our souls naked, we would feel less inhibited from baring our innermost selves. Of course, it was going to take a while, because with all that delicious food at hand, we were stuffing all the anxieties and fears down inside our gut.

The fifteen of us sat in a circle on top of pillows and cushions we had brought from home. Dr. Blackwell sat comfortably on his throne, on a brown leather chair, high above all of us, just to make sure we could experience the difference in power. The first hour went by in silence. We looked at each other and stared into the blank walls hoping someone would say something. The large clock on the wall seemed to be ticking more slowly than normal. I distracted myself by thinking about my job at the family clinic. I thought about my Hispanic clients in the barrio amid the violence of gangs and drug dealers. I wondered about the effectiveness of this group process when applied to my brown-skinned clients. I laughed quietly as I imagined their reaction. It would never make any sense to them to waste an hour of their time sitting around in silence.

Being the only brown-skinned person in the group, I was intimidated by the whiteness around me. I wasn't sure I could open my mouth and talk about my life. I was puzzled by Dr. Blackwell's ability to sit on his chair, looking so calm and cool, while we were twisting internally with tension. I was suddenly curious about whether he knew anything about Cuba. Maybe if he knew, he could understand my situation and not turn me so quickly into a diagnostic code.

Our visits to the food table increased together with our restlessness. Then, just as the clock marked the beginning of our second hour, a member of the group, Carl, spoke to Dr. Blackwell from his place on the floor: "This is a waste of time." Dr. Blackwell did not say a word in response. Carl waited a few minutes. Nothing was said. "Dr Blackwell, could you explain to us what we're doing here?" Again, Dr Blackwell ignored Carl's question. Carl's jaws clenched.

Then Nancy jumped in. "Carl, you look upset. You're breaking down. Do you want to share your feelings with us?" Carl remained quiet.

Under the pressure, another member, Liz, joined in. "Why don't we go around the room and say how we feel?"

Dr. Blackwell leaned back in his chair, making himself comfortable. We went around sharing our feelings like a herd of well-trained cows. My time came. Uneasy, my words came out as if squeezed out of my throat. I expressed my discontent with the process. Dr. Blackwell took the opportunity to push some points he knew were sore in my soul.

"Maybe you should go back to Cuba," Dr. Blackwell said. "You must have a lot of unresolved issues with Fidel and with men in general. Don't you? I could guess problems with trust." He leaned forward and looked at me as he waited for my answer.

"Yes, I have old scars from Castro's revolution, but that

doesn't mean that as a result I don't like men," I said, with a tone of anger in my voice.

"I can see that upset you very much."

"I'm angry about your assumptions."

"Maybe I hit a painful spot." Dr. Blackwell rubbed the back of his hand against his reddish brown beard.

"You did, but I'm not about to pour out my pain in here. This group doesn't feel safe to me with you as the leader. I'm sure you already have a diagnosis for my dysfunction. Is it Post-Traumatic Stress Disorder? Do I fit in that wonderful category? Tell me, Dr. Blackwell, is that how you see me?"

Dr. Blackwell continued playing with his beard. Uncrossing his legs, he searched in one of the pockets of his pants for a pouch where he kept his pipe and tobacco. In slow motion, Dr. Blackwell filled the wood bowl of his pipe. It was then I noticed his well manicured fingernails. This man, I thought, doesn't know about farm work or about the roughness of sugarcane leaves. He probably doesn't even garden. Dirt is a foreign matter to his touch. How could he possibly understand my experiences in the labor camps or my pain about losing my grandparents' farm? No way was I going to open myself to those memories in front of him!

For the three days of the group marathon, I remained silent. Dr. Blackwell managed to successfully poke into the traumas of the different members. There were all kinds of emotions brought to the surface, from sadness to rage. As an observer rather than a participant, I could see the dynamics at play. The purpose of the weekend had been accomplished, but in my heart I felt the sour and bitter taste of my loneliness. I was alone with my past experiences and the mistrust I had accumulated from years of oppression in a country where telling the truth could cost your life.

Dr. Blackwell was right about my mistrust—not of men but of people in positions of authority, especially teachers or professors. They were the ones who wounded me deeply with their constant humiliations and emotional abuse. All throughout the weekend, I thought of the teachers at the working camp in Cuba. They were the ones who destroyed my trust. Castro, even though a monster, was a distant figure, but these teachers had been present with their abusive whips for four years of my life.

The group process brought to me the realization that clinical psychology was not for me. I did not want to be part of a system that categorized people without regard for their individuality, race, class, culture, and spirituality. Behavior that deviated from the standards of society was defined as abnormal.

By the end of the semester, I found myself in a quest for a new university. It was then I heard about a doctorate program in transpersonal psychology at International College. A dear friend of mine introduced me to their classes and, without much hesitation, I asked to be transferred there. Once more, Oyá came swirling with her spirit of change. She took me under her multicolored mask and carried me to my new destination—a place where I found inspiration and encouragement.

For the first time in many years, I had the strong feeling that I was going in the right direction. With the freedom to design my own study program, I embarked on a journey of self-exploration and discovery. With the help of my mentors, Barbara Dobrin and Ed Elkin, I danced into a world of expressive arts. Then I moved into the world of cross-cultural healing as I studied Native cultures and their medicine.

On the advice of a friend, I signed up for a class on guided visualization taught by Dr. Beverly Galyean. She was thin and not very tall but she exuded an aura of wisdom and compassion. Her light brown eyes were warm and expressive. Dr. Galyean made us feel at home by the way she moved around the classroom and addressed students individually. She had the habit of placing her hand on your shoulder as she talked to you, a friendly gesture that instantly shortened the distance between pupil and professor.

The first day of class, I was late. Quietly, I sat on a chair by the entrance. Dr. Galyean stopped her lecture and said, "You must be Flor. Welcome!" I was surprised she even knew my name. Most professors hardly remembered how to say Flor, instead of Flora or Flo. Immediately I felt a strong connection to the stranger who, after a few seconds, began to feel like an old friend.

Dr. Galyean guided us in a meditation where we were supposed to meet our higher self. The concept didn't appeal to me. The idea of her higher self was foreign, but as she explained, "Your higher self can be anything you connect to the concept of a god or goddess." Well, I said to myself, that could be possible, but I never imagined God personally talking to me. I wasn't sure what God might look like. I knew about Jesus Christ, and about the orishas from Carmen and about the saints my grandmother had introduced me to, but a higher self was something different in the realm of my knowledge.

With skepticism, I closed my eyes and followed Dr. Galyean's hypnotic voice as it guided us through a maze of images. First a path in the forest, then the ocean. I could feel my own resistance to the process. Each time I anticipated the threat of my mind spacing out I forced myself back. I breathed deeply as Dr. Galyean suggested. I breathed and I breathed, and then I must have surrendered, because in my mind's eye I saw what looked like sparks of fire and lights. My hands were tingling—a sensation that quickly spread to my entire body as if every cell of my being had been awakened and infused with a life force. I found myself sitting on the moss-covered floor of a forest among tall cedars. I was a young girl, maybe five years old. Standing in front of me was an old tired-looking white man, who immediately transformed into a young and jovial mulatto dressed in red and black. He wore a straw hat and held a forked branch in his hand.

Even in my state of mind, I wondered about the appearance of this character and about his possible connection to the so-called "higher self." The mulatto, as if aware of my thoughts, smiled and tapped my head with his forked branch. It was then I had the realization that this man was a messenger of the gods. Without wasting any time, the mulatto talked to me and said, "I'm the guardian of all the gates. I hold the keys to all communication between the gods and humans. You'll always find me at entrances, doors, and pathways. You must ask for my permission. Otherwise, you'll make me angry and I can make trouble for you." Then he taught me how to salute him. He asked me to lift my right arm and to move my right foot to the side and to greet him. "Repeat the same steps with your left arm and left foot." When he was finished, the mulatto man whispered his name, "Eleggúa," and he disappeared.

Of course! How could I have possibly forgotten about him? Eleggúa, Eleggúa, I repeated in a low voice. Carmen, my Afro-Cuban nanny had told me about the deity many times. Eleggúa was the gatekeeper to all the orishas and, according to the tradition, one must ask for his permission at the beginning of any ritual.

After the guided meditation, people shared their visions. Some talked about meeting angels. Others had similar versions of an old and wise man. A few had Native American spirits, female and male, who communicated with them. I was moved by the openness of the group. There was an aura of respect and mutual understanding for each individual's beliefs. In contrast to what I experienced at the marathon group encounter, I did not feel alone among the Americans. The mood in this group was one of embracing our differences and perceptions. Dr. Galyean, with her compassionate approach, made us feel as if we were all part of a tribe of people in search of spiritual connection.

Dr. Galyean became my mentor. In addition to the classes I took from her at the University, I sought out her guidance in my spiritual journey. I met with her once a week and we talked about my dreams and my meditation practices. I looked forward to our meetings. My encounter with Eleggúa during the guided visualization exercise had opened many doors that led me into vivid memories of my childhood in Cuba. The faces of my Grandmother Patricia, the curandera, and of Carmen, my nanny who was a practitioner of Santeria, emerged from behind the curtain of the past.

Suddenly, I found myself standing at the edge of two worlds that contradicted each other and threatened to pull me apart. Yet, there was excitement about the mystery of my journey. Oyá was present in my dreams; her stormy appearances brought strong gales that made the ocean swell in giant waves, and hurricanes that uprooted trees and houses. The deity wasted no time showing me the changes within my psyche. Oyá was fierce in her desire to remove all stagnation and blockage that had held me back from a kind of death on multiple levels.

Oyá, with her nightly visits, gradually began the process of peeling away the layers of my dark mask. It ripped away the persona that was rooted in my deep desire to belong, and to fit into a society whose values and beliefs were so radically different from those in which I had been raised. Assimilation into the American culture had meant repression of my creative fire: the annihilation of unique traits that would make me stand out in a crowd of people; the taming of an inner fierceness that was not accepted by the norm.

One night, while I sat on my bed, propped against my pillow with a psychology textbook in my hands, Oyá visited me once more, this time outside the realm of my dreams. I was memorizing the physiology of the brain when all the lines on the page disappeared behind a curtain of fog. At first, I thought I was merely too tired, and I put the book aside so I could rest my eyes for a few minutes. As I closed my eyes, I became aware of a subtle sensation of tingling and burning at the base of my spine, like the fluttering of butterflies.

The image that came to me was that of a red funnel of energy that raced up my back like a spiral. I was scared. I never had experienced anything of that nature. My whole body trembled. My heart beat fast and sweat permeated my clothes. Maybe I was having a heart attack, but I had no pain in my chest. Death. I thought of death and I was terrified. I wasn't ready for that yet. I didn't want to go at age twenty-six. No, God! I prayed, but the prayers only intensified the heat and trembling. Then, everything turned bright red. I opened my eyes and I was surprised by the brilliance of colors in my room, as if I were at the center of a rainbow. I could see an aura of light around every single object. I closed my eyes thinking that this was my last vision of the world. I was certain that my moment to depart had arrived and that I was on my way to that place of "no return," that my grandmother had talked to me about before she went back to Cuba.

Not sure what to do, I waited for Oyá to come and pick me up. Instead of Oyá, the mulatto Elegguá appeared in front of me. He smiled and he tapped my forehead with his forked branch just once.

"Elegguá," I mumbled, "Elegguá."

"I'm here, my daughter. Your grandmother sent me."

"She did? Why?" I asked, not certain of my state of mind. Was I going crazy?

"My child, you must understand that there is no explanation for what is happening to you. Your Grandmother Patricia warned me about how American you're turning out to be when it comes to matters of the spirit. You must stay present to the moment. You must avoid so much thinking and processing. Those psychology classes are turning your brain upside down."

"I don't understand."

"Here. Give me that book," said the mulatto and he sat by the foot of my bed. He opened my physiology book and glanced through the pages with a bored look. "Ha! The brain! What a magnificent organ! This is all right, but you need to go beyond the structure and adventure through all the possibilities. Science is limited."

"All right," I said. "What is it that I need to know?"

"You need to let go of all the theories so that you can begin with a fresh mind, open to all the potential you have as a human being." Elegguá tapped me once more with his forked branch.

"But—if I do, then what?"

"Then you'll be like a child, curious and naïve, ready to explore the world with new eyes. You hear that?"

Not knowing what the mulatto was really talking about, but

certain that I was not to argue, I heard myself saying "Yes, sir. I heard you well." Like smoke, he was gone. I was there on top of my bed all alone, not sure of what was to come next. Without hesitation, I jumped to the floor and went to sit in front of my altar. I lit a candle.

"Grandmother, be with me."

I waited for an answer. I looked around my bedroom for some sign. I waited for my Grandmother Patricia to talk to me. I called the names of all my favorite orishas, of my beloved Carmen. I sat with my eyes fixed on the flame of the candle. Back and forth I rocked, with my arms wrapped around my knees. Where are my people? Have they abandoned me? I needed the comfort of their voices, the gentle touch of their breath on my shoulders.

I woke up to the warmth of the sun's light that filtered through the gaps of the window blind. The morning light found me all curled up in a fetal position in front of my altar. I had fallen asleep, and now the memories of the night were far in the distance but still in my mind. The candle I had lit was all burned, and the statues of my orishas were facing me as usual. In her silent way, Oyá seemed to be talking to me. She said, "You are not crazy. This is the way of the spirits. We swirl and we move across dimensions. We talk in voices to be heard from a place inside your mind and your heart, not with your ears. Pay attention and you'll never be alone again."

THREE

First Meeting with Don Tomas

BY SEPTEMBER OF 1985, I was ready to complete the final phase of my doctorate degree in psychology. In addition to taking classes at International College and working as a therapist at a mental health clinic, I had spent endless hours gathering data for my doctoral dissertation on the murals of East Los Angeles and their symbols. My days were a race against time. At night I would come back to my small apartment and write until one or two in the morning. I was ready to take a break from school and work!

For six months, I had been waiting for the opportunity to travel to the Yucatan. Going to meet a healer named Don Tomas was somewhat of an obsession. It all started one night in March. Due to exhaustion, I had fallen asleep in front of my computer. An hour later, I woke from a strange and vivid dream. As soon as I opened my eyes, I was compelled to write down information given to me by an unfamiliar voice. Whoever had visited my dream gave me the command: "Flor, go to Merida, in the Yucatan, Mexico. Go and find the small town of Piste. There is an old man, a curandero, who lives there, in the outskirts of town, in the jungle. His name is Don Tomas. This man is about 101 years old. He's five feet tall, with white hair and penetrating dark eyes. He's very wise. Don Tomas wants to see you."

"Fine," I said aloud, "like I have much time to look around for some old curandero in the jungles of Mexico." I got up from the chair and walked around the living room, trying to make sense of my dream. It must be the effect of exhaustion, I thought. I'm burned out! This dissertation is finally getting to me. In the bathroom, I washed my face with cold water. I laughed at the nonsense: a curandero in the Yucatan, ha ha ha! What a bizarre idea! The ringing of my phone brought me back. I rushed to answer the late night call thinking it could be an emergency.

"Hola, Flor. This is Angel."

"Oh, hi, Angel, What's happening? Are you okay?"

"Sorry I'm calling you this late, but I thought you might be up. You know, working on your dissertation."

"Yes," I said and thought about my dream.

"Flor, listen, are you interested in going to the Yucatan with me and Lisa?"

"What?" I said in disbelief, thinking that some joke had been played on me. "Yucatan? What about Yucatan?"

"Well, Lisa and I are leaving for Yucatan in two days on a business trip. We thought perhaps you might be interested in joining us as a translator."

"Well, that would be fabulous, but honey, I'm up to my ears with school and work. I can't afford to take any time off at this point. I can't. I'm sorry."

"I understand," Angel said.

There was a pause. I hesitated to tell Angel about my dream. Maybe he could look for Don Tomas. It was a wild thought but I had nothing to lose. I took a deep breath and shared with Angel the message I'd received earlier. Angel was not surprised at all. He was excited. "Hey, Flor, I'll do my best to locate this curandero. Believe me, if he's there I'll find him."

Angel left for the Yucatan and I went back to my work on the dissertation. Three days later, I received a call in the middle of the night. On the phone was the lively voice of Angel, calling from Merida.

"Flor, you won't believe it! I found the man. He lives in the town as your message said. This curandero is 101 years old. I was taken to his house, out in the jungle, by a taxi driver I met at the airport."

"Wait. Wait! Are you sure about this?" I asked in disbelief.

"Sure. He's the guy. Tomorrow, I'm going to take a picture of him, if he lets me, of course."

I hung up the phone. My body was shaking. Even though Angel reassured me several times that Don Tomas was real, I couldn't believe it. This was so mysterious and unbelievable.

Several days later, Angel and Lisa returned from the Yucatan with pictures and anecdotes of their trip and of their meeting with Don Tomas. The curandero only spoke Yukatec Mayan, so in order for them to communicate, they hired the taxi driver named Nico to be their translator. When they shared my experience with the healer, he smiled and said he knew, and that he was waiting for me to come and visit him. "I'm getting old," he said to Angel and Lisa. "She should come soon." During this first encounter with Don Tomas, Angel had asked for permission to record the conversation. He had made sure the machine was working but after he went back to the hotel and played the cassette, there was nothing on it, except for a loud noise.

Now, here I was six months later, my dissertation completed, and I had received another invitation from Angel and Lisa to go to the Yucatan. Excited, I prepared for the trip. As agreed, I was to meet Angel and Lisa at the Los Angeles airport. That afternoon, I left my place in plenty of time to catch our flight to Merida at 2:10 pm. Yet as soon as I entered the North 405 freeway, traffic was bumper-to-bumper, a long snake moving at less than five miles per hour. I got off the first exit and drove along the streets, thinking that if I went north for a while, the freeway would be less congested as soon as I passed the area of the accident. To my dismay, five miles later, the road was not any better. Sweating and anxious, I drove at this snail-like pace for more than an hour and a half. I cursed the L.A. traffic hundreds of times, and I made promises to all my orishas of fresh fruit and candles, if they got me to the airport for my flight.

It was 2:15 when I arrived at the airport check-in. The woman took a look at my ticket and said, "I'm sorry but this plane is ready to take off. The door was closed a minute ago." Full of frustration, I dropped my luggage to the floor. The lady must have felt my deep disappointment because, immediately, she suggested another flight I could take in twenty minutes.

Without even thinking about my options, I booked myself onto the next flight to Mexico City, where I would spend the night and then take an early morning plane to Merida. I grabbed my boarding pass and ran towards the gate of Mexicana Airlines. What a day! I thought, as I stood in line to get into the plane. Behind me, two men talked about a recent earthquake. I did not pay too much attention until I heard them say that Mexico City was a disaster. Rescue crews were still digging bodies out of the ruins. I panicked at the thought of spending a whole night there, but it was too late. The line was moving. I was on my way.

The plane took off and we left Los Angeles behind, with its perpetual layer of smog above the horizon. Exhausted from all the stress, my body sank into the uncomfortable seat. I closed my eyes and thought about Angel and Lisa somewhere in the skies, in another plane. Suddenly, I was hit by the thought of Earthquake City. Oh virgencita, what if another big one rattles the Earth while I'm there? My heart pumped faster!

One of the flight attendants came by to let me know that a message had been sent to Angel and Lisa, informing them of the new itinerary. I breathed a little bit easier, yet I was still puzzled by the circumstances. I couldn't help wonder how in a matter of a few minutes my whole travel plan had been rearranged. I took the situation as a sign of fate.

The arrival in Mexico City was chaotic. The airport was still recovering from the earthquake of magnitude 8.1 that had hit the city at 7:19 on the morning of September 19, 1985. Thirty-six hours later a second earthquake of a magnitude of 7.5 occurred. As I read in the paper, the quake destroyed as many as 100,000 housing units and countless public buildings. The city was in grief. The pain of all its losses was palpable in the zombie-like appearance and anxious gestures of the crowds. The airport itself was a microcosm of the outside world—a place of despair and overwhelming confusion.

It was past midnight by the time I collected my luggage and found my way out of the crowded maze. Outside, the city was dark from multiple power outages. Not knowing exactly how I was going to get to the hotel, I stood at the edge of the curb and oriented myself. A few seconds later, a taxi pulled right in front of me. The driver, a friendly short man, swooped my bags into the trunk of the car. He was quick to open the door and help me in. And as soon as I landed in my seat, he told me that the ride to the hotel could take us longer than usual. Many of the streets were closed. Mexico City was a mountain of fallen bricks and homeless people. The air had the smell of strange fumes—a combination of human stench and gasoline fumes.

"There are thousands of people without electricity," the taxi driver said. "The water is contaminated in many neighborhoods."

"What about in the hotels?" I asked.

"You're fine there. No problem."

As we drove through the streets, I had the opportunity to have a close encounter with the face of devastation and death. Houses were down. Streets were blocked in areas where working crews were repairing water and sewage lines. The people of Mexico City, like a busy colony of ants, were deeply immersed in the process of rebuilding their homes. I rolled down the window; a pungent odor penetrated my nostrils and filled my lungs. The taxi driver must have noticed my expression of my face because he turned to me and said, "La muerte. We're still digging out bodies from underneath the *escombros* [rubbish]. The whole city smells of death."

Finally at the hotel, I went into my room and I lay on the bed with my eyes closed. The impeccably white sheets smelled fresh. I was surprised this part of the world had escaped the stench of the rotting bodies. California seemed so remote from the foreign environment of Mexico. I couldn't help but think about the sequence of events that had brought me into this place of trauma and pain. I could feel the touch of some unknown force directing the destiny of this trip. And there I was in my hotel room, surrounded by ruins. Mother Earth had decided to shake off from her back the heavy concrete that had oppressed her crust. How vulnerable I felt as I entertained the possibility of another earthquake. Just the thought sent me spinning into terror.

Not able to sleep, even though my body felt tired, I went down to the hotel lobby. It was obvious that I wasn't the only one awake. It was near one o'clock in the morning but people were still roaming. Right across from the entrance, the bar was full. I walked into the noisy and smoke-filled room, not quite sure of what I was doing there. Among strangers, I was comforted by the sound of their voices.

I sat next to a group of men and women who drank beer and talked. I ordered a glass of red wine, which I thought could help me relax. As I waited, I tuned into a nearby conversation. One man shared the saga of his personal encounter with the face of the earthquake. He was still figuring out how he had escaped from underneath a crumbling wall in a downtown building. His wife jumped in with her own tale of survival when she was at the Museum of History and Anthropology and the building started to shake. Another man barely managed to pull himself from under a pile of bricks. He was lucky he only suffered minor scratches on his face and a broken arm.

By light of day, Mexico City was a mountain of broken bones. Above the horizon hovered a thick layer of smog. It reminded me of Monte Alban, city in the clouds, the sacred mountain where the ancient people of Mexico worshipped their gods. The so-called "Dancer Stones" are all that can be seen of the first, the oldest, works on the mountain. But when the Mixtec Indians come to Monte Alban to partake of the Sacred Mushroom, they say they can see the invisible remains of the temples and pyramids far surpassing those known by modern man. They say the Dancer Stones house the spirits of the ancients who still come forth and roam the countryside on the old Holy Days.

The Zapotecs of the old way laugh at the scientists who, with shovel and screen, try to find what they believe is truth. The old Zapotec says, "The scientists don't know much; they gather potsherds and dig into the sacred tombs. They find only material remains and that is not the people. The people, the Zapotec, are more spirit than flesh and so it has ever been."

Later that morning, en route to the Yucatan, I watched the ruins of Mexico become more and more like the "Dancer Stones," as the plane gained altitude. Among them, the spirits of the ancient ones were beneath the destruction, like dormant seeds of grass waiting for spring to cover the face of the earth. I leaned back in my seat and thought about the strength of the human spirit to endure catastrophes and trauma, and about the gift we are given over and over to be able to witness death so that we can embrace life. Perhaps this was the picture Don Tomas wanted me to see—a reminder of my vulnerability, a call to understand that at the beginning of every journey one must face the eradication of the old ways.

Suddenly, the picture was clear in my mind. Don Tomas as a wise man knew of my scientific training. All those years of school and research had contaminated my thoughts with the usual symptoms of objectivity and omnipotence. Like an ancient Zapotec, he wanted me to put my shovel and screen away, so that I could enter the spirit world with the innocence of a child. Therefore, Don Tomas had placed me in a position of having to witness the fragile body of Mexico. The ruins of a city at the mercy of the Gods! The earth had shaken off in a few minutes what had taken men hundreds of years to build. One cannot disregard such a powerful force.

On my arrival in Merida, I saw no sign of either Angel or Lisa. They were not at the gate. Confused, I walked towards the baggage station. I was beginning to worry, when I was stopped by a short man, who introduced himself as Nico, a taxi driver sent by my friends. The Mayan man was cordial and had a childlike appearance that made me feel at ease in the foreign place. He informed me that Angel and Lisa were at the hotel, recovering from the "gringo sickness."

"How could that be?" I asked the man somewhat perplexed.

"The food made them sick."

"So soon? I can't believe it," I said.

Nico took me to the hotel, a beautiful and peaceful place, near the ruins of Uxmal. There were many comfortable cabanas surrounded by colorful tropical gardens and native fruit trees of mango, guavas, and coconuts. I was reminded of my childhood home of Cuba, the lush green landscape bordered by the tall brush of the tropical jungle. From inside the cabana, I could hear sounds of the brightly colored birds and the penetrating call of a parrot sitting on the branch of a gardenia tree outside, next to the entrance.

Angel and Lisa were out of commission, with frequent bouts of diarrhea and vomiting. Lisa was actively working on their healing with the help of acupuncture needles and homeopathic remedies she had brought from Santa Barbara. They both looked quite pale and wasted. Angel told me that Nico would take me to see Don Tomas as soon as I was ready. Not knowing what I was about to get into, I needed reassurance about Nico.

"Don't worry," Angel said. "Nico is totally trustworthy. He's honest and he knows Yucatan like the palm of his hand. Nico has a friend, Antonio. They often hang out together. They're like brothers and they are very interested in your story of how you found out about Don Tomas."

"Well, if that is the case, you can tell them to pick me up this afternoon."

Nico showed up in the company of his friend Antonio. The young Mayan had a round face and warm, dark eyes. His tanned skin was the color of bronze. Right away, I was aware of Antonio's shyness and introversion. He remained quiet while Nico did all the talking. With little preamble, we walked to the green and white old taxicab. I sat in back, the two men sat in the front. With Nico at the wheel, we drove around the hotel and onto a highway, past the pyramids, on our way to the small town of Piste.

Thirty minutes later, Nico drove into a town of unpaved streets. The houses were modest and simple but colorfully painted with bright blues, greens, oranges and terracotta reds. Bricks and cement were the basic building materials and the floors were tile or dirt. I was surprised by the cleanliness of the people, who in spite of the rustic conditions wore white embroidered cotton clothes. Even the children were dressed in impeccably white outfits and leather sandals. Nico stopped the car in front of a small grocery store. The owner, an old man, greeted us with friendliness.

After picking up a few bottles of bottled water and a box of Coca-Colas, we were back on our way. From there on, the road was less than desirable. Big potholes made us jump up and down inside the car. Then Nico took a right turn onto another road that was narrow and bordered by the short brush, so typical of that area. It was hot and humid, but Antonio and Nico didn't seem to be bothered. I was the only one who perspired heavily. With every mile we moved farther away from any sign of civilization.

"We are not very far from Don Tomas's house," Nico said.

"Is he expecting me?" I asked.

"Of course he is." Nico exchanged a look with Antonio, who never said a word.

Twenty minutes later, Nico took another turn onto an even narrower road that ended right in front of a small hut built with palm tree leaves and clay. No one was outside, except for a black rooster and a couple of gray-white hens.

"This is the place." Nico came around and opened the door for me.

"He might be taking his siesta," Antonio spoke as he walked towards the hut.

I stood there facing the entrance and waited for Don Tomas

to come out. A few minutes went by and nothing happened, except I heard voices coming from inside. A small man walked out of the hut. His pure white hair, cut very short, contrasted with the dark brown of his skin. He wore a guayabera and white cotton pants. I figured this ancient-looking man was Don Tomas. Antonio shook his hand and, without wasting any time, the old one spoke. Even though I couldn't understand what he was saying, I could detect a tone of urgency.

Antonio turned to Nico. "We got to go back to town right away. Don Tomas told me my sister would die if you don't bring her to him."

"Well, let's go."

"What about me?" I asked.

"You stay with Don Tomas. He wants you here."

Antonio and Nico took off, leaving behind deep tire marks on the wet and orange clay of the road. Confused, I wondered how I was going to communicate with Don Tomas. Then an old woman emerged from the house and joined Don Tomas. Together, they walked towards me. The old healer was the first one to extend his bony hand to me. He was not much taller than I, perhaps an inch or so, but as I returned his greeting, my hand was held with the strength of a tall warrior.

Don Tomas had the vitality of a young man. He smiled at me, showing a row of healthy teeth. Then the old woman approached and said in a clear Spanish, "I'm Doña Mariana." She shook my hand and welcomed me. "Bienvenida a nuestra casa." I could hear traces of her native Yukatec by the way she enunciated "bienvenida." They signaled me to follow them into another hut, right behind the one I'd seen. This one was larger, just one spacious room. Inside, there were two hammocks, and right across, in the opposite corner, a small stove and some pieces of wood piled against the wall. In the center were a rustic table and four chairs.

Don Tomas motioned me to sit. I was amazed by how comfortable I was in the presence of these two elders. Only a few minutes and I felt as if I'd known them all my life. The air had a familiar scent of fresh herbs and earth, just like the smells of Cuba. Momentarily, I was transported. The voice of Doña Mariana brought me back. "¿Quiere café? I just made some before you arrived." And she poured coffee from a metal pot into three clay mugs.

I took a sip of my coffee, which was delightfully aromatic. Not too strong, it had the taste of sweet spices. Don Tomas watched from the corner of his eyes, careful not to be intrusive. At first, we drank our coffee in silence. Then, Doña Mariana asked about my trip. I shared my experiences in Mexico City. The old woman translated for Don Tomas. He said he was sorry for the people but not surprised. Don Tomas did not elaborate. We finished our coffee and Doña Mariana cleared the empty mugs from the table. There was a quick exchange of words between the elders, all in their native language. Don Tomas got up from his chair. He walked towards the door and gestured for me to follow him.

We walked to the other hut. Don Tomas went in first. Inside, I found a humble healing sanctuary. There was a small altar by the back wall where Don Tomas kept pictures of Catholic saints, candles, a jar filled with round crystals and a wooden cross. Hanging from a ceiling beam were bundles of dry herbs. I felt at home in this setting, which reminded me of the altars my Grandmother Patricia and my Afro-Cuban nanny Carmen had in their own healing rooms. Don Tomas took a bowl in his hands and, using matches, he burned some form of yellow-white resin. He turned to me and said, "Copal," about the only word I understood. Doña Mariana came into the hut and Don Tomas handed her the bowl. Soon, the place filled up with the scent of the resin, which resembled the smell of incense used in Catholic churches. The old woman ran the bowl up and down my body, smudging and blowing smoke all over me.

"This is sacred copal," she said. "It'll cleanse your body of bad *iki* [spirits] and of dark *iko* [winds] and of the tiredness from your journey here."

It was close to noon when Antonio and Nico returned with

Antonio's sister. The woman was frail and very pale. Don Tomas welcomed Quetzal into his healing sanctuary and asked her to sit on a chair across from him. As if they had planned it all, Doña Mariana pulled another chair and sat next to her husband. They closed their eyes and began to hum a prayer in a low tone that gradually became higher and louder. The walls of the small enclosure vibrated with the ancient sounds. I could feel my own body responding to the energies invoked by these elders.

The experience lasted for a few minutes. Don Tomas uncovered the jar that contained round crystals that looked like marbles. The healer took several deep breaths that he blew into the glass. He poured the contents into his opened hand and studied them carefully, then placed about ten of the crystals on top of a white cloth. Quetzal was still looking colorless. Antonio and Nico stood next to her. Doña Mariana went outside and brought back three eggs. Don Tomas spoke and Antonio lifted his sister from the chair into a standing position. She wobbled a bit as if she were nauseated. The old healer proceeded with the ritual healing of passing the eggs over the entire body of Quetzal. With swift and wide circular movements of his hands, he concentrated on the head and lower abdomen, while he chanted prayers.

After a couple of minutes, Quetzal rushed to the door of the hut and vomited a foamy yellow liquid from her intestines. Don Tomas cracked the eggs into a bowl and once more he observed the contents. He called us to come closer and pointed at two dark spots floating on the white of the eggs.

"Baal K'as," Don Tomas said.

"Algo malo," Nico translated for me. "This is what he found in her body."

As I understood, Don Tomas cleared the bad energy from Quetzal's body. According to the healer, there was a woman in town who was envious of Quetzal. This woman was after Quetzal's husband. She had cast some evil spell on Quetzal. So evil was this energy that it could kill her if not cleared right away.

After the healing, Doña Mariana prepared a green concoction from herbs and gave it to Quetzal with instructions to use a few drops in the water she drank. As strange as this situation was, I was not surprised. Don Tomas and Doña Mariana, although from a different country and culture, were no different than my Grandmother Patricia and Carmen. They believed in the same healing forces of the planet. For these people, their connection was to Mayan deities and spirits instead of Carmen's orishas and Grandmother's saints. It was all part of the same healing tradition.

Later that afternoon, when Antonio and Nico returned from taking Quetzal back to town, Don Tomas decided to take us for a small excursion to the ruins. Nico explained that the old man wanted to show me one of the sacred places, the ground for many ancient rituals. Without much preparation, we all hopped in Nico's car, except for Doña Mariana who wanted to stay behind. Don Tomas sat in the front. Antonio and I rode in the back. For almost a half-hour Nico drove his taxicab on a bumpy dirt road into a thick, low jungle. Finally, we arrived at a clearing where I could see a tall pile of stones that looked like a crumbled pyramid.

Nico and Antonio jumped out of the car and pulled out a big stone that sat on the side of the huge pile. A dark hole was exposed as they removed the mother piece. Don Tomas talked to them before Antonio turned to me with a question: "Are you afraid of dark and narrow spaces?" I searched in my mind for memories. The only thing I could think of was the time when I had been trapped inside an elevator for fifteen minutes. Except for minor anxiety, I had not been terribly affected by the experience.

"Well, then, we are going down into this tunnel. Don Tomas wants to make sure you can crawl on your belly for a while."

"Have you done this before?" I asked Nico.

"Yes, many times."

Nico's answer was reassuring. I took one more look at the black mouth of the tunnel. It was a bit intimidating, but I figured, if these people had done this before, I should be able to do it, too. Antonio began the descent into the cave, followed by Don Tomas. I was impressed with his agility. He was as strong and alert as a forty-year-old man.

"It's your turn," I heard Nico say right behind me.

I approached the entrance with reservation. I lowered myself to the ground and rested my belly on the cool and moist dirt. Head first, I faced the black entry to the subterranean womb, and slowly, I pushed my body into the narrow opening. I noticed a distinct smell of wet clay and minerals. The farther we moved in, the cooler and darker it was. I could feel the walls narrowing and pressing against my back. I panicked. I could hear my heart pounding hard, like a drum, inside my chest. Drops of sweat covered my face. I wanted to turn back, but how? There was no way to do so. Breathe, breathe, I said in a low voice.

"Chakmool," Don Tomas said. His words echoed inside the tunnel.

"Jaguar. This is the home of the Jaguar," Nico translated.

"What does that mean?" I asked. I imagined a large, spotted wild cat waiting for us.

"Jaguar lives here. Jaguar is sacred to the Mayan people."

The words of Nico reverberated inside the walls of my ears. Suddenly I had the feeling that we were not alone. Somewhere a giant Jaguar was watching us descend into the belly of his home. In the darkness, my mind raced with thoughts of death. What in the world was I doing in a place so remote from civilization? I thought of Lisa and Angel in their safe hotel rooms with no idea of where I was. But here I was in the womb of the underworld.

As we continued, the tunnel became even narrower. I could hardly move my arms to push myself forward. I couldn't breathe. I couldn't breathe! I couldn't hear any sounds. My head felt light. I was dizzy. I felt my body shrinking. I became a tiny baby pushing through the birth canal. The contractions of my mother's womb were like strong waves that pushed me to the shore. Every contraction brought me closer to the opening.

I was almost there but...then, a jolt like an earthquake. I was thrown into the air and I landed on a grassy pasture.

A helpless infant, I lay naked to the elements under a full moon. With my belly down on the wet grass, I shivered from cold and the shock of the landing. My back arched to the warm and moist touch of what felt like a tongue. A powerful stroke rolled me onto my back and I found myself face to face with a large black cat. Golden and fiery eyes gazed at me. Like the lens of a camera, the bright pupils opened wide and I was pulled into a cavernous world. Then I was pushed into a spiraling tunnel. It was dark! I couldn't see. I could only feel the downward and swirling motion of my body. Except I was no longer an infant, I was a man. Tall and muscular, I could feel the bulge of the tight and toned muscles of my strong legs, arms, back, and chest.

I was whirling down at amazing speed when I heard the voice of Don Tomas. This time he spoke to me in Spanish, "You have been called to the belly of Jaguar. You'll be born jaguar." And with these last words, I saw my body had been transformed into a wild black cat. I was a jaguar. My eyes could see through the dark veil of the night. With feline sensitivity, I was quite aware of the fine scents, sounds, colors, and texture of my environment. I moved on the earth, with the soft and smooth grace of the jaguar. I felt no fear!

The pull of a hand on my arm brought me back to the subterranean tunnel. I heard Antonio call my name and I opened my eyes to large stalactite columns. The picture in front of my eyes was magical! We had made it to a beautiful underground cave. The view was like nothing I had ever seen in my life. Drops of water fell to the earth from giant calcified structures. From a circular opening on top of the cavern, the rays of the sun shone through, illuminating the darkness. An underground lake of emerald green waters waited for me to step down from the narrow entrance. Don Tomas stood there. With his back to me and his arms wide open, he prayed. I listened to the Mayan words, not understanding, but feeling in my heart the depth of his reverence for this place.

"This is a sacred Xenote," Nico told me as soon as I stepped on the ground. "This is the place where our ancient people came to pray and to have ceremonies. We still do, but only those of us who believe in the old ways. These days not many Mayans do. They don't even want to be called Mayans. The white man brought shame to us. They mixed their genes with ours to create a mestizo race. More than that, they invaded and tamed our souls and spirit."

Don Tomas placed his hand on my right shoulder. With his other hand, he motioned for Nico to come closer. He spoke in a rhythmic tone, as if chanting old prayers. Yet he talked to me about the journey. Nico translated.

"Flor, you have forgotten who you were. Now you remember. Jaguar spirit lives in your heart. It is the flame that burns deep, very deep with the memories of many lifetimes. You've been living in fear. Not good! Fear dries your soul. It hardens your insides like the bark of a tree. This cave is the womb. The water from Xenote will soften you. It will cleanse and heal your body. Old man and old woman of creation are wise and they remember the old ways. They'll help you find your way back to spirit, back home to the jaguar family where you belong. Jaguar will teach you how to listen carefully and how to see in the darkness of the jungle."

As soon as he finished, he turned to Antonio who handed the old man a small clay bowl. Don Tomas lit some copal. The resin burned inside while Don Tomas chanted. He raised his hands towards the Xenote and somehow I had the sense that he was imploring the gods and spirits who lived in the cave. Antonio translated one more time, letting me know Don Tomas wanted me to bathe in the green waters of the underground lake. Somewhat reluctantly, I took my shoes off and walked into the emerald lagoon. The waters of the Xenote were refreshing and warm. I dived in and out feeling the silky touch of the lake on my body. It was deep and dark but I felt no fear. I swam and I floated, trusting that the lake would hold me in her invisible arms. "Oshún," I whispered and I thought of Carmen, my

Afro-Cuban nanny and of her orishas. Oshún, the goddess of the rivers. "Oshún, thank you for your soothing embrace and your sweet kisses. Thank you for your blessings. I am your child."

FOUR

Star of the Jaguar

THE TRIP BACK to Don Tomas's house took longer than I expected. The three men conversed in Mayan, not bothering to translate a single word for me. I was upset about their lack of sensitivity. I decided not to take it personally and focused on my experience at the Xenote.

"Hey, Nico, is my hotel on the way to Don Tomas?" I asked. I was feeling the need to have some space of my own.

"No, but if you want we can drop you off first. That's not a problem."

"No," said Don Tomas, "she go back to house."

I was dumbfounded to hear Don Tomas speak Spanish, not very well, but enough to make himself clear.

"She sleep at house."

No one dared to say anything. The rest of the journey was in silence with occasional interruptions from Don Tomas in his dialect. Upset, I leaned back in my seat and, with eyes closed, reflected on the day; the subterranean tunnel and its narrow walls pressing against the sides of my body. The inexplicable experience with the Jaguar played in my mind like the smooth walk of the big cat through the thick forest. As far as I knew, jaguars had a prominent position in Mayan myths and legends. According to one myth, the jaguar acquired its beautiful spotted coat by dotting mud on its body with its paws. All throughout Latin America, these big cats command fear and respect. Its name, translated, means, "a beast that kills its prey with one bound." This four-legged creature is the ultimate predator—it climbs, it swims, and it roams the dense forest with ease.

My experience with Jaguar inside the entrails of the cave had been a total shock. Why this vision? It was an enigma I couldn't decipher with my limited understanding of the culture and traditions. I was afraid to ask, for fear of making Don Tomas angry and yet somehow I had the feeling he knew about my encounter with the beast. I had a deep knowing that the old shaman did not want me to ask him any questions.

On our return, Doña Mariana prepared a modest but delicious dinner of refried black beans and chicken Pibil style with handmade corn tortillas. As soon as we finished the meal, Don Tomas signaled us to follow him to his healing room adjacent to the house. Packed inside the small structure, we sat around the wooden table where the shaman conducted most of his work. As usual, there was no explanation for this gathering. So, I waited while I watched Don Tomas uncover the clear glass that contained his divination crystals. He closed his eyes. I could see the gentle trembling of his eyelids and the peaceful expression of his face. Don Tomas was in a trance. Maybe he was making contact with his spirit guides.

The shaman's voice rose in a chant—old prayers spoken in Náhuatl. The intonations went from high to low and vice-versa. His words seemed to have the energy of the ocean, with big and small waves that reached into my heart, creating a rippling motion across and inside my chest. An image flashed inside my head. I saw how Don Tomas leaned forward, and with his right hand, barely touched a point in the center of my forehead. Fireworks filled the room! And I was thrown back into the presence of a large cat, a black jaguar that looked straight at me and roared with such a force that every single cell in my body rattled.

The intensity of this energy evoked a stream of childhood memories. I lay in bed in the healing room of my Grandmother

Patricia. I was sick and unconscious but I could hear her voice. She was talking to me about the roar of thunder and its power to dispel evil spirits that made me ill. "Negrita. Negrita." I heard her words echoing inside me. "Negrita, just think about thunder. Let its power clear all the darkness. Bring the light and the fire of thunder from the top of your head all the way down to your toes." My feverish body burned and I sweated until my clothes were soaked.

The roar of this black cat sounded like thunder. I trembled. The face of the feline seemed to me like the face of death. Jaguar was death. With its sharp teeth, ready to rip me apart, the cat moved closer, its eyes fixed on mine: golden amber spheres with the glow of the sun. The gaze of the beast was like a torch that burned tunnels into my being. Long and dark pathways filled with smoke and ghost-like characters.

Where was I? I couldn't see Jaguar anymore. I looked around. Now every shadow took on a different dimension. They were no longer ethereal and transparent. They were people. Old people with faces that looked as ancient as the earth itself. They sat around a stone table, on top of which was a large book of weathered pages. The marker was a white eagle feather.

"Welcome to the cave of Balam," said one of the elders who stepped forward to greet me.

"Balam?"

"Jaguar spirit," the old man translated.

"What am I doing here?" I asked.

"Come. We have been waiting for you. My name is Maximo. I'm an old Mayan scholar. We are the keepers of the Jaguar books. We invited you here via Don Tomas so we could talk. We have a lot of work to do and very little time to waste."

I was invited to join the table. Maximo was almost another version of Don Tomas, with gray short hair, dark eyes that had a warm and wise expression. His thin body was still strong and agile. His torso was half-naked. A cotton cloth around his waist covered him down to his knees. There were a total of four elders, two of whom were women. They waited for me to settle in my place.

"The Balames, or Jaguares son espíritos protectores." The old woman spoke. She was a small Mayan woman with a face that had hardly any wrinkles, but her eyes were ancient and deep as the insides of the cave we were in. "The Jaguars are there to protect the four points or corners of the horizon. They also guard people from the dangers of the dark energies. The Balames know how to stop the bad winds that bring illness and poverty to the villagers of the world. They are gods and goddesses in disguise and are endowed with supernatural powers. But you also need to remember that Balam once destroyed the earth, devoured mankind." She leaned forward "Mi nombre es Luna, Moon. The jaguares are very connected with the powers of the moon."

"You, my dear child." The other woman spoke and stood up. She held in her hands a black jade mask. Taller, with a square and strong torso with unusually wide shoulders, she was a warrior, even though she dressed in a black cotton dress embroidered with red Mayan symbols, in contrast to Luna who wore a simple and delicate white cotton dress. As she walked towards me, I could see the angular shape of her face adorned with jade earrings. Her eyes were glowing sparks in the darkness of the cave. She frightened me. "Yo soy Jaguar de la Noche," she said and showed me her mask. It was the face of a jaguar beautifully carved in black stone. The mouth of the creature exposed its fierce and sharp teeth.

"Don't touch it!" she yelled at me.

"I'm sorry. I didn't—" I apologized for my thoughtless action.

"That's a privilege one must earn."

Jaguar of the Night, as I translated her name, was as fierce as her mask. The sharp tone of her voice commanded instant fear and respect.

"You'll learn." This time it was the other male, younger than Maximo. "You'll learn if you trust your fear," he said. His thundering laughter echoed against the walls of the cave. The man got up from his place and stood right next to Jaguar of the Night. His black hair was tied back in a ponytail and adorned with Quetzal feathers. His arms, legs and torso were painted with figures of animals, which included a snake, jaguar, eagle and others I couldn't see well in the dimness of the cave. He wore a loincloth made of jaguar skin. A string of shells wrapped around his ankles rattled as he walked.

"I'm Jaguar Dancer," he said in Spanish and took the mask from the hands of Jaguar of the Night. He positioned it over his face and roared. I was struck by the chiseled beauty of his muscles. He could have been a gymnast or a body builder, perhaps a wrestler. He was old, maybe sixty, but he had the physique of a young gladiator.

Jaguar of the Night clapped her hands, and immediately, Maximo and Luna joined them in a circle. Luna beat a small, cone-shaped water drum of clay and finely stretched deerskin. The sounds echoed inside the cave with muted bits—the voice of Mother Earth. Maximo had a large conch shell that he blew in harmony with the drum. Jaguar of the Night moved in with the soft music of a wooden flute. How magical! I thought to myself, as I stood there befuddled by their concert. Then, Jaguar Dancer's body moved to the music while he held the mask over his face. At first, his movements were slow and gentle, like those of a snake slithering on the surface of the earth. I could see the man turning to snake right in front of my eyes. Just when I was getting used to this image, Jaguar Dancer leaped in the air with a roar that made my heart beat fast with fear. His eyes fixed on mine and now he was the black jaguar enticing me. He moved around like a big cat stalking his prey. I was his prey. I screamed. The echo of my voice resonated inside the cave.

The black jaguar moved closer. He opened his big jaws. Sharp white teeth shone in the dark. I panicked. My body froze from the closeness of a giant creature that threatened to devour me. Its large paws pushed me to the ground and I curled into a ball. The animal rolled me onto my back and stood there on all fours. So small I felt, like a helpless child waiting to be ripped apart, but instead, its large and red tongue licked my face with an unexpected and gentle touch. From prey, I became the cat's love object. I was a fragile cub being stroked by the wet and warm tongue of the Mother.

It was the hand of Don Tomas that caressed my hair as I came back from the cave. Dream or vision, I wasn't sure. I was disoriented and confused. I found myself resting flat on the floor of Don Tomas's healing room. Doña Mariana sat by my side, right next to Don Tomas. I looked around as I tried to make sense of what happened. Antonio was gone but Nico sat on a chair away from us.

"Star of the Jaguar." It was Don Tomas.

"What?" I said.

"You are 'Star of the Jaguar.' That's your name."

"My name?"

"Yes. Your name," Don Tomas said and he touched a point in the center of my forehead. "Here." He pressed with the tip of his finger on the same place. "You see the past and you see the future. You feel like Jaguar does. You are its daughter." Don Tomas spoke in clear Spanish.

Doña Mariana walked out of the room. Don Tomas signaled Nico to come closer. They both helped me up onto the chair where I had been sitting prior to all that happened. The old healer sat across from me and Nico sat next to him. Then, the shaman carefully gathered his crystals back into the glass where he kept them. He was quiet for a while. Occasionally, he spoke in his old Náhuatl language and paused so that Nico could translate for me:

"The old ones are worried about this world. Man with so much greed in his heart is destroying the land. When all the jaguars are gone, the underworld will be left at the mercy of the evil winds. Every day, Jaguar travels in and out of the underworld and mends the spirit of the world. Opposite forces such as good and bad are balanced, and the evil winds are stopped from making us sick. Modern man doesn't pay attention to the signs.

He's too busy! One day our planet will be barren. Then it will be too late! You came here because we called you for help. Like Jaguar, you know how to walk in-between the worlds of dark and light, the dead and those alive. Those elders you saw in the cave will work with you. They are spirit guides who knew you even before you came into this life. The Jaguar dance is a dance where life and death are woven together. When we dance we heal and we grow! We become one with the spirit. I'm an old man. Here, young people don't want to know about these ancient ways and I have no means to go places too far away for this tired body of mine."

Don Tomas got up from his chair and went to the door. He lifted his arm and pointed at the distance. He said: "Even the jungle is dying. Men who don't see the future cut off too many trees to make room for tall houses." For the first time since my arrival, Don Tomas looked sad. He walked back to his chair. "Star of the Jaguar, you have the gift of words and the means to walk among many. You must tell the stories. You must share your knowledge of the spirit world. Like Jaguar, you can move smoothly through the jungles of people's minds. Your job is to make known what is unknown. Ignorance, my child, is our worst enemy."

Don Tomas handed me a small leather pouch. I held it in the palm of my hand with curiosity. The old man was tired but his eyes were glowing with light. I could tell he was excited to be sharing all this information with me. As for myself, I was struggling with thoughts of the responsibility this name Star of the Jaguar represented. I wasn't sure I could measure up to the expectations of these elders. I wished I could be less alone in this path. I wondered about Don Tomas's life as a shaman. Did he feel alone, too? Did he have friends? Was he in contact with other shamans?

"Don Tomas, what is it like to be a shaman?" I asked.

"It is not what you people think. We shamans are *guerreros* [soldiers], always alert and ready to fight the unseen forces. We are the guardians of the gates between death and life. We are born to serve the gods. It is work that demands one to be humble. Sometimes, we are forced to be fierce and rude when under attack and invasion."

"What invasion?"

"Invasions from those who are hungry for power. They want what we have but they only use it to hurt others. Some of these attacks come from the world of the dead, from angry ghosts and evil spirits, who are restless and tormented! Many of them lived violent lives full of suffering while here on Earth and then, they refused to go to the other side. Their souls linger around us. They create trouble and sickness for those who are unprotected." He paused. "Here, open the pouch I gave you."

With hesitation, I opened the leather pouch. Inside were two crystals, one a clear quartz, the other a smoky quartz. Don Tomas took them from my hand and put them against the light of the candle that burned on top of his table.

"Can you see these tiny sparks inside the crystal? They are angels who will protect you any time you need help—dark and light, angels from both sides of the world to take care of you. Keep them within reach."

Indeed, there were many little lights. Unlike the round and clear marbles Don Tomas used for divination and healing, these crystals were long with a pyramid-like shape.

"You will need protection when doing your work. But this is just a minor step. These crystals are good so long as your faith in them lasts."

Don Tomas placed the crystals back in my hand and rose. He talked to Nico for a few seconds and walked away.

"Don Tomas wants you to sleep in this room tonight. He'll meet with you tomorrow morning. I have to go home and make sure my wife and children are fine, but I'll be back."

Before Nico left, he handed me a mat made of woven palm leaves and a blanket. I placed my portable bed close to the altar and away from the entrance. Since there was no such thing as doors in that area, most houses were open to the elements and to all kinds of crawlers, including poisonous snakes. I sat on the mat. I was tired but I didn't want to fall asleep. My head was full of images. The face of the black Jaguar haunted me. The wild creature was calling me to my dreams and I was resisting its call. I rested on the mat with my eyes wide open. I wondered if other people in the world were having similar experiences. I thought of how easy it had been for me to enter Don Tomas's world. From the moment of my arrival at Merida, I felt at home with the green lushness of the landscape, the hot and humid climate, the brown-skinned natives with their round faces and dark eyes.

Despite the possible dangers, there was a familiar feeling about Yucatan that allowed me to feel safe and trusting. At times, I even wondered about my openness to this journey in the company of total strangers whose lives were so different from mine. But there I was, and I had no regrets, because I was convinced that I had been guided to Don Tomas by forces beyond my comprehension. I did not miss California, my family or friends. It felt as if my spirit had been absorbed by the culture and the soul of the land. I was intrigued by my experiences with the mysterious Jaguar. Why this animal? I thought that perhaps it would help to look at this entire process as a dream. This wild feline energy was a part of me, an aspect of my psyche in need of integration.

I closed my eyes and pictured the cat as it moved through the jungle. Its movements were sensuous and agile. Untamed, the creature knew its territory—the scent of the earth and of other animals. Its biological radar was able to capture every sound of the forest. Its body was a tuning fork that vibrated with information from the environment. Every single cell in its magnificent anatomy was fully awakened to life. Yet, the large creature appeared relaxed. There was a feeling of complete abandonment about its ways that allowed the animal the freedom to simply be. This refined awareness gave it the wisdom and power to be the master. Jaguar was like the jungle itself. Its wildness came from a connection to the wild. Its ability to merge with the colors, textures, sounds, smells...made Jaguar fearless.

I thought about the words of Don Tomas and of his

prophecy that, when Jaguar is gone, we'll be at the mercy of the destructive forces of the underworld. It occurred to me that Jaguar is a reflection of the masculine and the feminine forces of the world, the Yin and Yang in us and in the planet. An overabundance of any one force could be harmful at any given moment in evolution—personal and collective. Therefore, the dance I had witnessed in the cave was a daily journey of renewal from darkness to light and back. Each morning, Jaguar becomes the Sun God traveling across the sky to the West, where he falls into the underworld to become the dark Goddess.

The extermination of Jaguar leaves us at the mercy of evil hidden in our unconscious as well as the blinding light of our pretentious consciousness. Either way, we must stop to think about our individual responsibility and contribution to the tipping over of nature's scale if we are to survive.

As for myself, I had been presented with the opportunity to restore the capacity to travel into my own underworld. There, I would find an abundant well of archetypal energy for healing my fragmented self, a part of me that over the years had been repressed and distorted by having to survive in a world of the material and technological. In my own struggles to be successful in a society that has forgotten to honor the spirit world, I became disconnected from the sources of life.

I was beginning to understand that the most important dramas in life take place in the invisible spirit world that surrounds us. Everything that happens in the physical realm is caused or determined by happenings in the spiritual world. Hardly anything has a physical cause. Death, life, disease, fortune and misfortune are all set by spirit dynamics. The dead come back to cohabitate among us. The world around us is peopled with voices, influences and spirits. We are never alone and yet there are plenty of lonely people on this earth. In part, we have forgotten how to tune in to this invisible world.

Tiredness won over my fear of the darkness. Despite my resistance and the sounds of crickets and frogs in the near distance, I faded and drifted into the dream. That night, I traveled back to the cave of Balam. My four old friends were there waiting for me. They asked me to join them at their table. Maximo called me by my new name "Star of the Jaguar" and told me that Jaguar was my teacher, my *Tonal*. Then Jaguar of the Night placed her mask on the table, right in front of me and asked me to take it. "No. No!" I screamed in my dream. But the elders insisted that it was mine to keep and protect from now on. The black jade was glowing in the dark. Terror invaded my whole being as I thought of the responsibility of being the keeper of such a powerful artifact. Jaguar Dancer, who sat next to Jaguar of the Night, must have sensed my fear because he got up from his chair and walked around the table to where I was. He looked straight at me and in his eyes I saw the eyes of the Jaguar fixed on mine. Then, he took the mask and he placed it on my face.

Fire traveled down my spine into my feet. I was burning, as if my body were being consumed by flames. Shaking, I rose and moved around the space feeling possessed by the spirit of the Jaguar. All of a sudden, I was taken by the energy of the Tonal in some form of spiritual intercourse that burned deep inside my pelvis. I was aroused and terrified all at once. Jaguar Dancer moved with me but his movements were a dance. He was Jaguar himself. He circled me, moving closer and closer. Now our bodies were pressed against each other. With his arms wrapped around my body, he continued his dance. It was a mating dance. Jaguar Dancer was no longer an old man but a young and strong warrior, who wore a mask, not made of stone but from a spotted jaguar pelt. His body fully naked was covered with paint of black and yellow. With gentle force, he took me to the floor of the cave. Our bodies were like two snakes entwined, slithering on each other with the fire of passion. Jaguar Dancer's erect member penetrated my insides in search of a dormant volcano. He went deeper into the chasm of my inner being until finally the explosion occurred and I shook and convulsed in ecstasy.

I woke up to the morning sun. I had no notion of what time it was. I was surprised I'd been able to sleep at all on the hard mat. My body ached and my neck was stiff. With effort I lifted myself up from the floor and stretched my back and arms. Outside, a couple of parrots bathed in water from last night's rain that had collected inside an old clay pot by the side of Don Tomas's healing room. Even though it was early, the air was already heavy from the humidity, and the temperature was maybe eighty degrees Fahrenheit. I was ready to step out of the hut, when Doña Mariana appeared by the door.

"I brought you some coffee. Did you sleep well?"

"Yes," I said to be polite but I was sure she could tell by the look on my face that I was not quite telling the truth.

"Have your coffee, and when you're ready, come and join us for some breakfast."

Doña Mariana and her quiet appearance reminded me of my maternal Grandmother Petra. She was soft-spoken and her hands were the hands of a woman who had dug in the heart of the earth for years. These hands were strong and wide with thick veins that popped from underneath the thick skin.

"Doña Mariana," I said as she was ready to walk away.

"Si."

"Do you have any grandchildren?"

"Five, but they don't live here. They moved to Merida where they can find jobs."

"Do you miss them?"

"I do, but there is nothing they want to do here in Piste. Living in this green jungle is for those who love silence. These days, young people get bored easily. They want to be in the city. You know, everybody wants to have electricity and running water. For us old people those things are bad. Too many lights make your mind fussy and confused. I get sick from the smell of gasoline from all those cars. I get big headaches."

"How about Don Tomas, does he miss his children?" I took another sip from my coffee.

"Don Tomas has no children. J'meen [shamans] have no children. The spirit of the forest takes away their fertility, so it won't interfere with their work. I know it sounds strange," Doña

Mariana said as she perhaps noticed my confusion. "J'meen don't live their lives in the same way others do. They are busy even at night when they travel to the dream world. Well...I better go now. I have things to do."

"Can I help?"

"No. Don Tomas doesn't eat any food that is not prepared by my hands or by his own hands. Please don't be offended. J'meen believe that evil winds that make you weak and sick enter through the food we eat, the water we drink, the air we breathe, even through the soil where we grow our goods. One must be careful."

Doña Mariana hurried out of the healing hut. Perplexed by her words, I drank my coffee and thought about how far away we have grown from these concepts. When in the States, I had no idea where the food I bought at the local grocery store came from. Here in the house of these simple people, everything was taken into consideration. No wonder we had so many problems with rare diseases of unknown causes. As my Grandmother Patricia told me when she visited us in California, the food we ate was, in her vocabulary, bagazo de caña, which means it had little nutritional value and lots of toxic stuff. Like Don Tomas, my grandmother, a j'meen or curandera with her own gifts, never allowed anyone to prepare her food. She never ate at restaurants, no matter how fancy or clean. She preferred to cook everything herself so that she could be certain of its freshness and integrity.

Later that morning, Antonio and Nico showed up just as Doña Mariana and I were ready to go out to the milpa to pick some fresh corn. Nico gave me a note from Lisa and Angel. They wanted me to know that their health had improved and they were on a short business trip to Cancun. Don Tomas came out of his hut where he had been by himself for at least a couple of hours and asked Nico and me to join him. Doña Mariana handed Antonio the empty basket she had in her hands and signaled him to follow her to the milpa. I was disappointed.

In my early childhood years in Cuba, at my grandparents' farm, I used to accompany Grandmother Petra to pick corn. It had been one of my favorite activities.

I could see that Don Tomas had been praying or meditating by his altar. The smell of the burning copal permeated the inside of the hut. There were offerings of fresh flowers and fruit that he had placed in front of his Catholic saints and Mayan deities. The white and tall candles were lit. The shaman invited us to sit across from him. Without preamble he asked me via Nico to tell him about the dreams I had last night. Not only was I surprised, I was hesitant to share them with the two men.

"I must hear your dream," Don Tomas said in response to my resistance. "Dreams tell me about the gifts you were given at birth. Your dream of last night is a story from the spirit world. It is the j'meen's bundle you came to me for—a bundle of dreams. As your teacher, I'm responsible for teaching you how to feed it, so that its songs and prayers never die. Ancestors get angry when one doesn't take good care of the dream bundle."

Don Tomas waited patiently for Nico to finish translating his words. Carefully, he observed the expressions of my face and body. All during this time when the shaman spoke, I was aware of my trepidation and ambivalence about this "dream bundle." How would I know what to do when on my own, away from Don Tomas?

Don Tomas interrupted my thoughts. "Your ancestors are the roots of this big tree of life. Our ancestors are our life force. They are the thick roots that feed and nurture our spirit and our dreams. Therefore, we must keep them alive and strong through our rituals and prayers." The old curandero tapped me on the shoulder with his right index finger. "You have been dying like a tree whose roots have been cut off. When you left Cuba you lost the thread to your ancestors. With no teachers to guide you and teach you the rituals, you got lost! The spirits around you don't have a place to be. There is no altar in your home to house them. Your dream last night is about remembering. You are called to remember your own ways of connecting with spirits. Dreams are story-tellers. They help you remember the keys to the spirit world."

Don Tomas's words gave me confidence to go ahead. With his eyes closed, the old shaman listened to my dream, and when I was finished, he did not wait for Nico to translate. Obviously, as on many other occasions, he had gathered the information he needed by way of his powerful ability to link directly with the images, not with the words.

"Jaguar is your spirit bundle. Jaguar is your Tonal, and now you are married to this jaguar. He is your first husband. He is your link to the ancestors and to nature. From now on, his energy will ride you every time he is needed. He will feed you with his vitality, but only if you return this gift by honoring him. Jaguar will help you remember the wild and the untamable in you. He is the part of you that was broken when you entered society. The most difficult task for us j'meen is to learn how to live in the human jungle. Because of our extreme sensitivity to the 'winds,' our bodies can become frail and sick if not protected."

"What about the mask?"

"Ah, the Jaguar mask." Don Tomas held his face with one hand and thought for a moment. "That mask is now part of you. It is not my job to tell you about it, but for you to find out."

Don Tomas didn't say a whole lot more. On his way out of the hut, he asked me to think about the nature of the hunter and hunting. It was an unusual request but again the curandero had his ways of teaching. Later that day I went for a walk. I took a narrow trail that led me into the low jungle. Not wanting to get lost, I marked my path by breaking branches. About a half-mile later, I reached a clearing and at its center was a big pile of stones. At first, I didn't think much of it, but as I approached the site, I discovered a few pieces of broken pottery scattered on the ground. I kneeled down to take a closer look. I had a strong hunch not to touch anything. "No," I heard a voice say inside my head, "this place is sacred." I pulled myself back and stood there facing the short pyramid. I heard a sound. It was the crackling of dry branches across from me. I froze and my eyes searched the circumference of the area. It sounded like an animal or a human moving through the brush. My heart raced in anticipation of an encounter with some wild and ferocious creature.

Then, the face of a deer peeked out from the thick wall of trees. Its eyes made contact with mine. With effort, I swallowed and began to relax. Not wanting to scare the animal, I did not move, but the deer leaped across the clearing knocking off some stones from the pile. Quickly, it disappeared back into the dense shrub. I was feeling blessed by the unexpected visit of the deer when my eyes rested on a small clay figurine amid the scattered round rocks. On closer examination, it was the head of a jaguar. It had broken apart from the missing body. I hesitated but finally I took it in my hands. Again, I heard what I thought was the deer coming back. While I waited, I made the connection between the mask of my dreams and that of Oyá. The deer had been the messenger or perhaps it had been Oyá herself. The clay head was a gift to me from the goddess of the wind.

FIVE

Snake Woman

INSTRUCTED BY Don Tomas, Antonio and Nico came looking for me at the hotel. It was close to one o'clock in the afternoon. They found me relaxing by the pool. As soon as I saw them walk towards me, I knew the two Mayan fellows were on a mission. Their greeting was brief. Nico informed me that the old healer wanted me to meet him at the cave of the jaguars in the middle of the low jungle. The thought of meeting these creatures outside the realm of my dreams was frightening.

"I know this place like the palm of my hand," Nico said.

"I understand, but can we do this tomorrow morning when it is less hot and humid?"

"No," Antonio replied, "Don Tomas is already waiting for us."

"Can you give me details?" I asked.

"Not really. You know Don Tomas. He never explains anything," Antonio apologized.

Nico drove us in his taxicab for about twenty minutes on the paved road near the pyramids of Chichén Itsá. We could see the magnificent temple, De Los Guerreros, with its tall, concrete columns decorated with feathered serpents, characteristic of the Kukulcan period. Amid the ruins is El Castillo, a pyramid built in honor of the wind god or feathered serpent known as Kukulcan.

69

The temple is structured to represent the experience of crossing the boundary between two different symbolic realities. First, the top of the pyramid, flooded with light, stands on a platform that is elevated above the realm of daily life. Second is the interior, like a mystical underworld, humid, compressed and dark. Every year, in the equinox of spring and autumn, one can see the shadow of the serpent, descending the steps of the building to the earth.

Kukulcan is also known as Quetzalcoatl, the wind god, Nico explained. The Mistec people called this god "Nine Wind," he said, as he pointed towards El Castillo. "In the equinox, the snake is seen coming down the steps of El Castillo pyramid. As the elders say, this is the day of the year when Kukulcan returns to the earth." Nico was a great storyteller, compared to Antonio, who remained quiet most of the time. Nico enjoyed sharing his knowledge with me.

"'Quetzalcoatl' means the Feathered Serpent. According to the ancient legends, the serpent is said to be the center axis above the World Tree. It is the line that divides heaven and earth. Before the Mayans disappeared, the priest in charge of the rituals was required to enter the spiritual world. During these ceremonies, the priest was able to talk to the ancestors and bring their messages back to the people."

"What about the jaguars inside the pyramid?" I asked.

"Jaguar is the god of the underworld and a messenger between the living and the dead. He is the lord of the jungle. A good hunter and protector."

Behind the temples of Chichén Itzá, we entered a narrow road, unpaved and bordered by thick low brush. As I pondered the information Nico gave me, I was able to make a connection with the deity Oyá and her role in the Yoruba religion with that of the Kukulcan god. Both deities were linked with the wind. They were each the go-between of the two realms.

Suddenly, I was aware that I had been led to this place to further understand the works of Oyá. Due to different cultural mythologies, she appeared under a different name here, but I was in a situation where I could learn about the nature of this warrior and dark goddess of my tradition. Given that I was not able to go to Cuba, I believe my Grandmother Patricia had choreographed her plan well, with the help of Don Tomas, a curandero like her.

The dirt road wound into an even narrower path. The old taxicab of Nico made its way over small stones and holes, which upset my stomach. I kept my attention on my breath and the limited view ahead. Nico turned into a clearing by the side of the road and stopped the car. "Here we are."

"Is this the cave of the Jaguar?" I asked.

"No, but from here we go by foot."

After Nico helped me out of the car, he grabbed water bottles from the trunk. Antonio joined us with a long machete. "When visiting the jungle, you always take this," he said as he touched the sharp and shiny blade. Antonio used it to open a trail. The brush was five feet tall and very thick. Under the hot afternoon sun, with humidity that made it hard to breathe, we moved through the lush forest.

Nico, right behind me, was never quiet for long. He was busy naming trees aloud so I could learn their names. Then he shared his childhood experiences of walking through this jungle. His father had taught him to track animals, such as deer and wild pig, which they had hunted for family meals and special celebrations. Nico emphasized the importance of using every part of the animal and of never hunting just for the sake of the sport, which, according to his ancestors, was a crime that upset the animal and the spirits of the forest.

Antonio continued his work of opening the path until at one point we connected to an already existing trail. He stopped to drink some water and to wipe the thick drops of sweat that covered his face. We were all sweating profusely. The underbrush was like a gigantic cauldron and we were cooking inside it.

"This a deer trail," Antonio pointed out. "If we follow it, we'll end up near the jaguar cave where Don Tomas is waiting."

"How far away?" I asked.

"Two kilometers. But from now on, we will be able to walk faster."

The image of Don Tomas making his way through this thicket amazed me. I was very impressed with the old man's ability to move around physically, with incredible agility for a centenarian. I attributed his condition to the peaceful life he had had. In Yucatan, people move at a slower pace. Their lives are still in harmony with the elements and the seasons. Farmers travel around the jungle growing their corn, squash, and beans in their milpas. Mayan campesinos see the milpa as a sacred place. After a few years of cultivation, the land is allowed to rest and replenish so that the vegetation may grow back. As I learned from Nico, curanderos like Don Tomas are responsible for rituals that ensure the health of the land, communicating with the dueños or spirits of the earth. A good relationship between farmer and the dueños is believed essential for a healthy harvest. Simple and ancient farming techniques form the basis of their agriculture.

As we moved through the path, Nico said; "One must never forget to pray and to ask for permission to go into the forest, or to cut trees." He looked back to see my reaction. "If you don't, the spirits may be angered and one can get sick or suffer terribly. Also, there are bad spirits that live in the milpa, in the mountains, in the rain, in the ancestral ruins, and in the jungle. These dueños are merciless when provoked."

"Did you ask for permission before we entered this place?" I asked, concerned.

"Move back!" Antonio yelled. I saw his arm coming from behind me. With incredible speed, his large machete cut through the air and landed on the ground with a sharp and firm blow. I looked down and saw the elongated and thick body of a snake that had been cut in half. I froze in place, totally unable to utter any words. The body of the reptile was still wiggling. Antonio moved forward and with the tip of the hatchet poked into its body. I guess he wanted to make sure it was dead. A wave of sadness wrenched my insides and a dull pain radiated from my lower back all the way up into my neck. My legs felt numb.

"You're lucky," I heard Antonio said.

"Itz' a k'an. A rattlesnake!" It was Nico, who had moved closer, so that he could take a better look. "Snakes are messengers of the Lords of the Earth and the guardians of the day."

In our walk, I had been distracted by my thoughts. Unaware of the danger, I had taken the lead on the trail while Antonio went to inspect a bird's nest that sat on a low branch of a tall tree. All I remember is Antonio making a comment about the nest and seeing him go towards a large tree, ten feet away from the path. It was when he rejoined us that he saw the serpent, two or three feet in front of me.

"Are you okay?" Nico asked.

"I'm not sure. Why did you kill it?" I still felt the pain of the sharp blow in my own body.

"That was a deadly snake and you were about to step on it!" For the first time, Antonio's eyes met mine with fierceness. I could tell he was not pleased with my doubts. "If you get bit by a snake like that in the middle of this jungle, you'll be dead before we can get you some help."

"Yes, but—why kill it?"

"It was the only thing to do."

"That beautiful creature was minding its own business. We were the intruders," I said with anger in my voice.

Antonio didn't reply. He shook his head and started walking.

I could tell the men were confused by my reaction. I struggled with my own feelings. My anger was perhaps unjustified but it was like a hot coal burning its way through my spine. I had a strange sensation of feeling my head disconnected from the rest of my body. I was having a difficult time making my legs move. An odd sensation of heaviness filled my abdomen and lower extremities.

Nico waited for me to recover. He was patient but his eyebrows frowned when he looked at me. I glanced at the severed body of the snake. The bright colors of the skin were now turning pale and its open eyes were opaque and lifeless. Its spirit was no longer there. It had disappeared into another dimension. I kneeled down for a closer look. My eyes went to the wound. Fresh blood still oozed from the cut. I felt an impulse to touch the body. It was cold. I ran my finger down the slender and scaly skin, my own body started to tremble. My mind became fuzzy and images of an earlier time in my life flashed inside my head.

The stream of images was so intense that I was forced to sit down. I was dizzy. Thick drops of sweat ran down my face. The memories went back to when I was fourteen, the time of my arrival in the United States. Having left Cuba without any hope of return in the near future, I became very depressed. I was lonely and extremely homesick. I missed my extended family and my friends. I was like a tree whose roots had been cut off and I was dangling in the air.

Now the snake was there to remind me of the extreme severance I had gone through, during that period of my life. The separation from my culture, people and spiritual upbringing had left me numb, desolated and very sick spiritually. I saw the snake as a symbol, as a sign. I thought about the words of an old teacher, a woman named Sheila Moon I had met at a Jungian psychology conference. This woman spoke about the Beautyway, or the myth of snake woman—a journey of the heroine and of her initiation as a medicine woman. It is the myth of the feminine descending into the underworld and it parallels the Kukulcan myth. Both journeys are important in the healing and therefore restoration of a balance of opposites.

According to Moon, the Navajo believe that mental and physical health depends on getting things back into balance. Beautyway is a downward spiraling into the underworld where opposites meet in order to restore harmony. This is a descent into unknown aspects of the self—the shadow where we encounter scary, dangerous, and fragmented elements that must be brought to the surface and befriended if one is to live in balance.

I looked at the halves of the serpent in front of me. The

sharp blow of patriarchy on the feminine had been perfectly re-enacted by Antonio. With precision and dexterity, head and tail had been separated. It was a mirror of my own body, of the disconnection I had experienced for years within the underworld of my own psyche. With sadness, I realized that I was not alone in my journey. The known and unknown faces of women paraded in front of my eyes. We were the daughters of Coatlique, the lady of the serpent skirt, the giver and taker of all life, who wears a necklace of skulls around her neck as a reminder of the inevitable destiny each of us must face—that time when we return to her serpent arms. Coatlique was there at my feet, enticing me to hold to my memories of what it is to be a woman. She had made a sacrifice so that I could remember my path. It was not possible for either Nico or Antonio to understand my feelings. Patriarchal, they had only seen the threat of death and not of birth.

I followed Nico on the open trail. Antonio was ahead, searching for the so-called Cave of the Jaguars. Now as I walked through the thick jungle, I could feel the hot breath of Coatlique burning my entrails. Like Oyá, she moved through the forest with the agility of deer and jaguar. Like Oyá, she was there to teach me how to negotiate with the world above and the world below. She was Snake Woman with her lessons of how to shed the old skins of acculturation and decades of social training. I had been a caged woman, who had forgotten about her fire and about her wisdom. The trail to the jaguar cave was itself a large snake leading me to the womb of my forgotten instincts.

"Here. We are here!" I heard Antonio say.

Amid trees and rocks was a cave. I trembled at the thought of a large cat roaming in the vicinity. Smart as these creatures are, they could easily turn us into a fresh and juicy dinner. I could see no sign of Don Tomas. But nothing surprised me. After all, I was in the middle of nowhere, basically, with strangers, two men I knew very little about. My mind spun with crazy ideas— kidnapping, rape, death... Hold it! I said to myself. You're going over the edge.

"Where is Don Tomas?" I finally asked.

"He said he would be here," Nico replied.

"What if something happened to him? He's old."

"No. No. I don't think so. Don Tomas has been here many times. He knows this place." Nico walked towards the cave. He called for Don Tomas. There was no response, only the echo of his voice in the distance.

"Well, let's find a place to camp," Antonio spoke for the first time since the incident with the snake.

"Camp?" I asked. "Aren't we going back to town?"

"It's getting dark. It's best for us to stay here. This is not a friendly site when the sun goes down. One cannot see as well as the wild animals."

I was annoyed by Antonio's authoritarian attitude. Who was he to decide whether I wanted to spend the night there, and where was the old man? Suddenly I became very suspicious of both Nico and Antonio. What kind of plan did they have in mind?

"Hey, you guys, I don't know what's going on here but I want to go back to town. Where is Don Tomas?" I demanded.

"We don't know. He was supposed to be waiting for us in here," said Nico and he played with one end of his black mustache. "He will come. I know Don Tomas."

With his machete, Antonio cleared a new trail by the side of the cave. I was angry with them. I was at their mercy. Not knowing where we were, I began to feel anxious about the night. I was furious with myself for blindly trusting these two men. Just because Angel had recommended them didn't mean a thing. All the good feelings I once had for them had been replaced by a tremendous level of discomfort. I even wondered if Don Tomas had any knowledge of this trip.

Nico followed Antonio on the new path. He ignored me as well. I looked around. The cave was intimidating. I imagined that the jaguars would return at night and that was the reason for us to camp someplace else. I thought about my choices. I could try to retrace my way back. At least I could go back to where the car was parked, but I was afraid of getting lost or confused by another deer trail. I stood there, aware of my profound fear of the jungle and its dark veil. I could almost hear the whisper of Oyá from behind the thick wall of trees. Her face, a mask of horror and death, enticed me to feel my dread, the chilling terror of the hunt where I was the prey. I could smell the breath of the predator's energy all around. I could feel the zigzag of Snake Woman's body on the surface of the earth. Coatlique with her invisible dress and deadly bite was there, so close that I could hear the loud and penetrating rattle of her teeth.

In the distance, I heard Nico's voice. He was calling for me to join them. Once more, I examined my choices. Defeated, I gave up on my plan to desert. The men didn't make any comments when they saw me behind them. They must have sensed my inner strife. I walked in silence.

"You know," I heard Nico say in his normal jovial tone, "the guardians of the woods are known as cuyos. They are beings who wander in the jungle at night. The cuyos make weird noises and throw stones when they want to be noticed by those who enter their territory. I know people from town who have gone hunting and they have been scared to death by the cuyos. One friend of mine told me how he was chased out of the forest by cuyos. He was sitting by his fire when a shower of stones poured down into the flames. He couldn't see anyone, but he heard all these sounds coming from the woods. Strange and wild sounds! When I was a child, my grandfather used to tell me stories about cuyos, who stole children from the village. They would enter people's houses at night and take the young with them."

"So," I said, "what is the secret to keeping the cuyos away from us?"

"They like cigars and copal."

"Did you bring some?"

"Of course." Nico patted the front pocket of his shirt. "I would never travel in the jungle without plenty of offerings."

I laughed when I saw a bunch of cigars sticking out of his pocket. For a moment I had forgotten about the snake. It was hard to resist the charm of Nico and his stories. Antonio, though, was another case. Machete in hand, he kept forging ahead, with no apparent regard for my feelings. By this time, the sun had set below the horizon and it was dark. We walked in search of a place to camp. I decided not to ask any questions and to mind my own business. I was preoccupied with the long night ahead in the company of these two Mayans. I noticed the vegetation was not thick and lush in this area, but still I stepped on the ground with the awareness of all the dangerous crawlers underneath the low brush. After a while, I noticed how alert my whole body was to the sounds and smell of the thicket. Despite my worries, I relaxed.

Finally, we arrived at a clearing which Antonio decided was a good place to spend the night. He disappeared into the woods, and a few minutes later came back with a bundle of dry branches. Ordered by Antonio, Nico went for more wood while Antonio started a fire. I was still very upset about having to spend the night in this unknown and eerie place, especially because no one ever consulted me about this decision and Don Tomas was nowhere to be seen. Nico came back with dry wood he had gathered. He dropped the pile on the ground and went back for more. Irritated with the way the men had ignored my feelings, I decided to address Antonio directly. "What are we doing here and where is Don Tomas?"

"I'm following instructions from Don Tomas. It's not that I like to be mysterious. To be honest, I'd rather be at home with my wife and my children. This is not fun for me, either, but Don Tomas insisted that we bring you here and wait for him. Do I know what the old man had in mind? Of course not! Medicine men don't talk about their plans."

"Nor do they tell you about these sorts of business." It was Nico, who was back with another big bundle of wood he dropped by my feet.

"This is crazy! I don't understand. What is the point of being here in the middle of nowhere surrounded by jaguars and snakes?"

There was no answer, Nico disappeared back into the forest, and Antonio continued making a fire. I wanted to check what time it was only to realize that my watch was no longer on my wrist. Probably it had fallen somewhere on the narrow trail. I stamped the ground with my right foot. I was mad.

Antonio got up and looked at me from the other side of the fire. "Here, keep my machete with you." Leaning over the fire, Antonio handed me his machete and walked away in the same direction Nico had gone. I waited for a few minutes to see if he was coming back, but Antonio didn't return.

"Great! This is great!" I yelled as loud as I could.

Time went by. In the darkness I quivered with fear. The pitch-dark veil of the jungle was as black and impenetrable as the obsidian blades of the sacrificial knives I had seen in pictures of Mayan culture. The jungle at night was an underworld of indiscernible monsters. I held the machete in my hands. In Cuba I had been forced to learn how to use it to cut sugarcane when I was taken away from my family and placed in labor camps. I knew well how to hold this tool and how to swing it in the air with firmness and precision. But what could a simple hatchet do for me if I were confronted by a big and ferocious jaguar? The jaguar knew his territory and how to hunt in the dark night. I was easy prey, with no sense of smell trained to detect his proximity. With no good ears to hear his silent walk on the floor of the forest, I would be dead meat before I had a chance to lift the machete.

SIX

The Jungle

TIME WENT BY without any sign of Antonio or Nico. It had been at least two hours since I saw them last. At first, I figured they were looking for wood. Then, I began to panic at the thought that they had left me there in the middle of this gigantic jungle. Why? Were they trying to teach me a lesson? This was a cruel game I didn't understand. By now I was convinced that Don Tomas was not involved.

I was quite aware of how vulnerable I was. I knew that I needed to stay put by the fire until morning light, then I could retrace my way out. I was angry with myself for trusting them. "What an idiot!" I said aloud, and I sat by the fire. The thought of jaguars nearby made me tremble. Then I remembered the cuyos. Oh my God! I didn't have any cigars or copal. I looked around but I could only see what was inside the circumference of light created by the fire. I couldn't let the fire die. My life depended on its vitality. I glanced at the pile of wood Nico brought before he left. It was not enough to keep that fire burning for long. Yet the idea of leaving what I felt was my safe spot to venture into the forest to gather more wood was not appealing, either.

I sat there with the hope that Nico and Antonio would come back, but as time went by, I became aware of the futility of my wishful thinking. They were gone! Soon, I was going to run out of fuel. I stood by the fire strategizing my next move. Machete in hand, I walked towards the edge of the clearing. One more look and I quivered at the thought of moving forward into the dark web of trees and bushes. I waited to hear any sounds. The silence of the jungle was as noisy to my ears as the heavy traffic of the city. It was the type of stillness that penetrates one's mind. The earth itself appeared to be awakening beneath my feet, so strongly that I could feel the energy from the Mother tingle throughout my body with a kind of touch that was raw and primal.

Never in my life had I felt more alive. Every cell of my body was fully alert to the surroundings. Everything around me seemed to be dancing with life—from the comforting call of the crickets to the fine whisper of the soft and warm breeze, to the gentle movement of branches. Suddenly my vision was as sharp as what I imagined a jaguar's was. I could see into the night with surprising clarity. I could smell the freshness of the soil—a musty scent of earth mixed with the spicy aroma of grasses. The aroma from this wilderness tasted like a good wine that had been aged in the belly of an oak barrel. It filled me with ecstasy, and gradually, it melted away the thick armor of inhibitions and fears that had kept my body frozen for years. Now I was alive in all senses of the word.

The sounds of the jungle became louder. It was as if God herself had turned up the volume so that I could hear her voice—the rumble of river followed by drums. A mixture of earthy tunes that had Mayan and African rhythms. In the background was the rattling of seashells intermingled with the penetrating calls of conch and melodic flutes. As if that were not sufficient, the enchanting voice of a woman came from the depth of the forest. The words of her song turned to echoes from the past. It was the voice of my Afro-Cuban nanny Carmen. She was calling me, "Niña. Mi niña. Don't be afraid. Oyá is here with you." Then I heard my Grandmother Patricia, "Negrita, you are not alone! Remember my Oyá story. She is the hunter! She is the deer! She knows the forest."

"Grandmother, Carmen! Where are you? Please come to me."

"Negrita. We're here."

"Where?"

"We're here in the forest."

I was standing there at the edge. It seemed as if the boundaries in-between realities gradually dissolved in front of my eyes. Out in the jungle, there are no illusions. Only the elusive truth of the night, with its terrifying mask, prevails. Life itself becomes a fine membrane where forms lose their rigidity and turn to fluid shapes.

All around me I could feel the contractions created by the pulse of death and life. The jungle, dressed in her attire of black and silky cloth, was a large womb ready to swallow me in her moist canopy. It was an invitation. It was a call for me to surrender to her leafy embrace. How could I resist such a cry of love? Yet fear stood in my way. I was a city girl. My mind had been trained to rule over my body and now I was a crippled being among creatures with highly developed senses.

"Negrita, call Oyá. She is your teacher in this jungle." It was the voice of Grandmother Patricia.

"Niña, Oyá is a sorceress. Here in the woods, one must become invisible. You are not to act like a person. You need to behave as an animal. Moreover, you must become a hunter."

These were not the words I would expect to hear from Grandmother Patricia and my nanny Carmen. I had no memories of these two women as hunters. But I guess in their own way they knew about the "hunt." As healer and sorceress, they navigated the realms of another type of jungle, that of the spirit world.

City life had stifled my ability to engage in deep play with nature. I realized this experience was an opportunity to shed the tough skin of society's training and to reconnect with the savage in me. Jaguar and snake medicine represented a different type of consciousness I needed in order to become the hunter.

As I stood in the center of the jungle, with a new awareness of myself and of the environment around me, I realized the hunt was about to begin. I had the choice of becoming hunter or ending up as prey. This dance was a prance of courage needed to transcend daily routines and responsibilities. Free of burdens and restrictions, one could navigate other dimensions. Like a painter sitting in front of her blank canvas, one had to wait for an opening of the mind, for that moment when imagination presents us with a fleeting image.

There is a dance that takes place between the elusiveness of the image and the stealth of the painter. The artist waits for the right time when her keen mind's eye is able to freeze the image and her hand lifts the brush into the air, ready for the kill. In watching and stalking, the painter and the hunter make their imagination a friend. It becomes a mating dance where the painter and the image, or the hunter and the prey become one. In the act of fixing the image on the canvas, the painter sacrifices a part of herself and so does the hunter in killing his prey.

Now I was one step closer to understanding the essence of the jaguar dancer of my prior vision. And finally, I was able to grasp the teachings of the exchange between Antonio and the snake earlier in the day. "The hunter," I heard a voice say from within. "The hunter learns to play the role of the animal." Oyá, with her magnificent sorcery, is able to transform herself into the hunter or into the prey. She, with her incredible capacity to shift forms, is able to move from one role into the next, right in front of your eyes. Oyá teaches the hunter about animal wisdom. I, as the hunter, came to the forest to meet with her, to learn about a kind of knowledge buried in the old part of my brain.

"Oyá, Coatlique, Jaguar, can you hear my call? Please, come and teach me. I'm a huntress in the dark."

There, with my machete in hand, I waited for an answer. The images of Oyá in the forest dressed in her deerskin, with her antlers ready for the hunt, her fierce eyes searching for the prey and her hooves digging deep into the soil—Oyá was there amid the trees, with all the wisdom she had brought from the ancestral land. I felt her cloth, so finely woven with the fibers of all the ancestors, wrapped around my body. Above me, the moon shone with her silver rays through the trees, and I heard the voice of Coatlique. She was rattling her way through the forest. Coatlique was there to protect me and I heard her say, "Here, dress your body with my skin and you'll know what it is to be snake."

My eyes opened to the night firmament. The bright stars greeted me when I woke from my dreams. I had lost track of time. The sounds of the jungle filled my ears, and the scent of wet grass and earth was sweet and invigorating. I ran my hands along the surface of the ground and touched drops of rain on the low brush. How long had it been since I attempted to cross the threshold of the forest? I was still alone. The fire was extinguished, and smoke spiraled from the center of the pit.

Flat on my back, I could feel the right side of my body was numb and my left side ached. I had the sensation of sharp needles poking through my flesh. Maybe I had been bitten by a snake. That's it! And now its fatal poison traveled through my blood with its paralyzing medicine. In the dark, I lifted my head, which felt heavy and hurt. A wave of nausea forced me back to my resting position.

I closed my eyes to still the images spinning inside my brain. I was flooded with memories of my childhood in Cuba. I was a young child, four or five. The revolution had upended the safe environment of my home and family. Terror, like a sharp knife, stabbed the inside of my guts. I saw myself at fourteen, the loss of my country, my extended family, my culture, my spiritual roots and tradition.

I turned my aching body and rested protectively on my right side in a fetal position, curled in pain. It was then I remembered that during a healing session, Don Tomas had said, "The right side of the body has to do with health and success. The left side carries illness and failure." As Nico had translated these words, he had said: "Don Tomas wants you to pay attention to the aches and pains of your own body."

Now, I was sure the message he had given me was in

preparation for this time. Because later that day, Don Tomas invited me back inside his healing hut and talked to me about the Ool, which according to the Mayan tradition, is the vital spirit or energy that governs health, strength and emotional balance. It is the life force in our bodies. Don Tomas went on to say, "The Ool can be affected by strong emotional trauma and result in a sickness, whose root is fear."

At that point in the conversation, Don Tomas touched me on the left shoulder with his finger. "This kind of fear illness is what we call susto and evil eye." He reminded me of the many times I had been given the evil eye as a child. I was surprised he knew of my early experiences with mal de ojos. I didn't remember ever sharing that information with him.

"Evil eye was not the worst of your problems, but it set a pattern of weakness for harmful energies in your body and it has affected your Ool. Your grandmother Patricia, what a curandera! She protected you, but when you left Cuba..." Don Tomas stopped and went to consult his sastún, or divination crystal. "It is here!" he said with a serious expression. "It is here! The trauma of leaving Cuba really jolted your Ool. Without your family, your community, your people and their spiritual practices, you were a lonely prey to evil wind and to the spiritual illness of fear, susto." Don Tomas looked into his sastún one more time. "Your grandmother asked me to help you and I will." Don Tomas turned around and he left the healing hut.

Now, crippled with my spiritual pain, full of questions that I knew the old man did not want to answer, I was curled on the floor of the forest, like a helpless child in the leafy arms of the mother. Where was Don Tomas? Where were my grandmother and Carmen? Where were all those people I loved and whom I was forced to leave behind in Cuba? I was alone and afraid. My mother had been afraid too. I could see myself in the watery womb of her belly. My mother had been afraid of having me. She didn't feel prepared. She had been afraid to connect with me and even afraid of loving me because she was afraid I was going to be taken away. Inside her belly, I could feel my mother's fear.

She had passed it on to me at birth.

There was a thread of fear I could trace all the way to my mother's womb and even to the outside world around my mother's belly. I could go back to the years that followed my early dreams and nightmares of guerilla militia invading our lives. The neighborhood where I grew up was terrorized by the fear of spies checking for any signs of counter-revolution in our family. My father suffered the rage of having to live a life in prison, his wild spirit tied to the soles of his feet as he walked the streets of my hometown dreaming of a free world on the other side of the ocean.

Don Tomas was right! When I left Cuba, my soul became restless in search of the roots I had left behind. Without my people and the nurturance of my culture, I was naked and exposed to the evil winds. I had no anchor except for the memories of those who loved me once. Fear raked my insides and I lived a life protected by the pale colors of a new American identity. Was I Cuban? Was I American? I was both and I was neither. I was alone. I was lonely. Fear was my only companion. It was an incurable illness I fought every day as soon as I opened my eyes. Fear, always fear with its smell of bitter herbs, exuded from the pits of my arms.

I twisted from pain. A sound from the jungle captured my attention. I recognized the growling of a large cat. "Oh my God!" I cried. I heard the growl closer to me and I froze. Fear! I was afraid, but of what? The jaguar was my ally, as fear had been for so many years. We were one with each other. I paid attention. I listened for the sounds of the jaguar walking towards me. It was circling me but I couldn't see the animal. I waited. I couldn't move. My body did not respond to the commands from my brain. I was the cat's prey. Soon I'd be shredded to pieces by its strong paws and devoured by its sharp teeth.

I waited, resigned to a violent death. It was in that process of surrendering to my fate that I began to feel some peace. "Come on, Jaguar! Come and face me. I'm here!" I imagined Oyá, the orisha of death, taking me into her arms. The deity's face was a dark mask. The deity took me with her, we went across a river and then we arrived at the ancestral island. There, she placed me on the ground and covered me with a black cloth. This was not so bad, I thought to myself. The cloth felt like another womb. The fabric itself was vibrant and hot. It was full of life. Then I heard the voice of Don Tomas. He spoke to me in clear Spanish. "Flor, this is your chance to erase old pain from your life. Let go of your fear. Every single thread of that cloth is a link to your ancestors. You'll find protection in these fine but strong lines. They have been woven into the fabric of your Ool."

A new sound coming from the forest brought me back from what I figured had been a dream. It was the hiss of a rattlesnake. Again, fear rose inside me, and my body shook. I coiled on my side in the hope that snake would move past me, without noticing my presence. I remembered what I heard once from an old Lakota medicine man in Santa Barbara. The wise man said: "Snakes won't bite you if you stay calm and fearless." Oh well, not so simple, but in the face of my encounter with the rattler, breathing deep inside my lungs was my only choice. I breathed and I forced air inside my chest.

Without much warning, the cold body of the snake slithered around the side of my head. I breathed and the snake moved across my forehead and its long body traveled down the center-line of my body with a rippling motion that compelled me to gently uncoil my body from a tight fetal position. The snake found its way to my chest, belly, pelvis, thighs, legs and feet, and I was left with a sensation of tingling all over. My skin was as sensitive as I imagined the skin of a newborn to be. I lay there on my forest bed. For the first time, I was free from my fears. The jungle had become a familiar place. The hunter in me had emerged with confidence. The animal in me knew in her bones the territory where I was. Without much thought, I got up from my position and stood there face to face with the darkness. The night was no longer impenetrable. It had turned transparent to my eyes! Silky to my touch! It was a safe womb that palpitated with the heart of the jungle and its creatures.

I looked around in search of Jaguar and Snake. I was certain of their presence even when I couldn't see them. I realized that this was the game of the jungle. This was a dance of invisible partners and shadows. This was the ultimate play where hunter and prey become lovers in a sacred act of death and rebirth.

Like Snake, I'd shed the skin of my fears and witnessed my susto being devoured by the strong mandibles of Jaguar. Oyá, with her fierceness, had given me the gift to feel in my own body the paralysis of my psyche. She, the warrior deity, had shown me the way to fight the inner monsters that for so long had assaulted my mind and my spirit. This was not the kind of fight one fights with weapons. It is a journey into your own inner jungle. There are no enemies other than you, yourself, with all your torments and projections. It is here in this underworld of the human dungeon that one crawls through the maze of the restless soul. It is here one encounters the fragmented parts of the self that pain and trauma had separated. Once shattered, the psyche becomes an infected sore that feeds from sadness and anger.

Oyá was with me. She allowed me to swim in the black river of her body. The African deity found her way into the island of my unconscious and flooded me with the vital power of my ancestors. In an act of severance, she tore to shreds the black cloth of my social reality. She left me naked so I could be in touch with my instincts. Oyá, the great black Goddess of death, spirit of the wind, was there with her disruptive spiritual winds to teach me about the unpredictable and transformative powers of nature. She had placed me face to face with my own mortality and humility. I had died within my illusions of safety. The hunter in me emerged with a renewed sense of destiny.

Don Tomas had been wise not to teach me with words. From the moment he met me he understood the sharpness of my mind and my great ability to surpass the unknown, as well as my deep need to control unpredictable events. Don Tomas, himself a hunter, had strategized his moves. He had managed to place me in a position where I could learn about the hunt.

The old shaman had understood the troubles of my

imprisoned Ool. He knew that in my efforts to assimilate into American ways, I learned how to intellectualize my experiences and to ignore the voice of my instincts. In Don Tomas's world, one is taught to pay attention to the subtle signs that are seen not by the direct eye but by the indirect gaze. It is a dance where one learns to move with the flow of patterns rather than keep control over these innate rhythms.

Certainly logic has a place in life, but the body, with its genetic and emotional intelligence, is the link to our ancestral and spiritual roots. The way one sees oneself and the universe is colored by perceptions accumulated over many generations. The world is not linear and rigid. It is a fluid and elusive dance.

From my nanny Carmen, a Yoruba priestess, I learned that Oloddumare is the owner of all destinies and of creation. The breath of Oloddumare is the circular flow of all existence, of life and death. As a child I heard Carmen say, "Oloddumare is ashé, the blood of all life. Niña, listen carefully. Your ashé was given to you by your ancestors and it is your job to give good ashé to those who will come after you. You must honor your ancestors and you must pray to the orishas because orishas bring ashé to us people on this earth. When you pray to orishas and they answer you back, you are dancing with old and timeless stories of human beings. You are tuning into the ashé of these ancient ways of being. It is nothing you do with your mind. You can only feel it, and when you're in it, you are then moved by these forces. They take you into the realm of who we really are."

Don Tomas understood my biggest problem was the doubts I'd had about the existence of Oloddumare and of the ancestral world. My departure from Cuba at the age of fourteen left me without the guidance of my elders. I was cut off from the culture and the traditions that nurtured these spiritual values. In my new home in the United States, Oloddumare became a distant concept. Without the proper rituals, I had been disconnected, with no ashé to feed my soul.

As Don Tomas explained to me, all those years in exile, without a spiritual community to guide me and help access the ancestors, had weakened my Ool. The Mayan healer had helped me restore my connection to the ashé. He had placed me in a position of having to go back to myself. There I was, walking through this magnificent jungle at dark and feeling at home with the terrain and the environment. I was there, roaming through a territory inhabited by poisonous and wild creatures, and yet I felt immune to the danger. I was confident in my ability to feel and to smell its proximity. My own reclaimed wildness was nothing to play with. This primal aspect of me felt like an engorged river; its raging waters had set me free from an oppressive dam. The giant roar that for so long had been caught inside my throat was as powerful, if not more, as that of the Jaguar. I was exuding ashé from the pores of my skin. Oloddumare, the orishas and the ancestors were all with me.

The first rays of the morning sun found me all curled up next to the fire, now extinguished, that Antonio had built before he and Nico disappeared. I could feel no trace of anger towards them. They had done as they were told by Don Tomas, the old fox shaman of unpredictable character. I had no doubt that this night in the jungle had been the plan of the healer's mastermind. Hard as it had been, I could not think of a better way to learn about one's ability to transcend fear.

So absorbed was I in my own thoughts, I didn't hear the arrival of Don Tomas and Doña Mariana. There, standing a few feet away from me, were the two elders. Don Tomas's dark eyes smiled at me. He was dressed in his impeccably white cotton pants and guayabera. Doña Mariana wore a deep blue cotton dress embroidered with black and red flowers. They looked festive, as if they had come to celebrate the victory of my survival in the jungle.

Doña Mariana spoke for the two of them. "We brought you fresh coffee and tortillas. Are you hungry?" The old woman placed the food on the ground, next to the fire pit. "Don Tomas wants to know if you're feeling okay."

"Tired? I didn't sleep well," I replied, not knowing what else to say.

I poured myself some coffee while the couple made themselves comfortable on the surface of the earth, right next to me. I took a few sips of the aromatic and deliciously flavored hot coffee. I took my time with the tortillas. Strangely enough, I wasn't very hungry.

"Antonio and Nico are coming for you soon," Doña Mariana said. Don Tomas nodded. "They'll take you back to the hotel. Your time here is over. Angel and Lisa are waiting for you."

I had forgotten about my two friends. I wondered if they knew anything about what had happened to me. I doubted it, but at this point it didn't make a bit of a difference. It wasn't coincidental that we were in different directions on this journey to the Yucatan. The minute I missed my plane in Los Angeles, I knew this trip was going to be full of the unpredictable.

"Don Tomas wants you to know he's very happy you came to us," Doña Mariana continued. "He wants you to remember him and he wants you to come back soon."

I looked at Don Tomas, whose gaze held mine for a few seconds. I was moved by the warmth and kindness I felt coming from his heart. There were no words to express my appreciation for his care, his time and his teachings. Don Tomas had embraced me as if he had known me all his life. The humble nature of his personality, together with his wisdom, had returned my faith in humankind. My spirit had been renewed and nurtured by his wisdom.

"I will come back," I said.

Six months later, I returned to the Yucatan. This time I stayed with the couple for six weeks in their humble hut. They treated me as a daughter. Don Tomas allowed me to witness many healing sessions he performed for the locals. With patience, he spent endless hours talking to me about the importance of his work, the prayers and rituals. Antonio and Nico were my allies, extremely generous with their time, translating and taking me places.

At the end of my journey, we were sad about my return to the United States. Don Tomas expressed his gratitude to me, as well as his concerns for the inevitable extinction of the traditional healing practices in the Yucatan. With the introduction of modern Western medicine into the country and the high influx of tourism, ancient practices struggled for survival. The younger generations were ashamed of their elders, their customs and traditions.

Don Tomas knew his time to travel to the ancestral land was coming soon and with it, he had to face the reality of having no one to take his place in his community. He was aware of the challenges I was about to encounter on my return to Los Angeles. As a wise elder, he knew my role in the world would be different, but he was confident that I had the wisdom to share his teachings in my own way. He blessed me good-bye, and as he did so, I was deeply moved by the love and the respect I felt coming from his heart. As he placed his hand over my head and quietly chanted the ancient Mayan prayers, I could hear in the background the voice of my Grandmother Patricia. She was there with Don Tomas.

SEVEN

The Blue Crystal and the Man in Black

BACK IN LOS ANGELES, I missed the scents of the jungle and the company of my Mayan friends. Antonio and Nico had been by my side as faithful and loyal companions. After so many weeks in the quiet and peaceful environment of the Yucatan, I was disturbed by the fast pace of the world around me. I struggled with the noise of the city crowds and the thousands of cars on the freeways. At times I was forced to stop and pull to the side of the road so that I could collect myself and recover from the dizziness caused by heavy traffic.

The jungle had turned me into a wild creature that now suffered from phobias of bright city lights with their flashy neon signs, overpopulated neighborhoods with their streets covered by paper and empty beer cans. Like Jaguar, I could detect the smell of unhealthy humans, their bodies saturated with fat food and chemicals. So strong was the stench of their flesh that I would feel nauseated when in close physical proximity inside the malls. Headaches, blurry vision and feelings of disorientation followed my short visits to the thick human jungle.

With its concrete surfaces devoid of vegetation, Los Angeles was the underworld of modern society. Pollution had turned the skies into a constant gloomy brown mass that burned the eyes and hurt the lungs. I tried my best to adjust to the constant

95

atmosphere of people rushing to work. Their harsh expressions made me appreciate more than ever the soft and friendly lines of the Mayan faces, and the relaxed environment of the small towns where people took siestas and ate their meals without the pressures of a clock ticking fast.

Moved by the desire to start my own private practice as a therapist, I proceeded with my studies to obtain a license as a Marriage, Family and Child Therapist. I was eager to leave the traditional setting of the family clinic where I had worked as a counselor for more than eight years. My goal was to create a holistic practice—a combination of alternative healing and conventional therapeutic techniques. Los Angeles was the perfect place for me to practice because of its large population of Hispanics with their diversity of traditions.

For many Hispanics, the idea of talking to some stranger about personal problems is unheard of and never considered an option. They would rather consult local healers and priests. There is an understanding that emotional disturbances are not treated as separate from the family, or the community, or spiritual beliefs.

As I learned from my Hispanic clients at the family clinic, they expect a therapist to be some sort of holistic practitioner, someone who is capable and well equipped to dwell in their cultural traditions and values. They required of me the ability to go beyond the spoken language and to grasp the subtle realities hidden in their stories, dreams, body language, and daily experiences.

Unfamiliar with the process of therapy, my Hispanic clients equated my work with that of the curandero, and therefore, they expected me to behave as such and to be knowledgeable of the magic and healing skills they were accustomed to in their countries of origin. It was not unusual for them to talk to me about their experiences with mal de ojos, the evil eye, or *susto* [fright]. Oftentimes the clients brought with them remedios that had been given to them by a local herbalist to cure a child's upset stomach, insomnia, nerves or any other disturbances. And I knew not to contradict the advice given by these healers, not if I wanted to be trusted by the community.

The evening before the licensing exam, I decided that instead of going to my study group, I would stay home and relax, light the candles on my altar and ask my favorite deities for help. By the time I went to bed I was confident of my knowledge of the material. I was ready to step into my new role as therapist. I imagined what my Grandmother Patricia thought of me in this position. I thought of Carmen and of Don Tomas. I thought about my parents and of my Cuban relatives and friends. Like the parents I saw in the clinic, none of them had a clear idea of what therapy was all about. In essence, many of them thought I was studying to be a doctor in physical therapy, which made sense because the word therapy in Spanish translates to *terapia*, which has to do more with occupational or physical therapy.

In the case of my parents, they struggled with the task of having to explain to their friends what I had been doing at the university for so many years. I could hear the words of my father as he told his friends with great pride, "My daughter is a doctor." There was a remark that always followed: "Not the kind of doctor you see when you're sick but a doctor of the mind. She figures people's problems and all the messes of the mind." It was always funny to see the expression on their faces, "Oh, that kind of doctor." Being "that kind of doctor" gave me quite a reputation with my parents' friends. Soon, I was consulted for all sorts of problems, from headaches and marital conflicts to spiritual possessions. In any case, even though I understood my parents were proud of my accomplishments, I was forced to set limits on their innocent promotion of my profession. I asked them not to give my home phone number to their friends.

Around six A.M. on the day of the test, I was awakened by a dream so vivid and clear that I felt transported. I was in the Yucatan, at the house of Don Tomas. The old healer rested inside his traditional hammock. He looked tired and pale. Doña

Mariana was by his side and when she saw me, she greeted me with the words, "I'm glad you came. Don Tomas has been waiting for you." I walked towards Don Tomas and positioned myself next to the hammock, opposite Doña Mariana. The healer barely opened his eyes. Then he reached out with his right hand and touched my arm.

"Blue crystal," he whispered. "Blue crystal wants to be with you."

Then Don Tomas showed me a perfectly round blue crystal. The crystal sphere was radiant on the palm of his hand. In ceremonial fashion, the healer took the crystal close to his mouth and blew air onto it several times. He asked me to move closer to him. I could tell Don Tomas was very weak. He was dying, I realized with deep sadness.

"Don Tomas," I said and tears ran down my face.

"There is no need to be sad. I'm tired. I want to go home," he said in Mayan and Doña Mariana translated. "It's time for me to join my ancestors but you...you must carry on the energy of the blue crystal. It will teach you what I can no more."

With these words and with the magic of his shaman's fingers, Don Tomas inserted the crystal into the center of my forehead. I was infused with feelings of warmth and of peace. I looked at Don Tomas to thank him. His dark eyes held my gaze for a few seconds, then he turned to his wife. Their eyes locked in a brief exchange of private emotions. I looked away and when I turned back, his eyelids were closed. His face, wrinkled by the years, had a serene expression, as if in a deep sleep. The shaman was on his way to the land of the ancestors. I could tell his spirit was now free and happy. He had lived a long life, and his aged and fragile body was no more than skin attached to bones. Don Tomas, the healer, had consumed all his vital energy.

In the dream, Doña Mariana and I gave his body a burial. I, as the young woman, dug the wide and deep hole in the Yucatan soil. As I did this, I felt a great sense of gratitude. I felt blessed by the opportunity to carry and place the body of my teacher in his final home. Doña Mariana was sad and told me that she needed to wait for her time. "It'll be a few years," she said, "but I have things to do and...you do, too."

I woke up from this dream in a fog, as if caught in-between two worlds. My vision was not very clear. My head felt light. The images of Don Tomas were so present that I believed he was there in my room. I was puzzled by the idea of this crystal in my forehead. What was all that about? So absorbed in the dream, I didn't realize time was running. I looked at the clock and panicked, it was past seven! Oh my, I was going to be late!

In a rush, I put some clothes on, combed my hair, brushed my teeth and ran to my car. Fortunately, I didn't live very far from the university. I could be there in fifteen minutes for the eight o'clock test.

When I arrived, groups of people were gathered outside the building. One of my friends, Kitty, who was also taking the test, greeted me. "Where were you? I called this morning to see if you wanted to catch a ride with me."

"I had this dream...oh never mind, I'll tell you later." I noticed Kitty was looking at me with a funny expression. "What's wrong?"

"Have you looked at yourself in the mirror today?" she asked.

"Yes. Why?"

"No, nothing. Never mind," Kitty said.

"Come on. Tell me."

"I don't want to embarrass you but...I think you're in big trouble. You're wearing blue jeans and a sweater."

"Oh no! I don't have time to go home and change."

"What's going on with you? Are you okay?"

"I can't explain right now. People are beginning to go inside. Let's go."

Suddenly, I felt as if someone had poured a bucket of cold water over my head. Kitty was right. Everyone there, including her, was dressed in a business-like suit for the test. The night before, I had taken out of my closet the clothes I would wear in the morning, but I had forgotten about that. The dream had thrown me off balance or else I was still inside the dream or in some sort of trance. Whatever the situation, I had no choice but to take the test and hope for the best.

When I walked into the room, the woman at the door handed me the test. Turning away, I could feel her gaze fixed on my back. Other students gave me a glance. As soon as I sat in place, I concentrated on clearing my mind. I said some prayers. I called on my favorite orishas and once more asked for their help.

The multiple-choice test was long and difficult but I finished on time. After returning the sheet with the answers to the woman who sat at the front desk, I walked outside. Kitty was still inside. While I waited for my friend to finish I wondered if Don Tomas had visited me during the night. Perhaps the old healer had died and the dream had been his way to send me a message. The blue crystal he inserted in my forehead was some sort of gift he had left me. I was still in a daze, not quite awake, not even in my body. It was as if I were far away in the Yucatan. I could smell traces of the burned wood, so typical of that area. I could breathe the scent of the jungle and the smell of wet soil after the afternoon rains. The air was humid, even though I was in California where it is dry and cooler.

Suddenly I was very tired. I lay on the grass. With my eyes closed, I revisited my dream. Then I was hit by the realization that Don Tomas had died the night before. Like my Grandmother Patricia who had sent me a crow with the message of her passage, Don Tomas had left me in charge of this blue crystal I knew nothing about. My forehead tingled and my frontal lobe pulsated like a quasar. I heard the voice of Don Tomas. He said: "A curandera doesn't wear a three-piece suit. A curandera is invisible to the outside world. She walks on the Earth with the gentle touch of the winds. She is like a ray of light ready to take the form that is needed to do her work. People will see their own reflection. A curandera's body is a mirror of their darkness as well as their light."

A swirl of dust was uplifted in the air, right in front of my eyes. For a brief second, I saw the image of Don Tomas. He waved at me, then disappeared like a puff of smoke, leaving no trace behind his silhouette. I called his name. There was no answer. Puzzled, I looked around to see if anyone else witnessed what I had seen and heard. I was alone, except for a small squirrel chewing on a pine nut, a few feet away from me.

"You squirrel! Are you Don Tomas?"

The squirrel did not move. Frustrated, I rubbed my eyes. Maybe I had fallen asleep or maybe all this had been part of my imagination. Perhaps the stress of studying for the test had gotten to me. How could I possibly find out what had happened? One thing was clear: Don Tomas had been there. I totally agreed about the three-piece suit, because even though I had bought one, the idea of wearing such a garment to work was not appealing. Whether I was a curandera was something to be argued. For sure, the old man was telling me I was different from the rest of the group. Not better, but different because of who I was and where I came from. I was, by nature, a therapist with a cross-cultural perspective.

The blue crystal symbolized a gift to see beyond the boundaries of traditional psychology. People are more than what their behavior and their emotions expressed. They have a soul and a spirit. Don Tomas had been eager to show me the multiple dimensions of the human psyche, and how the complex dynamics of a simple individual interact with the rest of the universe. We do not function in isolation, nor do we exist as separate from all those who were here before us. The fabric of the present has been woven from the fibers of the past.

The squirrel was still there. She now had her vivacious eyes fixed on me, while she held on to the pine nut. Then the nervous creature dug a hole in the ground where she could place her treasure. Once more, I heard the voice of Don Tomas: "Trust that all you have gathered is in a safe place inside you. It will be there when the time comes for you to use it. Do not be afraid of scarcity because there is abundance in the world of spirit."

A few days later, I received the first sign of support. In my office at the Mental Health Clinic, I was absorbed in writing a report for one of my cases when I felt a presence in the room. Even though the windows were closed, a warm breeze blew into the space. The leaves of the ornamental plant that sat in a corner moved with the gentle air. I noticed a glow of blue light. At first, it was just a sphere of energy that gradually elongated into a female silhouette. I could not distinguish any facial features, but I was able to tell that she had long hair and that she wore some sort of free-style gown. The deity stayed there almost as if she were waiting for me to address her presence. I didn't know what to say. I was afraid she would leave.

"I'm here to stay," I heard the deity say with words I was not sure were coming from the corner or from inside my head.

"Who are you?" I asked.

"Don't need to know yet. With time you'll get to know me but for now let's say that I'm your helper. I see you have lots of work to do and little time for it. Look at all those files! I guess you call them clients. What a strange word! And those notes you write. What are they good for? Does anyone take the time to read those pages and pages of life garbage? Well, I guess you have to make sure you keep records of their troubles just in case someone gets interested in the future."

"It is part of being a professional. You know, we need to write down observations and treatment plans," I replied with some defensiveness.

"Of course."

I was about to ask the blue deity for her name when I was interrupted by Lidia, one of my co-workers, who happened to walk by my office. The blue lady did not move from her corner. Uncomfortable, I turned away and faced Lidia. I waited for a reaction, but Lidia did not seem to be aware of the presence in the room. Relieved, I took a deep breath.

"How are things going?" Lidia asked.

"Oh, just fine."

"You look kind of..."

"Ah, don't worry. I'm okay. I was finishing a report."

"By the way, this morning I took a call from the elementary school. They have a child who needs to be evaluated by a Spanish-speaking therapist. I was going to stop by the school this afternoon but I have a full schedule. How is yours?"

"I'm busy but...what seems to be the problem?"

"The boy has been afraid to go into the school bathroom. He told his teacher that there is a scary man in there. Even when accompanied by a male teacher, who checked every corner of the room, the boy is insistent that this man is there. The school thinks he is hallucinating."

"Well. Maybe it is true there is a man in there," I said and I looked at the blue lady in the corner of my room. The deity winked at me. "I'll drop by the school later."

As soon as Lidia left my office, I went back to my dialogue with the spirit lady. "You must go and see that boy now. He needs your help. If you wait until the afternoon he'll be gone."

"Why?"

"Don't ask why. Just do it. You'll know when you get there."

Puzzled by her insistence, I grabbed my briefcase and the keys to my car. Then when I turned to the corner, the blue lady was gone. I paused for a few seconds, trying to make sense of this situation.

By the time I arrived at the school, the children were lined up in front of their classrooms to go to lunch. I went directly to the office where I was greeted by the principal and his assistant, a Hispanic middle-aged woman, Maruca. Without any preamble, they tackled the subject.

"Oh my, are we glad to see you! We had another incident this morning during the morning break. Luis wet his pants in the classroom. He refuses to go into the restrooms. He said that this man is now coming into the classroom as well. What is going on here? We are ready to refer him for a psychiatric evaluation. We were just waiting for the school psychologist to get the papers ready."

Mr. Henderson, the school principal, was in his late thirties. His bright blue eyes were fixed on mine, as he waited for my response. Maruca handed me a manila folder. Inside were a few notes written by the boy's teacher, Ms. Gonzalez. I took a couple of minutes to look at the information. According to the teacher, two weeks ago during the lunch hour, Luis came out of the bathroom screaming. He was very frightened by the presence of a man he described as wearing a black suit and hat. Luis had experienced the same encounter for the last few days. None of the other boys in the location at the time had seen the so-called "man in black."

"Where is Luis?" I asked.

"I'll send for him," Maruca said and she pushed the intercom bottom.

"Wait! Is he at lunch?"

"Probably."

"Let's check the bathroom first."

"Any reason for that?" Mr. Henderson asked.

"No. I just want to check the place."

Maruca guided me to the location, while Mr. Henderson stayed behind. In silence, we walked fast across the grassy yard. When we arrived, there was a boy getting ready to walk in, but soon as he saw us, he ran away. I stood at the entrance, not quite sure of my intentions. The room was clean, with the exception of some water that had been splashed onto the floors, right underneath the sink. I looked around searching for any signs of the man in black. I looked inside the individual stalls. I moved around the space sensing the energy there. I couldn't detect much of anything, except for a corner. As soon as I got closer, I experienced a cold chill.

"Come, Maruca. Come and stand in here."

The woman was hesitant at first, but then she followed my instructions.

"Do you feel anything?" I asked.

"Umm...I'm not sure. Well...umm, I feel a cold breeze."

Then, as if the man in black wanted me to be sure of his

presence, I felt the pressure of a hand on my shoulder. I saw a faint glow of light that quickly disappeared. I took it as a hint that it was time for me to leave the place. On the way back to the office, Maruca said that when she was in the restroom, she had the feeling of being watched by someone.

Luis was waiting for me in the principal's office. He was small for his age, with curly dark brown hair and big hazel eyes that looked at me with fear. He sat by the Maruca's desk and nervously he tapped his knee with a pencil. His white T-shirt was stained with tomato sauce. I pulled a chair and sat across from him. Luis's body language told me he was uncomfortable.

"Luis, you don't need to be afraid of me. I want to help you." The boy looked at me, then turned his gaze to the floor. We stayed in silence for a few seconds. Without lifting his face, the boy mumbled some words. "I see that man in black in the bathroom, but my teacher doesn't believe me. She thinks I'm lying. My friends, too, they think I'm a liar. The only person who believes me is my Grandmother Lupita."

"Your Grandmother Lupita, that's good. What does she think about this man?"

"Mama Lupita, like me, sees people that others don't see at all. She tells me this man in black is not a good man. He's dead! He was killed a long time ago in a gang fight but the man in black doesn't know he's dead. He wants to go back to his gang and do the street fights again. Once, he showed me a big knife that he hides inside one of his boots. I got really scared when I saw the shiny blade so close to my face. He poked my cheek with the sharp tip of it and I ran back to the classroom. Man in black said his name is Chato because his nose is kind of flat from a time when he got into a fight and the other guy broke his nose. He told me that the other guy never lived to tell the story. Chato stabbed him in the chest and he cut his heart into two."

Luis looked at me. Thick drops of sweat ran down his pale cheeks. I reached out and touched his hand. I was aware of the boy's anxiety as he waited for my reaction. For days now he had been treated as a crazy kid, except by his Grandmother

Lupita. I had the certainty that Luis was telling the truth about the ghost in the restroom. Also, I knew it was not going to be easy to convince the authorities. They were ready to refer him to a psychiatrist for an evaluation.

"Luis, I believe what you're saying is not part of your imagination."

"You do?" The boy relaxed in his chair.

"Yes I do, but I need to talk to your grandmother. She could help us."

It took about a half-hour for his grandmother to come to the school. A woman dressed in a modest dress with blue and white flowers was brought into the small office where we waited. Maruca introduced the lady to me as Doña Guadalupe and left us alone. The lady had a dignified appearance. Her long, graying hair was combed into a single braid at the back of her neck. By her dark cinnamon skin and her piercing black eyes, I could tell she was a Mestiza. The mix of the Mayan and the Spaniard blood was visible in the chiseled lines of her moon-shaped face.

After introducing myself, I invited Doña Guadalupe to sit right next to Luis. The young boy was quick to take his grandmother's hand into his. As soon as I explained to Doña Guadalupe the reason for her visit to the school, she became quiet. I could tell by her looks, she was suspicious of my intentions. I didn't take it personally. In my years of experience of working with the Mexicans of the area, I learned how protective they are of their spiritual beliefs. They were very well justified in their fears of Americans calling them superstitious.

"Doña Guadalupe, I need your cooperation. Luis is in danger of being placed in a hospital. The school doesn't believe there is a ghost in the restrooms. They think he is suffering from some mental problem."

"No. No. Mi Luis is not sick!" she said, "I'm not going to let them take mi niño. I know that loco of El Chato is there in the restroom. He has lived in there for at least a year. Everyone in El Barrio knows that. Ask the other people around and you'll see I'm telling the truth."

"Doña Guadalupe, I believe you. I felt the presence of this man in the restroom a little while ago. I'm sure he's there. What do you know about him?"

"Man in black was killed a year ago. You know, in a gang fight. He was shot four times in his chest, but the maldito had enough energy left to crawl to the boy's escusado. Most people in the neighborhood think he actually died in there and his evil spirit has been haunting this place. Not everybody sees him. But those who have seen Chato say he is angry and thirty for revenge."

Doña Guadalupe paused, and right at that moment I saw the Lady in Blue float into the office. She positioned herself next to Luis and placed her luminous right hand on top of the boy's head. She said, "He'll be all right. You ask his grandmother to take him to the barrio's woman healer." Then she disappeared.

"Doña Guadalupe, do you know of a woman healer in the barrio?"

She took her time to answer my question. I believe she was as surprised as I was. She nodded without ever mentioning any name. I knew not to inquire further. It was clear she wanted to protect the identity of the local healer.

"Take Luis to her, she'll know what to do."

A week later, when I returned to the elementary school, I was greeted by Mr. Henderson with the good news. According to Luis's teacher, the boy had not had any incidents of "hallucinations" in the restroom. The principal was curious about my meeting with Doña Guadalupe. To that I simply said, "It's confidential, Mr. Henderson." And I walked away before he had a chance to ask any more questions.

EIGHT

Ghostly Characters

E LVIRA WAS twenty-two years old, a native of Guatemala who had arrived in Los Angeles three years before, in 1981. Like many undocumented Hispanic women who reside with relatives here, she moved into the living room of a one-bedroom apartment where her cousin, Rafael, lived with his wife and three children.

The dark circles under Elvira's eyes were a sign of many sleepless nights. With no set bedtime, the young members of the family never went to sleep before eleven. Rafael and his wife Alicia watched T.V. late into the night. On weekends, relatives and friends of the couple visited, and after a long evening of talking and drinking, they were forced to camp out in the tiny living room.

These were the nights when Elvira, unable to close her eyes, would dream of her home in Guatemala. The house there was small but she'd been happy and hadn't minded sharing a room with her two sisters. Elvira longed for those years before the guerillas became the terror not only of her village, but of the whole country. The political turmoil in Guatemala took away her family and her home. One dark night in December, 1980, when Elvira was fifteen, her parents and her brother Carlos were killed. The guerillas kidnapped her sisters Libia and Marta.

Elvira managed to escape the attack. Suddenly, she was an orphan and a homeless young woman on the dangerous streets of the capital. Elvira headed for the United States.

In preparation for my first meeting with Elvira, I read the report from her social worker. It said Elvira had been picked up from the streets by a policeman and charged with prostitution. He had seen her come out of a local bar in the company of a Latino man. They walked to the man's car where the officer found the two of them in a compromising position in the back seat of an old Chevy. When interviewed, the Mexican man accused Elvira of prostitution. He said he had given the woman a fifty-dollar bill for her services. The officer found the bill inside Elvira's purse.

Elvira arrived for her appointment with me on time. She dressed modestly in a black skirt and a gray blouse. Her shiny black hair was cut shoulder-length and she wore little make-up. As she sat on the couch across from me. I could tell by the slight twitch of her upper lip that she was nervous, which was not unusual given that she had been through the courts and many interviews by authorities, who had questioned all aspects of her life. She had also had to face the constant threat of being deported.

Noting her discomfort, I told her that I was not "one of them," that I had no association with the courts, the police department, or the social worker. I was a counselor and as such I was going to do my best to help her figure out her situation. Also, I took the opportunity to ask for her cooperation and honesty. Elvira nodded but did not say a word. She waited for me to continue.

"Elvira, I've read the report," I said. I thought to myself that the woman sitting across from me did not quite fit the profile in it, but I had learned from experience not to draw early conclusions. I waited a few seconds for Elvira to speak.

"Ms. Fernández, I know you're not going to believe me but I'm not a prostitute. Mario is someone I met a year ago. We went dancing a couple of times. That night he came to see me at the bar where I work as a waitress. You know, I don't have a green card. It's hard to find work without papers."

"I understand, but in the report..."

"Officer Galindo lies!" Elvira was visibly upset. "He has been after Chucho, the owner of the bar. He wants to close his business. He has some kind of personal vendetta. They come from the same town in Mexico and, according to Chucho, that officer was in love with his young sister. She rejected him and ran away with another guy. Since then, Galindo has been after Chucho. Now that he's a cop, he has power with the authorities in this town."

I wanted to believe Elvira's story. It was not unusual for people there to be harassed by the police. With almost no rights to protect them, a great deal of abuse occurred. Elvira's story was no different from many others I had heard. I checked my notes and took a sip of coffee. It was then I noticed the presence of the blue lady standing across from me. There she is, I thought. Now what? She floated towards me and touched my shoulder. I heard her say: "Let's get to work. This girl needs your help. Put that report down and pay attention to your gut feelings."

I wondered if Elvira could see the blue lady. "Don't bother, she can't see me," I heard the blue lady say. It was obvious she could read my thoughts, although I had doubts about whether my imagination was playing tricks on me. And I was not comfortable with the presence of this spirit in my office. It was like having a co-therapist in the room, except she was bossy.

"Listen, I'm here to help. Don't waste my time." The blue lady meant business. "I brought someone I'd like you to meet. His name is Fermin."

As soon as the blue lady said the name I saw a glow of light that gradually took the form of a ghostly male figure. He stood right next to Elvira, who sat unawares, with a somber expression in her eyes.

"My father would die of shame if he knew about this problem," Elvira said as if she knew of his presence in the room. "My father was a good and honest man, a farmer with strong values. Ms. Fernández, if he was alive, he would never approve of me working at the bar. He was proud of us girls and he wanted the best for us. When he died, my world crumbled. That night, when the guerilla men broke into our house, is a constant nightmare. They killed my mother first and then my father. I was in my room when I heard the gunfire and my sister Marta scream "asesinos!" I was so afraid, all I could think was, Elvira, run! I left the house through the back door and hid in the woods until it was safe for me to come out. On my return, I found my brother Carlos dead by the entrance door. He was shot five times in the chest. My two sisters were gone! I was so terrified. I couldn't bear the thought of facing my dead family. I must have been in shock because I turned around and left my home and my village."

"I'm Elvira's father," the ghostly figure said from his corner. "I am here to help my daughter."

For a moment I had the feeling I was crazy. What was going on? I was in some sort of twilight zone, a place in-between worlds, where humans and spirits were talking to me at once. I remembered the story of Oyá and of her great ferry going back and forth from the land of the dead and this world. Were these appearances the works of Oyá? I wondered about Elvira's sisters. Where were they?

Unaware of her father's presence, Elvira went on with how much she missed her parents, brother and sisters. She couldn't understand why she was left alive. Every day, she thought about going back to Guatemala to find those criminals. Elvira's face turned red with rage. She cursed the guerilla men. Finally, her words turned to a quiet moan. Fermin moved closer to his daughter and he embraced her in his ethereal arms. She must have felt it, because in a very instinctive way she brought her own arms around her chest. Like a little girl, Elvira rocked her body back and forth until she collapsed into the couch.

"Elvira, do you ever feel your father's presence near you?" I asked.

"Sometimes I hear his voice and feel his hands on my

shoulders. He talks to me and tells me he's fine and that my mother is there, too. My father comes in my dreams and he looks just the way he used to, so full of life. I reach out for his hand but he disappears and I wake up. I feel so alone in this world."

Elvira shared that since her parents and her older brother Carlos were killed, she had suffered from terrible nightmares. One night, a loud knock woke her up. At first, she thought it was one of the children, but they were asleep. She waited for another thud but instead she saw Libia, her older sister, sitting right next to her on the mat.

"I was certain she had escaped the guerillas. But like my father, she was gone in a split second. The next night I heard the same tap on the wall. This time both Libia and my younger sister Marta were on the floor across from Elvira's mat. But, oh God, when I looked at them, their faces and their bodies were covered with blood. It was horrible!"

Elvira rubbed her hands nervously. She opened her purse and handed me an old photograph. The three girls stood side by side, arms around each other. They were not very far apart in age, between ten and fourteen. What a tragedy! I thought to myself.

Soon after, I heard the voice of her father again. "My girls need help! Libia and Marta are dead. Those killers gang-raped my daughters. They tortured them with their knives. They cut pieces of their bodies while they laughed and joked."

"What kind of help?" I said aloud.

"What?" Elvira said with surprise.

"Never mind. I was talking to myself."

Across from me, the ghostly figure waited for my answer. I searched my mind for what I could do to help his daughters. The individual therapy session with Elvira had turned into a family gathering. And there I was, like a ferryboat, carrying messages from one world to another. I was aware of the uniqueness of my situation. This was a great opportunity to test the skills I had learned in Yucatan. But I wasn't sure I was ready for the challenge. I had doubts about my capacity to be an intermediary and Don Tomas wasn't here to help me.

"I am here," the blue lady said. "Remember that crystal Don Tomas inserted in your forehead? Well, I'm the essence of that crystal. I'm his gift to you. You can see what others can't. But don't let it go to your head. The ego, that famous word of Freud, can only get in your way and prevent you from doing your work. So be humble. This is just the beginning of our long journey together. Your doubts are not welcome!"

"You're hard on me," I said.

"Yes, don't test me. Go back to Elvira."

Elvira placed the picture back inside her purse. She spoke about her intuition. She was almost sure that her sisters had been killed by the guerillas, but she was confused by their nocturnal visits. She talked about how, on the night she was arrested by Officer Galindo, she had asked Mario, her old boyfriend, for some money so that she could consult a local psychic, a Mexican woman, who communicated with the dead.

"Did you see her?" I asked.

"No. There has not been a chance for me to do anything but go to courts and see social workers. You know they won't believe me if I tell them what the fifty dollars were for."

"Probably not."

Nor would they believe me about the presence of the blue lady and Fermin in my office. I could understand Elvira's fears. Our belief in this world of spirits was a cultural experience and a very private one. If I told the clinical director about my interaction with the dead, I'm sure she would listen with hidden judgment and suspicion.

Even though Elvira and I were both Hispanics, there were differences in the way we talked and related to the world. People from Guatemala speak slowly and softly as compared with Cubans who talk fast and loud. Elvira's energy was like a slow foxtrot and mine was more like a rumba. I became aware that in the course of our dialogue, I had moved into her rhythm, not consciously but intuitively. This made me think of the importance of this dynamic in therapy—there is a dance that flows from each one of us with distinctive movements and vibrations. Perhaps spirits inhabited a plane with its own frequency and it was up to us to figure a way to get across these dimensions.

"Ms. Fernández, you must tell Elvira I'm here." Fermin's voice brought me back.

I looked at Fermin and thought, why don't you tell her yourself?

"Elvira is in too much pain. She won't hear me. She gets scared. She needs to know that both of her sisters are dead."

"Ms. Fernández, are we through with our meeting? Can I go now?" Elvira asked.

"No, Elvira. Wait! Listen to what I'm going to say. It's going to sound eerie, but your father is here. He is standing next to you."

Elvira turned around. She looked confused.

"I know you can't see him. That's why he came to me for help. He has been here for a while now. He wants me to tell you that your two sisters are dead."

"How can I trust that you're telling me the truth?" Elvira stood up. She was upset.

"Please, sit down."

"Her nickname is Nanita," Fermin shouted from his corner.

"Nanita. Your father used to call you Nanita."

Elvira turned pale. Slowly she sat back and rested her face on the arm of the couch. Then Fermin wasted no time. "You must help us free our souls from this torment."

I searched my mind for what I could do. Of course, there was nothing in the hundreds of psychology books I had read. I turned to the blue lady—my only possible helper in this situation. She took her time to respond. But when she did, she was firm and spoke with authority. "Tell the young woman to go to the local priest. He is to perform a series of masses for the restless souls of her family. Nine masses to be exact. Tell Elvira to pray for their rest."

I repeated the message to Elvira, who lifted her head and

paid close attention. By the time I finished, the expression on her face had softened. I could tell she had been relieved of a heavy emotional burden.

"I love my papa. Would you tell him I love him and that I miss him?"

Her words turned to sobs. Across from me, Fermin cried silently as well. With his ethereal arms, he reached out to Elvira and embraced her in a blanket of bright blue and green light. I sat there feeling in my own heart the blessings of his love. What an amazing opportunity to be a witness to this healing that had changed, not only Elvira, but my own life as well! Once more, this experience was a confirmation of the existence of another world hidden behind the veil of death.

Without any warning, Fermin left the room. I reached over to Elvira and held her hand. She welcomed my gesture with a quiet understanding of the connection we now shared. What had just taken place in the safe environment of my office was nothing we could explain to the outside world. Yet we knew it had been real and powerful. We were not the same people we had been before the session.

For the next three months, Elvira returned to my office weekly. Fermin did not visit us again. Perhaps he was pleased by the fact that Elvira had done her job. The local Catholic priest conducted nine masses in honor of each member of the family. Elvira was feeling reassured by the absence of their nocturnal visits. The court had closed her case and she was now free to continue her life without constant interference by the authorities. With the help of a friend, Elvira found a job at a local food-processing factory. The new employment provided her with a salary stable enough for her to move out of Rafael's house into a two-bedroom apartment she shared with a woman friend.

During our last session, Marta and Libia showed up unexpectedly. The first sign of their presence was subtle—a flickering of two tiny golden lights across the room. A few minutes later, the glowing masses moved near Elvira's shoulders where they became attached to the magnetic field of her aura.

Finally, I could see the lights taking the form of two women. I recognized their faces from the picture Elvira showed me during our first meeting. Unlike what Elvira described, Marta and Libia did not appear to be in pain. The expression on their faces was peaceful.

Instinctively, Elvira closed her eyes. She appeared serene. From this meditative place, Elvira spoke to her sisters. She talked about the night of the massacre and about all the years when she had waited to hear from them. She told them all about her feelings of guilt for being alive. Elvira's voice sounded strong. There was no hesitation. As I listened, I was convinced she had finally come to terms with the death of her sisters. Now Elvira could get on with her life.

Across the room, the three sisters were embracing each other. They were younger. I felt grateful for the gift Elvira and her family had given me. There was hope for our existence on this planet. After all, we were not alone in our misery. Those we loved and who had died were there behind the thin and transparent veil that separated the two worlds. They were there to hold us and to carry us through the difficult times.

As I hugged Elvira good-bye, I thanked her for her presence in my life. Healing, I realized, is never a one-way process but a circle. Life does not end when our bodies cease to breathe but continues on in other dimensions unseen by the average eye. How naïve we are to believe that we are alone in the absence of people. We have many companions ready to help, but only if we are open to their unexpected and loving presence.

NINE

The Tin Man

R EADY FOR MY FIRST home visit of the day, I stopped
the engine of my 1991 Toyota Tercel in front of the modest
house of my client, whom I'll call Guillermo Palmero. He is
a Cuban immigrant, known by the nickname of Tin Man. A
Cuban exile myself, I was looking forward to this meeting with a
somewhat legendary patriarch.

Two palm trees grew at each side of the entrance gate, and a
tinajón, or clay pot, rested at the edge of the narrow brick walk.
I could smell the fragrance of the yellow and red roses as soon
as I walked in. Near the west corner of the porch was a tall
gardenia and next to it wild jasmine that curled around one of
the posts. Bright red bougainvillea nearly covered the entire wall
facing the street. Gladiolas, lilacs and daisies were abundant all
over the front yard, like the gardens I had seen in Cuba when I
was child.

An old woman, barely over five feet, introduced herself as
Antonia Palmero and greeted me at the door. Seventy or so, she
had a few wrinkles for her age and warm brown eyes.

"¿Tú eres la Doctora?" You are the doctor? Antonia said in
Spanish. Without waiting for an answer, she asked me to come
into the living room.

"Siéntate." She directed me to a beige leather sofa placed

119

against the white wall next to the front window. On top of the center table was a porcelain base with artificial flowers. Thin and translucent curtains hung from the windows. There were two large oil paintings of Cuban landscapes. One depicted the famous Morro, built by the Spanish conquistadores. The other was of the Cauto River running through vast green valleys. On a corner shelf, the statue of La Virgen De La Caridad Del Cobre stood proudly next to a bouquet of fresh yellow roses.

Large indoor arecas gave the area a warm and humid tropical feeling that took me back to my maternal grandparents' farm, to the hot afternoons when grown-ups waited for the air to cool off. Sitting outside on the porch, men and women would sip sweet and aromatic Cuban coffee from tiny porcelain cups. Only the men smoked cigars, but I do remember my Grandmother Patricia rolled her own tabacos and smoked them with great delight.

"My daughter Cristina was going to be here today, but she had to work. You know how it is when you're not your own boss," Antonia said. She sat on a smaller couch opposite me. "Cristi is very worried about her father. He's getting worse. He thinks aliens are visiting the house at night to steal the guavas from the tree in the backyard. Last night he didn't sleep. He spent the dark hours sitting by the back door waiting for them to show up. It's so sad."

"I'm sorry, Señora Palmero."

"Por Dios. What am I doing? I haven't offered you any coffee." Antonia got up from her seat.

"No, no, don't worry. I'd like to see Mr. Palmero."

"He is on the patio. Come with me."

I followed Antonia through the immaculate dining room and kitchen. The fresh smell of Pine Sol was still in the air, evidence of the hard work Antonia had done before my arrival. It reminded me of my own mother's obsession with cleaning. Then, as I stepped out the back door, I saw Mr. Palmero, comfortably sitting on a wood chair right next to the garage, a large brown cigar in the corner of his mouth. He wore a big cowboy hat, a long-sleeved blue shirt with his gray khaki pants and shiny leather boots. Oblivious to my presence, Mr. Palmero was engaged in some sort of conversation about banks stealing money from people.

Guillermo Palmero was well into his early seventies. He was thin with a healthy mane of white-silver hair. Occasionally, he would spit out a ball of tobacco, then clean the saliva trapped in his elegant and well-trimmed mustache with a soiled handkerchief he had pulled from the back pocket of his pants.

"Guillermo, Guillermo, there's someone here to see you."

"Good morning, Señor Palmero," I said and walked towards him with my hand extended. He ignored my cordial gesture. A ball of tobacco flew out of his mouth and almost hit my leg.

"Por Dios, Guillermo, can you be more respectful?" Antonia yelled.

Guillermo pulled the big cigar from his mouth and rolled it between his fingers while he frowned at me.

"You must be one of those *viejas* [women] from the bank." He pointed towards me with his cigar.

"No, no, Señor Palmero. I work for a family clinic. The Department of Social Services asked me to visit you. I'm here to see how you're doing. A complaint has been filed against you for harassing a gentleman in front of the grocery store last Friday." I said this in a rush, as if anticipating the ejection of another brown missile. Guillermo stayed on guard. He held the cigar in his hand, and he looked directly into my eyes.

"A complaint? I should knock out his teeth. He's a Communist! He's one of Castro's spies. Don't you people know that? They're everywhere in this country." Guillermo shifted his position on the chair so that he could cross his legs. "Bring me some coffee, Antonia."

Antonia disappeared inside the house. I took the opportunity to search through the police report. On Page 2 were notes of a detailed declaration from Rosa Miramar, the owner of the grocery store. When questioned by the attending officer, she referred to Guillermo as the "Tin Man." Rosa said she had known Guillermo for many years and described him as a hard-working man, honest and jovial, who in the last year or so appeared to be losing his mind. According to her, the old man visited her store every day, he teased her about her big derrière and he drank two or three Cuban coffees before leaving.

"Do you know Rosa Miramar?" I asked him.

"Of course I know Rosita. She is a good woman, unlike her lazy drunk husband. He doesn't do shit, except for chasing the young pollas who come to the store. He is a welferista with no cojones. But, Rosa! I love Rosa. You should see her big and round fondillo. Carajo, I dream of her every night. If only I was younger, but you know...I'm an old man now with no looks and no money."

At first, I couldn't help feeling offended by Guillermo's language. But then, I reminded myself how most Cubans are direct and plain-spoken.

"She calls you 'Tin Man.'"

"She's not the only one," he responded with a somber look. "You know about the banks? Well...shit, they're doing what Castro did in Cuba."

"Why do they call you Tin Man?" I tried to steer Guillermo away from his paranoid thoughts.

"Tin Man. The Tin Man. I became the Tin Man when I came to this country. It's a long story...but those banks, I went to talk to the president of my bank yesterday. He's that tall güero with a moon-face full of freckles. I believe he has connections with Castro."

I tried one more time to get him to focus. "Maybe he does, but I'm more interested in hearing about how you got the name of Tin Man. Can you please tell me about it?"

"Why do you want to know? Who cares who Tin Man is! He's part of another time. He had dreams. I was forty-five years old when I arrived in this country. Tin Man wanted to become rich, wealthy as he was in Cuba before that cabrón took everything away from us, just like the banks."

Antonia returned from the kitchen with a tray and two tiny

porcelain cups filled with steaming and aromatic Cuban coffee. Having grown up in a Cuban family, I knew not to reject the friendly gesture. Even though Cuban coffee was too sweet for my taste, I gulped it down while Guillermo sipped his slowly. He paused and turned his gaze to the kitchen entrance.

"That woman has güevos." He meant Antonia had balls. "She's candela! She's the one who keeps this household running. You know? She cooks three meals everyday. Not that kind of frozen shit, but real food. No one can make black beans as tasty as she does." He shook his head. "Mi vieja is getting old." There was a tinge of sadness in his tone.

"She keeps the house spotless," I said and Guillermo did not respond. "So, Tin Man was a dreamer," I tried to bring him back.

"Here you go again! Why in the hell do you want to know about that? Tin Man is gone. He's gone. Se lo llevó la corriente. Do you hear me? He was drawn in the river of life. Are you a CIA agent? Because if you are one of those...you're knocking at the wrong door. Tin Man was an honest guy with balls, big cojones. He came to this country without a penny. His pockets were empty...but, chica, he would die of hunger before taking any food stamps. He hated those marielitos! They're a bunch of vagos! I told Rosita I'll be more than happy to kick them out of her store. Those mugrosos waste the day *comiendo mierda* [eating shit]. They never worked in Cuba and they don't want to work in this country, either. Why don't you go to Rosita's store and put those marielitos to work?"

Guillermo's face had turned red. His light honey-colored eyes were almost ready to pop out of their sockets. He stood up to search for something inside his pants pockets. After finding what he was looking for, he disappeared into the back of his garage. I heard what sounded like the door of a refrigerator open, then close. Tin Man came back with a fresh cigar in his mouth and a yellow lighter in his hand. As he lit his tabaco, I noticed how large and strong his hands were. I admired the net of veins, like engorged rivers. The callus, scratches and cuts were signs of his hard work. Dark dirt colored the bed beneath his fingernails.

"I might as well tell you all about Tin Man. These days nobody seems to remember him. Not even my children. They're too busy with their lives." He looked at me, searching for a reaction. For the first time since my arrival, Tin Man had dropped his defenses to make eye contact with me. Deep from within the darkness of the old man's opaque irises veiled by cataracts, I saw tiny sparks of his fierce but kind spirit.

"When I came to this country in 1969," he said, "I had all kinds of dreams for the future. I was so lucky to be free from Castro. You know that *hijo de puta* [son of a bitch] stole my life, just like those banks are trying to take my money, my blood. He's like those aliens, because there are aliens from a planet called Frion. They come at night and steal the guavas from that tree." Tin Man pointed in the direction of a tall guava tree in the northwest corner of the backyard. "I see those aliens every night. Chica, you should see them. They have ugly heads that look like watermelons. Huh! They have no hair and their eyes are like those of the bullfrogs I used to catch when I was a child. But chica, the strange thing is that these aliens have long, bushy black beards like those of the Cuban revolutionaries."

"Tell me about your dreams," I interrupted.

"Well, when I first arrived in this city, I got a job in this factory where I worked on a line. Oh man, it was hell. Hey, how can I tell you about this? You haven't even told me your name. You might be one of those aliens in disguise. They said those aliens could do that. You know? They can make themselves look like people. I heard it on the news the other day.

"My name is Flor Fernández."

"Fernández? Are you from the Fernández family who lived in Camagüey?" Tin Man asked with a smile, as if happy to make a connection with someone familiar from his past.

Cubans love to make those connections. Usually, the first question asked when you meet someone is, where in Cuba are you from? And if by any chance you happen to be from a known place or family, you are immediately taken in as a friend and invited to dinner. Unfortunately, that was not the case in this situation. My relatives were from a different province.

"I don't know the Fernández family of Camagüey."

"Well, you look like them. Fita Fernández, who could be your aunt, was like a sister to me. We went to the town dances together until she married Eufemio Cardona. He was a jealous man. He ended up at the working camps with me before we left Cuba. Poor infeliz, he spent his days crying and thinking he was going to die from working so hard."

It was fruitless to try to convince Tin Man that he was confused, but I knew about the working camps. My father had been in one for more than two years while waiting for permission for us to leave Cuba. The men there were called *gusanos* or worms, for the sole reason that they wanted to be free again from Castro's dictatorship. They were subjected to forced labor under inhumane conditions. The water they drank was often contaminated with fecal matter. The food was rotten and rationed to a few spoonfuls of rice and a small cup of bean soup. I was lost in my own thoughts, when I felt the tap of Tin Man's finger on my right shoulder.

"Here, have a cigar. As a good Fernández you would appreciate the taste of my Dominican tabacos." And before I had a chance to react, Tin Man pushed one of his big cigars into my mouth.

"I...don't smoke cigars," I mumbled.

"Carajo, chica, what's the matter with you? Are you like those gringos? They whine about the dangers of eating meat, sugar, rum and...to these people everything is bad for your health. They won't even let you smoke in their houses. Here in my house there are no such rules. To me that's a whole bunch of mierda! Every one of us comes to this world with a date to die. You die when that day comes, no earlier and no later." Without giving me time to respond, Guillermo pulled out his yellow lighter and lit the cigar that hung from my mouth. Not wanting to offend Tin Man, I sucked and puffed smoke from the cigar. A few seconds later, my whole body shook with intense coughing. Once when I was eight years old, I smoked a cigar I had stolen from my father. I became so sick that I couldn't hold my head straight for a few hours. Now my gut twisted with nausea as it had many years ago.

Tin Man grabbed the cigar from my mouth and threw it away. Without saying a word, he disappeared inside the garage and came back with a chair for me. "Here, sit down. You look like life has been sucked out of your body." Tin Man had a twinkle in his eyes.

Having been trained as a therapist, I tried not to overanalyze the situation, but I was certain that his behavior had not been an innocent act. He was letting me know this was his territory and that my presence was invasive and provocative. Tin Man was not the type to follow rules. He had his own ideas about what makes the world move.

"I'm sorry, Mr. Palmero." I sat on the chair, angry and embarrassed over my behavior. Enough of Tin Man, I thought to myself, and I opened the manila folder. I glanced over the information just to buy time.

"Señor Palmero, let's talk about the incident at the store."

"Well, that factory I was telling you about was a place from hell," Tin Man said without any regard for my words. "For a long time after I stopped working there, I had nightmares about this fast line of plastic chairs coming down at me, like an avalanche of rocks falling from the top of a mountain. I worked there for a couple of weeks. I tell you, I never in my life dreamt of working in a chair factory. I hated every minute of the day, from the moment I punched my time card in, till that second when the clock marked the hour to go home." Tin Man looked down at his half-burned cigar. The horizontal wrinkles on his forehead deepened and curved downward. I wondered how much longer he was going to stay with the story.

"One night I was awakened from my nightmares and I saw a shadow in the bedroom. I pinched my arm just to make sure I was awake. A tall figure of an old man was walking towards me.

He sat by the foot of my bed. I didn't know what to think about this man. All I knew, he was not of this world, because when I looked at his body, he was sort of transparent, and there was a glow of light around him. An angel, I thought to myself, but... No! Coño, angels don't wear cowboy hats and boots, and this guy was dressed like a rodeo rider. It scared me a bit. I said ay mámá. What is this? I was ready to call Antonia who slept next to me, when the fantasma grabbed my feet and asked me to stay quiet."

"'Hey, don't say a word, you chicken shit, I ain't going to hurt you.'

"His words sounded as real as I'm talking to you now. 'What do you want?' I said. I was shaking inside.

"'Listen, you Cuban cowboy,' he said. I was surprised this ghost knew that about me. 'If you don't quit your job in that plastic melting factory, you'll be dead soon. Dead as a poisoned rat.' And then, coño, the ghost pulled the big toe of my right foot. 'Tomorrow, we're going to do some work on getting you an old truck.'

"'An old truck for what?' I said.

"'Hey you, boy, there is gold, gold on the streets of L.A. You just got to look around and find it. I'm an old miner of the west. I know every square inch of ground in this town. There is copper, tin, aluminum, brass...You name it and it's there. People throw away the precious metals we had to work so hard to get out of the mines when I was a young man. Now, you don't have to do any digging. It's just there, lying on the sides of the street, freeways, roads, but they call it junk. So junk is our gold. I can fill your pockets with money from recycled junk.'"

Tin Man spoke to me, "You know, chica, I didn't know what to believe. The old man, or ghost, never told me his name or where he came from. The next morning when I woke up, I thought I had been dreaming, but when I sat on the side of my bed to put my shoes on, I saw prints of red dirt on the beige carpet of the bedroom. I followed these tracks all the way to the kitchen, and then, I lost them! You know there is no red dirt in this city. Not the kind of bright red soil I've seen in the old western movies, canyon dirt."

For the first time, I saw the face of Tin Man brighten up. He even looked younger. There was a gleam coming from the depth of his eyes. He didn't seem to be lost in a world of delusions. His mind was coherent and clear as that of a young man. Tin Man got up from his chair and went inside the kitchen. I wondered what he was doing. A few minutes later, he returned with two tiny cups of coffee.

"Here, try this. Antonia is not the best coffee maker. Her coffee is too bitter."

Too bitter, I thought to myself, as I remembered the sweetness of Antonia's coffee. I prepared for the shot of molasses Tin Man handed me, and I gulped it down, trying not to taste the syrup-like fluid inside the tiny porcelain cup. It reminded me of my mother's, the strong and sweet pots of coffee she left for me on top of the stove, during those nights I had to study for finals when I was an undergraduate student at the University.

"That day," Tin Man continued with the story, "I didn't go back to the chair factory. Instead, I went and I got myself an old beat-up 1960 Chevy truck that I fixed with the help of my good friend Mario. Antonia spent the day screaming at me and saying I was crazy for not going back and for spending the rent money on a piece of 'shit'. You know, chica, Antonia has always been a sour orange. She thinks the worst, and that's why she never learned how to drive a car. Because the minute she sat in front of the wheel her mind ran wild with all kinds of catastrophes. So basically I told her to leave it alone, and when she didn't, I got in the truck and went to the streets.

"I wasn't sure what to do next, and for a moment I felt like Antonia in front of the wheel. What if this deal didn't work and we didn't have money to pay the rent and buy food at the end of the month? I had small children with big mouths at home. I stopped the truck mid-road, and I said to myself, you got to have cojones and do this, or else you'll die like that ghost said. I called on my favorite saint, mi Santa Barbara. You know in santería, she is Changó, the orisha of thunder and fire. When I was a boy, mami, who was somewhat a santera, told me that any time I was in trouble to call Changó for help, and then to make sure to offer her a red apple. So I said, Santa Barbara, it is you and me now finding this gold that old cowboy ghost talked about last night. So here we go, and I stepped my foot hard on the gas, and the old truck responded like the fast mare named Luz I had when I was twenty-one. We were into something big, because I felt the fire burning inside. Luz means light and I decided to name my truck Luz, too. Qué mierda, I figured this truck was my horse in this modern city."

For a moment, I imagined Tin Man riding his old truck on the busy streets of Los Angeles. With his big cigar in the corner of his mouth, he searched for trashed treasures at the turn of every curb: aluminum and tin cans, abandoned broken refrigerators, washing machines, dryers, and stoves. The piles of unwanted garbage became the source of Tin Man's vision to change his destiny from factory worker to self-employed businessman.

"The ghost cowboy visited me again one night, and he gave me a lesson on how to separate all the metals I found trapped inside the rusted appliances. Soon, the backyard of the house was covered with piles of precious metals. Once a week, I loaded Luz with pounds and pounds of tin, brass, aluminum, iron, copper, and we went off to the junkyard. Sure enough, that ghost was right. Money was flowing into my pockets as if I had magnets sewn into the cloth. Antonia couldn't believe what was happening. After my second trip, I handed her five clean hundred-dollar bills and she panicked. 'Are you selling drugs or what?' she accused me. It took her a while to realize that business of recycling was a gold mine."

Tin Man became pensive. He seemed lost in the glory of his past, in the subterranean tunnels of a world that now was as distant as his beloved island of Cuba. Tin Man took his cowboy hat off and placed it on his lap. Like a trophy of war, he held on to it with an air of pride and dignity.

"That's the story of Tin Man," he said. Suddenly, he looked

older and more tired. There was a shadow of sadness on his face.

"You know chica, the aliens who steal the guavas from my tree at night are not so bad after all. They are just curious about us. But Castro is a sonovabitch! He stole my life. His revolution was a sham to fill his pockets with all our money, just like the banks in this country. Those rateros are sucking away what is left of my light, of my blood. Tin Man is history! I'm an old man no one respects. Even Rosita from the grocery store believes I'm just a crazy man. She won't admit it but I can tell what she's thinking inside her pretty head, every time I walk into her place."

Tin Man leaned forward to grab a worn-out, black leather wallet from the back pocket of his pants. He took his time searching through pieces of wrinkled paper till he found what he was looking for.

"Here, Mija. You take a look at this picture." I was moved by Tin Man's affectionate tone of voice. He talked to me now as if I were one of his children. To this old patriarch, I was just a human being with an empathetic ear. He did not care about my professional background or the ethical rules of my job. To him I was Flor Fernández, his new friend. I could tell he was saddened by all the losses he had experienced in his life. More than that, Tin Man was deeply hurt by his invisibility in a world that saw him as a crazy old man.

"Hey, muchacha, is that cigar still bothering you?" he asked.

"Yeah, a little bit, nothing to worry about."

The man in the photograph was handsome, with black hair and light brown eyes. Thick eyebrows, an elegant and fine mustache that adorned the tan skin of his face, and a smile disclosing a perfect line of teeth. I held the small photo in my hand, while I lifted my head to look at Tin Man. I felt compassion and sadness for him. Time had shown little mercy. The winds of change had swept away his charms with the force of a strong hurricane. Tin Man was himself, like a trashed appliance, abandoned on some street corner, his metal guts corroding under the elements. Poor man, I thought to myself, his spirit buried under the debris of his departure from Cuba has been forgotten in exile. Over the years it had rusted like a piece of iron.

"How old were you here?" I asked.

"Twenty-eight. I've kept this picture in my wallet since I left Cuba. Thirty years in exile feels like a kick in your balls. Every morning before I went to work I would look at it and remind myself of who I was. This guy in the picture was full of hopes and dreams. In Cuba, he was a well-respected businessman. Just to show you, if you stop at any little town, and say you knew Guillermo Palmero, people would treat you as a friend, without any question."

Tin Man put the picture away and became quiet, as if absorbed in memories of a distant time when life smiled at him and promises were like the wild flowers that grew in the Cuban sabanas. I thought of my father, like Guillermo Palmero and like many other Cubans, who had left their native island in search of freedom and better fortune. Suddenly they found themselves amid the melting pot of a foreign land. The fight for dollars took them to unknown territories of unfulfilled goals. They became nameless and faceless.

"That's how well known I was in Cuba," Tin Man said. "I could go from one end of the island to the other. Friends waved at me from every corner of the town." Tin Man rolled his cigar in his fingers. He was lost in some happy memories. He scratched his right eyebrow and said, "Don't think of me as a vain old man but...women followed me all over. You know the Tropicana, the famous nightclub in Havana? Well, I had no problem getting two or three beautiful rumberas to sit at my table. My friend Paco used to say, 'Guillermo Chico, qué brujería les echaste.' Paco was convinced I was into witchcraft."

Tin Man's voice changed into a somber tone. "Here, I'm nobody. I have no real friends. My children laugh at me when I tell them not to get any credit cards. They say, 'You know nothing about this world, Papi. You're living as if you were still in Cuba.' And you know, maybe I am, but I know my business,

and banks are not going to take away a penny from my pockets
with their high interest and tricks of 'you buy today and pay
tomorrow.'"

I asked how many children he had.

"Three, all grown and gone. Cristina, my oldest, lives nearby.
She is the one with a better head on her shoulders. She went
to the university and got some kind of degree in...I don't know
what, but she makes good money. Javier is the middle one and
he is a *cabeza loca* [scatterbrains]. He moves around from job to
job and never has a peseta in his pockets. Arturo is the youngest
and he's been in school forever. He changes his career every time
he goes to the bathroom. I think he's a Communist and works
underground for Castro. He has been in Cuba twice, not to visit
the family as other Cubans do, but to go to some conferences,
and you know what that means. He is into all that mierda of
cutting off the embargo and helping the Cuban economy."

Tin Man was no different from all the Cubans of his
generation. They smell betrayal in the air. Anyone having a
slight association with the Cuba of today is considered a traitor.
His paranoia ran thick in his veins, an infectious illness that
propagated like fire in a forest. Castro was a demon not to be
trusted. After all, in 1959, he had promised a revolution that was
going to change the country for the better. It was supposed to
eradicate the poverty from a decaying economy and the political
corruption that Batista and those before him had created. But
instead, Castro ended up selling their beloved island to the
Russians.

Like many veterans of war, Tin Man had never recovered
from Castro's revolution or from the emotional wounds he had
received in exile, unable to acculturate into the mainstream of
society. Perhaps his obsession with extra-terrestrials had its
roots in the fact that he felt an alien himself. Tin Man was a
lonely warrior who stood alone, amid piles of broken dreams.
He had spent most of his life banging on and cleaning metals.
Somewhere in his journey, Tin Man began to build his own
spaceship, a vessel he would later use to escape the torment of

his wounded soul. He became an alien to most people he met, his family and even to himself.

"I'm a ghost nobody wants to look at," Tin Man said, as if he had read my thoughts. "The other day, Antonia, mi vieja, told me I'm not the same man she knew, 'You're a stranger to me and to your children. Who are you? You're not the Guillermo I used to love. Chico, something happened to your brain. You're as alien to me as those aliens you talk to. Guillermo, the real you is probably rotting underneath a big pile of tin cans.'"

Tin Man lowered his face and avoided my gaze. He looked defeated. Though paranoid ideas flitted in and out of his consciousness, he had a remarkable ability to stay within his dark and confusing reality: that of a man stripped of his identity. Now at the end of his life, he was faced with a long maze of doubt and failure. In spite of his success in the metal recycling business and his acquisition of a couple of pieces of real estate, Tin Man never reached his goal of recovering the man he had left behind in Cuba.

I looked at my watch. I was running late for my next appointment. I felt torn. Tin Man had captivated me with his mannerisms and stories. It was as if he had the magic of a Cuban kind of manhood I had experienced in my own father, though not enough to understand it. Tin Man knew life in a way I couldn't relate to. Being away from my beloved Cuba for so many years had created a veil over the vivid images of my childhood. My own insatiable need for knowledge and for becoming part of the American culture had re-cast my identity—neither Cuban, nor American. I was both and I was neither. But Guillermo Palmero was a criollo man. He was pure in his practical and elemental connection to life and to the old ways of his culture.

"Mr. Palmero, I'd like to come back," I almost pleaded.

Tin Man looked at me from head to toe. I didn't feel uncomfortable. For a few seconds he didn't say a word. Then, he reached out with his left arm, and he placed his hand on my right shoulder. I shrank a bit at the warm display of affection and friendship.

"Chica, you can come and visit anytime. You don't have to call before, like the gringos do. You're welcome at my home anytime."

"Thanks," I said and went to shake Tin Man's hand but the old man stood up quickly. Instead, he hugged me with a strong and brief embrace. I was taken by surprise. Without any time for me to say a word, Tin Man walked away, towards the guava tree. He was back to his conversation with the aliens and thieves.

"You guys from Frion better stay away from my tree," he said. He turned and waved at me. "You come back soon. I'll show you a few tricks about how to roll a cigar."

I thought about Tin Man's words: "a few tricks about how to roll a cigar." What made Tin Man think I would be interested in such thing? After a few steps, I remembered the cigar factory in my Cuban neighborhood. In the rainy afternoons of the summers, we kids of the barrio sat by huge piles of cured leaves of tobacco and listened to stories read by Eduardo, the house reader. A great storyteller, he entertained the workers with his readings from novels. It was such a delightful experience to hear the characters come alive in his vibrant voice.

Even after the revolution, when good literature strangely disappeared from the bookshelves of the town's library, the tradition was kept. Tin Man was part of that romantic generation of tabaqueros, inspired by the romantic lyrics of Cuban writers. A Cuban cigar was a piece of art, with the flavors of sweet sugarcane juice and the sweat from the hands of many men and women, who like Tin Man, carried in their souls the essence of the Cuban soil and its people.

My experience with Tin Man brought me in touch with the alien within. A part of my own identity was lost in time and space. Like the aliens who stole guavas from his tree, I was a robber myself, not of guavas, but of Cuban dreams that with their sweetness would nurture the forgotten roots, the connections to my native land, to the spirit of my people. I was as much an alien as Tin Man was. We both shared the longing to belong and the grief of our losses.

TEN

Power Animals

MY EXPERIENCES in the Yucatan broadened the spectrum of possibilities for me, personally, and professionally, in my work as a therapist. Don Tomas had introduced me to the Tonals, the nature spirits that live in the trees, the lakes, the rocks, the mountains, the animals. As he'd explained to me, each Tonal has its own power, its own dance, music and songs.

They are wise teachers and guides, and as humans, we are responsible for maintaining a connection to these nature spirits. Without a constant exchange of knowledge between them and us, the growth and evolution of our planet are hindered. We become alienated from nature and from each other.

The curandero emphasized the present lack of respect for nature as reflected in the pollution of the air we breathe, the water we drink, the oceans, and the extinction of old forests. Being out of touch with Tonals had turned us into destructive and insatiable consumers. Don Tomas said: "We are lonely and sad people devoid of spirit." Then, he looked at me and added, "It is time for you to dance your power animal. Jaguar has waited for you too long. She has walked on this earth with you from the very first breath you took. Don't make her wait. She is your Tonal and you must grow closer to her spirit and to her wisdom."

I was told how, at the second we're born, there is a power animal that is born with each of us. This animal represents the powers, attributes, and knowledge that we bring with us. In the process of living our lives, we meet many other Tonals that come to assist us with the work we were sent to do in this world.

During my first trip to the Yucatan I had the opportunity to work with Jaguar as my main Tonal, but when I returned to the United States, I felt removed from the essence of the jungle and its creatures. Faced with the concrete landscape of Los Angeles, I was at a loss how to implement the knowledge I had acquired under my mentor. Although I kept my own personal connection to Jaguar, I was anxious to share the many gifts I'd received with the rest of the world.

My first contact with Jaguar as a helper in the context of my work happened unexpectedly. I was on the witness stand in one of the rooms of the Los Angeles Court House when Jaguar leaped into my consciousness. It happened at a moment when I was being attacked by the opposing counsel—a person with no professional integrity. As I recall, the attorney was a middle-aged man with dark hair, a large mustache and piercing blue eyes, and he was right in my face. Even though I had complained about his proximity and the judge has cautioned him to keep his distance from me, the aggressive man persisted.

I could not risk being intimidated. The safety of the eight-year-old boy who sat across from me depended on how well I presented the evidence of his sexual abuse. This child, since the age of four, had been repeatedly molested by his maternal uncle. Arturo, as I will call him, was removed from his home and placed under the care of foster parents. The mother had refused to get her brother to leave the home. She was in denial of the sexual assault. Even when presented with medical evidence of severe scars in Arturo's rectum, she had refused to accept the reality. Now she was there to request the return of her son. With the uncle still living in the house, there was no doubt in my mind that Arturo was at risk of being re-molested. Even though the uncle had attended therapy for the past six months, he had never admitted to the charges.

Once more, I was cornered by the counsel. I moved back in my chair. Standing in front of me, Mr. Rubin, as I will call him, rested both of his arms on the wood railing of the witness stand. He leaned towards me. He was so close I could smell the stink of chewing tobacco on his breath. I glanced at the drawings I had gathered from my sessions with Arturo, clear indication of the persistent assault the young boy had suffered from his uncle. I handed the drawings to the judge.

Mr. Rubin backed away from the stand and returned to his desk while the judge examined the drawings. As I observed him from the corner of my eye, the counsel was busy making faces at me. I laughed. I had never encountered anyone like him. Dirty tricks and intimidation were his arsenal for victory. The judge concluded his examination and asked the court clerk to record the drawings as evidence in the case. Mr. Rubin fired away with his next strategy, that of destroying my credentials, with the implication that my educational training was questionable, since I had attended a university not accredited by the APA. He proceeded to attack the integrity of the drawings by pointing to the possibility that I had misled Arturo and implanted such images in his mind.

At this point, I realized that with no witnesses or recordings of my sessions with Arturo, we were losing the case. Arturo's attorney was young and inexperienced. The case had been handed to him five minutes before his court appearance. With so little time to examine the evidence, "Mr. Corral" was not prepared to help Arturo.

I looked across the courtroom to where Arturo's uncle sat on the bench. He looked relaxed and remorseless. For a brief second, my eyes met his and I couldn't help feeling angry. Right next to him sat Arturo's mother. She looked down at some papers she pretended to read. Across from his mother and uncle, on a separate bench, Arturo sat next to his foster parents. In a protective gesture, the foster father had his arm around Arturo's shoulders.

I knew best not to allow my emotions to contaminate my professional perspective, but how could I not? Arturo had shared details of the abuse: how his uncle waited for Arturo's mother to leave the house every night; the minute she left for work, he abused Arturo. It was inexplicable to me why this mother did not pay attention to her son's cries for help, to his irritated and bleeding rectum. Arturo's teacher was the one to notice his discomfort in the classroom. As Mrs. Quintero told the authorities, Arturo couldn't sit still in his chair and when she asked what was wrong, the boy complained of pain in his bottom. She wasted no time and the school nurse confirmed her suspicion.

Mr. Rubin continued his attack. Now he was on to the subject of my professional training and whether I was really an expert on the matter. I knew I needed to buy some time so that I could get together with Arturo's attorney and strategize. I thought of Don Tomas's words: "You are Jaguar. Feel your strong paws on the earth." Could this nature medicine work? Could I trust my Tonal to help me in this situation? I had nothing to lose.

I took a deep breath and I concentrated on the image of the strong and wild cat I had met in the Yucatan. At first, it was difficult to stay focused with all the noises in the room. I tried harder. I remembered the light brown eyes of the creature. Spark of fire. My body warmed up and I could feel heat rising from the tip of my spine all the way to the top of my head. Gradually, I saw myself transformed into the black Jaguar. The instinctual nature of the animal surfaced with a palpable sense of survival in the foreign environment of the courtroom. Suddenly, my sense of smell was bombarded with the stench of human sweat and offensive perfume. Fear was in the air like an impenetrable curtain of fog. As Jaguar, I could sniff and feel the emotions of each individual around me.

My jaguar vision allowed me to see the nervous twitch on the face of Mr. Rubin. Underneath his bravado mask was a restless, insecure and fearful little man. I laughed inside. Mr. Rubin, I thought to myself, you're nothing but a greedy pig. With this thought, I saw myself leap into the air. I was going for his throat! For a few seconds, I experienced everything in the courtroom as frozen in time, except for the fast motion of the giant cat as it struck Mr. Rubin's throat. There was no visible sign of the attack. For all those in court, unaware of my experience, the flow of events never altered.

Oblivious to the attack, Mr. Rubin approached the judge. He stood there a few feet away from me. With his right hand, he reached over and fixed his tie and stretched his neck. This was some sort of power dance, I read in his gesture. I waited, and then, the unexpected happened. Mr. Rubin went to address the judge, but as he opened his mouth, not a single word came out. Confused, he tried again. This time, a raspy and almost inaudible voice was heard. Mr. Rubin cleared his throat unsuccessfully. A sudden case of laryngitis had claimed his vocal cords.

I cannot say that I was happy over Mr. Rubin's episode of laryngitis, but I was relieved when the judge postponed the trial. For the next few days, I prayed for Mr. Rubin's recovery and I worked with Mr. Corral in the preparation of Arturo's defense. We did go back to court and Arturo was ordered to remain in the foster home. The uncle was convicted and sentenced to two years in jail. The mother was mandated to continue in therapy for another year.

A year after the incident with the Jaguar in the courtroom, I was invited to participate as a presenter at a women's camp. The opportunity to be out in nature and to teach about power animals was exactly what I had been waiting for. The atmosphere of the camp was one of trust and receptivity. The women who signed up for the workshop were ready to journey.

We began the day with a brief introduction to the Tonals. I did not want to intellectualize the process. Rather, I wanted these women to dive right into the realm of the nature archetypes, with the help of trance and dance. The group of at least fifteen members had brought their own musical instruments, mostly drums, rattles and flutes. As I stood in front of them, I noticed the pristine beauty of the landscape that surrounded us—tall pine trees and cedars around a clear lake. I was appreciative of the richness of the land and the presence of the nature spirits around us.

The women stood in a circle. Some of them had their eyes closed. Other looked around and into the trees with anticipation. The sound of my drum was soft, like the heartbeat of Mother Earth. With a simple prayer, I invoked the powers of the land to be with us.

"Here we are, Mother Earth. Please open your arms to us. Let us move with the rhythm of your songs. Let us dance from our hearts." I asked the group to follow the beat of my drum. "Follow your breath and be aware of your own body. Let your body move with the elements of air, earth, fire, and water. As you do so, invite your Tonal to come and join you in this dance."

Slowly, the women were moving and dancing. It was not long before their power animals claimed their place in the circle. Some women were opening their arms and flying. They were eagles and hawks, ravens and crows. Others were slithering on the ground emitting the hissing sounds of snakes. One woman had turned into a bear. Another was a monkey, and not too far, swimming in the imaginary waters, were dolphins and whales. There were a deer and a mountain lion. The magic was working! The group of humans was now a gathering of Tonals.

The drumming and dancing went on for about an hour and by the end, all inhibitions had melted away. The women had fully claimed their bodies. Their sensuous and earthy movements and the strength of their sounds were indicative of their vital connection with their power animals. They had transformed into their Tonals!

During the afternoon, I sent the women out into the woods. They were to go and deepen their relationship with their Tonals as well as gain some understanding of the "medicine" or the power of their own animal. They were to come back to the group with their bodies painted and with a gift or message they could offer others in the form of a dance, a poem, a song, or a story.

I sat on a log while the women were out into the woods. Five minutes after they had left, I was approached by one of the members. I could tell she had been crying. She said to me, "I can't do this. The whole process brought out for me a lot of painful dynamics with the church. I'm a nun." I was not surprised. I thought about what to say.

"Were you able to connect with your power animal?" I asked.

"Oh, yes, I did, I was visited by a beautiful deer with large antlers. That's the problem. You see, intellectually I can envision that deer, but when it comes to my body I immediately lose the connection. I have spent too many years in denial of my physical being, of my body's reactions and feelings. The church taught me well to repress all that is sensuous and pleasurable. Fifteen years at the convent have molded me into a disembodied creature."

"Well, what would you like to do?" I asked.

"I'm afraid of this process," she said and looked down to her shoeless feet. "It helps not to wear shoes. I haven't done this since I was a child. I cannot even tell you how good it feels to walk like this on the forest. The soles of my feet have been hungry for the warmth of the Earth and the gentle caress of the grass."

"It must be your deer nature coming back to life," I said. I felt compassion for the woman, whose name I'll keep confidential. We'll call her "Deer Woman."

"If I continue in this journey, I might not be able to go back to the convent and that is frightening to me because that life is all I know."

"That's certainly a risk and only you can decide on what the call is."

Deer Woman appeared confused. So many years in the convent had taught her how to follow directions but not how to make her own decisions. Now she stood face to face with the challenge of whether to trust her inner knowing or to walk away. I could tell she had come to me for an answer, but I understood that part of her was to open the door to her intuition, to her deer medicine.

"I know I must go back to the forest and search for my deer," she said.

"Then you must go and only return when you're ready. Come back when you can dance deer for the tribe."

Deer Woman turned around and walked away into the forest. She was a small woman, in her fifties. I couldn't help wonder what her life had been like inside the convent and about the many years of indoctrination and daily prayers to a Father God. Mother Nature with her Goddess face was a different story. Her journey was one that required from us full intercourse with her earthy body.

I went back and sat on my log, but not for long. A few minutes after Deer Woman had left, another woman showed up for help. She complained of not feeling comfortable with the Tonal she had met. She wanted to know if it was okay to change power animals. Her expression reminded me of that of a child who was unhappy with a new toy. I almost laughed but I held back. I realized we live in a world where we are trained to discard things or people without any questions. We had mountains of trash in the fields.

"What Tonal came to you?" I asked.

"A frog! A little green frog! I don't like frogs!"

"Well, what's wrong with frogs?"

"I just don't think frogs are powerful. I wanted my Tonal to be an eagle or a lion or even a hawk."

I looked at Frog Woman with disbelief, but I was aware of how in our world power is defined in patriarchal terms. Of course, she would want to have an eagle instead of her small and what might appear to be a vulnerable and less powerful creature. After all, for eons, women had been abused, raped and oppressed. I could understand why this woman wanted a Tonal that could protect her from strong and large male predators.

"Don't underestimate the power of a tiny frog," I said.

"I want an eagle, not a frog," she said with a childish

expression.

"I'm not a car salesman. You're in the wrong workshop," I said and I got up from my log to get a drink of water. Frog Woman followed me.

"When I was a kid, I was teased by my friends all the time. They called me 'frog eyes.' I don't want to be a frog."

I turned around to face the woman and, sure enough, she did have frog eyes!

"Children can be very cruel. I'm sorry about all the teasing but...frogs have their own medicine. Maybe frog could help you soothe your childhood pain. Think about the power of little frogs to bring the rain. Maybe frog will help you cleanse your soul from old scars. Call frog to refresh your spirit so that you may see the reflection of your true self."

With these words, I walked away from Frog Woman. I went and sat by the lake. I did not see Frog Woman again until later that afternoon when she came back totally transformed. I could not quite believe what my eyes were witnessing. The woman had changed into a frog. She had painted her entire body green. Somehow, she had managed to get hold of a pair of water goggles and a set of diving fins. I wondered if she had brought this equipment from home of if she had borrowed it from other campers. In any case, she was a frog.

With great delight, I sat back on my log and prepared for the final dance of the Tonals. All the members of the group were back in their Tonal costumes. Some of them appeared to be in a trance. They moved in a circle, beating their drums, playing their flutes, shaking their rattles. I realized they were ready to present their gifts to their newly-established community. What a gift their presence was! Almost with surreal undertones, they manifested the energies and elements of nature. What a great opportunity it was to witness the transformational power of the ancient ritual I had learned from Don Tomas!

One by one, the women danced their Tonals. First, a sensuous snake slithered her way on the surface of the earth. Roaring, a big grizzly made her way into the center of the gathering. She was fierce and proud. Then, Deer Woman leaped into the circle. She was graceful and gentle. Deer Woman's eyes were filled with compassion and serenity. She was no longer confused or appeared to be afraid. Reconnected with her deer essence, the woman had opened her heart and her body to the sacred spirit. She was sacred.

The energy of Wolf followed deer, a woman in her mid-forties stood in front of her sisters. She was silent and nervous. I could tell she was shivering from fear. She was not wolf, she was caught in her human struggles. She felt powerless and fragile. She had painted red her entire pelvic area and, on her abdomen, she had drawn a large black circle. Stripes of red and black paint decorated her face, legs and arms. She was naked in front of us. She was strong in her vulnerability. Tears ran down her cheeks, mixing with the pigments of the paint.

The sounds of the drums, flutes, and the rattles stopped. Only the whispering of the gentle breeze could be heard until the moment when she broke into sobs. Like an arrow, the woman's pain ripped away any layers of resistance and she spoke. At first, her voice was low but gradually, she gathered her strength. Her words became the howl of the wolf. The story she told us would explain her fears.

"When I was six years old," Wolf Woman said, "My father came into my room one night. He pulled down the covers and he lay on the bed next to me. At first, I was comforted by his presence, then he touched me and...you know, he touched me down there. It didn't feel good but he told me I would like it. He was my daddy and I trusted him but he came back the next night. I was scared. I said, 'Daddy, please don't...,' but he didn't stop. He came back again every night. He waited until Mom went to sleep. He told me not to tell my mom because it would hurt her. I was confused."

Wolf Woman covered her face with her hands and she cried some more. The rest of us waited in silence. Wolf Woman's tears were the bitter tears of many women who have been victimized. Wolf Woman's words were the words of the many women I had witnessed crying in the safe space of my office. They were women. They were little girls whose innocence had been crushed by the hands of men they trusted. Wolf Woman, like these others carried the pain of the betrayal deep inside her pelvis.

"My father stole my childhood!" Wolf Woman shouted. "He robbed me of my sexuality! All my life I have been in pain when I could have lived in pleasure." Then Wolf Woman began to move around inside the protective circle of women. She moved like Wolf. Gradually her body took the essence of the wolf energy. The pained expression of her face turned fierce. She howled with her piercing black eyes as if she were in front of her enemy. She exposed her sharp teeth, ready to rip the skin of her predator. She leaped into the air! I could imagine Wolf Woman tearing to pieces the body of her father.

The women in the group, who up to this point had remained silent, joined Wolf Woman with the sound of their instruments and their voices. In her dance of destruction and revenge, the body of Wolf Woman gained stature. She looked taller and stronger. Then her motion came to a sudden stop. Wolf Woman stood in the center of the circle, with her gaze fixed on the ground and her nostrils flaring from rage. She reached over her belly and began to caress the pale skin of her abdomen as she spoke with a soothing tone. "My body is my body. The body of the Earth is also my body. Let there be no more rape of this land. I reclaim this body as my body with all the feelings and sensations. I am a sensual and a sexual being."

As I looked around, the rest of the women joined Wolf Woman. Together they chanted the words "My body is my body. The body of the Earth is also my body. Let there be no more rape of this land..."

The women joined hands and danced with their feet grounded on the earth. As they moved, the circle became a tight hug, a wave of female energy rocking the shores of our souls. Quietly, I got up from my log and found a place in the circle. I felt privileged among the courageous women. A deep sense of appreciation permeated my being. As I danced, I thought about the women in my own family and wondered about their pain. The energy of the group was contagious and invigorating. The more I moved, the fuller my hips felt. Heat rose from my pelvis into my belly, my chest and finally into my throat. The roar of black Jaguar broke through the walls of resistance. My heart leaped with joy.

One year after the workshop, I received a letter from Deer Woman. She had left the convent to joint a community of ex-nuns dedicated to the propagation of world peace. For the first time in her life, as she wrote, Deer Woman was happy with her choices. She had found her "Deer Medicine" and was sharing it with the many she touched on her travels.

As for myself, I returned to my office in the city with a renewed sense of purpose. Fearless about venturing into the forest of the psyche, I began to work with the Tonal energy in the private setting of my practice. In an amazing act of synchronicity, clients began to bring their Tonals to our sessions. Suddenly the animal world was my best co-therapist.

When ten-year-old Alfonso walked into my office for his weekly appointment, I could feel he had not come alone. Resting on his right shoulder was a majestic eagle. I took a glance at the bird and I relaxed in my chair. Alfonso had been coming to see me for about three months. His teacher had referred him for counseling because he appeared distracted and depressed and was falling behind in his work. Alfonso was shy and well-mannered and he spoke only to respond to my questions.

In our sessions, he had done many drawings of monsters that appeared in his nightmares. These creatures of long and hook-like fingers terrorized Alfonso. They chased him and threatened to rip his thin and fragile body to pieces. Alfonso was the youngest of five children and the target of teasing and rough play by his older two brothers. The father had struggled for years with alcohol abuse and the mother was a well-intentioned woman overwhelmed with responsibility.

Alfonso sat across from me on the carpeted floor of my office. As usual I pulled the crayons and drawing paper out of my desk drawer so we could begin our work. But this time Alfonso expressed his desire not to draw today. He looked tired, even though it was early morning. His face was pale and his eyes were sad.

"Alfonso, what's the matter?"

"I don't feel well. My stomach hurts. I don't want to do any pictures today."

"Well, what would you like to do?"

"I don't know. I'm tired." He crossed his arms over his chest.

"Show me where it hurts."

"Mi pancita." He pointed at his belly.

"Why don't you lie down? Let's see what's happening with your pancita," I said as I handed him a pillow. "Close your eyes, Alfonso, and take a deep breath. Imagine your belly is a balloon and that you're breathing air into it." Alfonso followed my directions. He was used to the guided imagery exercises where we went places and explored his dreams.

"It hurts more when I breathe."

"Just keep breathing," I commanded in a gentle tone of voice. "Your belly is like a road with many turns. Follow the curves to that place where you think the pain is."

"It is right above my belly button. I see the monster. He has an egg-shaped head like those aliens from the movies. He's ugly! He wants to catch me and take me with him to his planet."

"Alfonso, don't panic. It's going to be okay. Think about an animal you like."

"I see an eagle. It's a big bird with powerful claws!" Alfonso cried.

"Ask for help," I said now, understanding the presence of the eagle I had seen when Alfonso came into my office. The eagle was one of Alfonso's power animals.

"Woo!" Alfonso said. "The Eagle flew right to the monster's

head. It's so strong. What a bird! Just now, it grabbed the monster by his head and it's carrying it to the top of a tall tree where its nest is. I can see the eagle ripping the monster's face, feeding the pieces of flesh to a young eagle there. The monster's screaming for help but nobody's coming. He's a bad creature. He has no friends."

"Alfonso, how is your stomachache?"

"It doesn't hurt anymore. I feel fine. The eagle took care of the monster that was giving me the pain."

"Where is the eagle now?" I asked.

"Right on top of the tree, finishing up the monster. The eagle wants me to go there. It wants to show me his baby...but I can't climb that tree, it's too tall."

"You can do it, Alfonso. You can go up if you imagine yourself as a young eagle with powerful wings. Try to imagine that."

"No, I can't. I'm afraid of falling from the tree."

"Try. Just think of yourself as an eagle."

Alfonso struggled for a few seconds. It was hard for him to see himself as the eagle. I encouraged him. I could sense his internal fight with fear. Alfonso curled up in a fetal position. He wrapped his thin arms around his belly. He appeared younger and more fragile. I cheered him on to try one more time.

"Alfonso, you can do it. Don't let your fear win. Eagle can teach you to free yourself from your fear. It can show you how to fly above the mountains. Imagine your arms turning into strong and large wings."

Now Alfonso was quiet. I could tell he was trying hard to see those eagle wings. Slowly, Alfonso stretched his body and he opened his arms. He moved them as if he were soaring in the air. He was flying! He had become the eagle.

"I'm on top of the tree!" he screamed with joy.

Alfonso came back to see me for a few more sessions and we continued the work of strengthening the connection to his power animal—the eagle. Alfonso, like most children his age, was very open to this type of healing. Motivated by his vision of the eagle, he eagerly searched for books that informed him about the powers of his eagle. Through this journey, Alfonso discovered his native-American roots. Taken by his son's interest in eagles, his father, a Cherokee, remembered the words of his grandfather: "Son," the old man said, "Your name is Red Eagle." From that moment on, Alfonso and his father became closer. The Cherokee father taught Alfonso how to make an eagle shield for protection.

Alfonso became less timid and his nightmares stopped. He told me the eagle shield hanging above the head of his bed protected him from any bad spirits. I was curious about the introduction of the word "spirit" in his vocabulary. The boy told me his father had talked to him about bad spirits who could come into your dreams if you don't take care of yourself and how his great grandfather has been a powerful medicine man who knew how to fight these evil spirits. Alfonso now knew that eagle medicine ran in his family and that he was safe under the guardianship of this power animal. As he said, "My father told me I'm a member of the eagle clan."

The combination of Tonal work with art therapy, dream work, journal writing, body movement, and rituals is one of the most effective ways to bring individuals in touch with their creativity and the healing power of their bodies. Most women who have chosen to work with me have done so out of their need to explore healing techniques that are alternative to the traditional models of clinical psychology. They come in with an open mind and heart.

I'll share the case of a client, whose name I'll keep confidential, a 32-year-old woman who struggled with depression for most of her life. For the past three years she endured the impact of chronic fatigue. A professional artist, she had not been able to produce a single painting for more than two years. The fatigue typical of this syndrome had eroded her physical and emotional well-being and, as a result, her creativity.

During her first visit to my office, Carmen looked fragile and pale with dark circles under her eyes. The energy field around her body was thin. Because of my ability to see auras, I can read the emotions of people and I can locate more or less where the problem is in their bodies. In the case of Carmen, I was able to tell right away that she was not in touch with her pelvis. As I scanned her, I saw dark-gray pockets of energy around her hips, her lower back and her abdomen. To me this was a sign of trauma. A blockage of energy had occurred as a result of physical and emotional injuries.

Unaware of my thoughts, Carmen confirmed that she had had a hysterectomy at age twenty-eight. From the time she had her first period, she had experienced severe pain and heavy bleeding accompanied by headaches and nausea. As she said in this first session, she hated her menstrual cycles and her body altogether for giving her so much suffering. After the surgery, Carmen was relieved for a while but then she began to feel empty, her whole being felt empty as if a hollow tube were growing inside her belly. To her surprise, she found herself grieving the removed organs. She missed the pain and the moodiness that gave her a sense of being alive.

"I'm dead," Carmen expressed in a sad tone of voice. "I am broken. I'm a defective woman with no sexual desires. But again, who can think of sex when I can barely feed and bathe myself? Every single move takes monumental effort. I'm sick of it!"

Carmen was not a victim. In spite of her fatigue and depression, she had searched out all forms of help from Western to naturopathic medicine and even Chinese doctors. To her dismay, all the drugs, acupuncture and homeopathic remedies didn't seem to alleviate her misery. Not able to work anymore, Carmen had arrived at a point she called "the place of dead ends." And now she sat across from me in my office with the hope that I could help her. She had heard about my practice from another client who described me as a shaman. As soon as I heard the word "shaman" I was concerned. In a second,

I was prompted to correct the mistake. I explained to Carmen that I was not a shaman but I was familiar with shamanic healing practices.

I wanted to make sure Carmen understood the differences between being a shaman and a therapist with knowledge of shamanic work. The New Age movement and the revival of an interest in ancient forms of healing had attracted power-hungry individuals, very prone to misrepresent themselves to the public. The idea that one can take a workshop on Native-American healing and therefore become a healer has been abused. Many so-called "healers" carry around medicine pouches. And there are so-called "soul retrievers" who, for a fat fee, will travel into the underworld and retrieve your soul. To me, being a shaman is a lifetime apprenticeship. When Carmen came back to my office for a second visit, she shared a dream she had the night before.

"In my dream, I see my body inside a coffin. Standing next to me, there is a young woman dressed in white. Her wavy hair is long and shiny. I can see her eyes are bright and full of life. She tells me it's time for me to wake up. I'm confused by her words because I believe I'm dead. In my mind I'm thinking there is no way for me to move. My body is stiff and cold. I have no energy...but the woman insists that I must try to get up. Then the woman leans forward and touches my belly with her hand. At first, I don't feel anything but then I feel a current of heat moving inside. It feels like my vagina is on fire! My whole pelvic area is hot. I look down and I see a snake. I panic! The woman commands me to relax and to breathe. I do my best but I'm afraid of the snake inside me. I wake up."

I encouraged Carmen to close her eyes and to go back into her dream. With hesitation she explored the imagery. She told me this young woman was that part of her that had not given up and wants to live. Then we moved to the snake. Here, Carmen was not so sure. She opened her eyes and said, "I'm terrified of snakes."

"Carmen, let's try again," I said. "You must face the snake."

With some resistance, Carmen returned to the underworld

of her belly. As I looked at her aura, I could see the snake coiled at the base of her spine. I asked Carmen to focus on that area. She followed my instructions. It took a few seconds for Carmen to connect with her body, but finally she was back into her dream.

"It's a very large snake," she told me. "The snake is now moving inside me. It has piercing black eyes and a sharp tongue." Carmen was trembling. Drops of sweat covered her forehead.

"Carmen, let your pelvis move with the motion of the snake. Don't fight it!"

"I'm trying."

After a few minutes of struggle, I saw Carmen's hips barely undulating. She was there in the realm of her Tonal. Carmen told me the snake was traveling along her spine and that she could feel waves of energy inside her belly. Along with the motion, she heard the voice of her art teacher criticizing one of her paintings. Carmen recalled the many times her father told her "Art is a waste of time." Then, as if that weren't enough, she remembered the constant put-downs by her mother and her insistence on Carmen losing weight. She remembered the day when her mother caught her masturbating, after which she was forbidden to be in her room with the door closed.

"Old rage has been the killer of my energy," Carmen said, still with her eyes shut. "I was always a threat to the world around me: my parents, my schoolteachers, the church. I was a sensuous child with lots of fire, but over and over they managed to strangle my spirit. I became that dead body inside the coffin in my dream—a frigid cadaver!"

For the next few weeks that followed our session, Carmen dedicated herself to seriously explore the snake Tonal she had met in her dream. Her daily dialogue with the snake in the form of journal writing and drawings brought not just great insights to the nature of her chronic fatigue but improved health. With a renewed level of energy she had not experienced for years, Carmen returned to her art. The symbol of the snake was a primary character of her paintings. The lady of the Serpent

Skirt, the Goddess Coatlique, came to occupy the place of honor.

As Carmen explained, she had adopted this goddess, Mother of all Aztec deities, as her Snake Mother and helper in reclaiming her fire and creativity.

"I chose Coatlique because she knows about life and death. Even though I'm not Mexican, I have always been attracted to the culture. Coatlique is for me a reminder of the molten lava inside my pelvis. In her obsidian mirror, I see reflected the face of death and the promise of the unknown future. My struggle with chronic fatigue has been a close brush with death but it has also allowed me to be reborn to a true self."

In addition to doing her art work, Carmen signed up for a Yoga class where she explored the connection of breath with the movement of stagnant energy in her body. Through this process, Carmen became connected to the sources of healing and regenerative powers of her snake Tonal. Carmen was no longer afraid of snakes. She understood how her snake was an ancient totem of women and shamanic power.

ELEVEN

La Cubana

I WAS FINISHING a report that was due in court the following day when I was interrupted by the voice of Lalita, my secretary, coming through the intercom. As she announced the arrival of my next client, I heard the loud voice of a woman in the background. The strong Cuban accent vibrated through the line of communication, interfering with Lalita's words.

"I'll be out there in just a moment," I said and glanced at the appointment book that rested on top of my desk. Dora was the name of my next client, a Cuban lady who had been referred to me by a local attorney. Two days before, I had spoken to Dora by phone. At that time, she had been loud and clear when she told me she did not believe in therapy and nor was she in need of a shrink. Dora was only coming because of a "crazy woman" who had gotten her into trouble with the law. So, with her words in mind, I prepared for an encounter with this character.

And there was Dora, a large woman of round and voluptuous body, sitting comfortably on the couch. Her dress was a free-flowing gown of orange and red flowers on a black background. Dora's black and curly hair was shoulder-length. She had aged well. At fifty-five, her skin was smooth as that of a thirty-year-old woman.

Extending my hand, I introduced myself. The woman took

her time to rise from the couch and, once on her feet, she sized me up. Her moon-shaped face and her brown complexion were the perfect frame for her light hazel eyes and her bright red lips. "My God, Doctora, for such a large name you have, you're a very short woman," she said. Without making any comment, I reminded myself of the tendency Cubans have to be direct to a point that oftentimes borders on pure rudeness.

I invited Dora into my office. As soon as she stepped in, she proceeded to advise me on the arrangement of the furniture. "This couch needs to be near the door." Dora went around and pointed out how one of the pictures on the wall was too high and another one was too low. Mesmerized by her audacity, I listened, aware of her discomfort. Finally, when Dora was satisfied with her comments, she sat on the large chair across from me.

"You seem very young," she said and waited for my response.

"Let's talk about the issue that brought you here," I said.

"Let's get one thing clear," she said and leaned forward on her chair. "I'm not the crazy one. If anybody should be here, it's that woman. I told my attorney that I don't want any of this on my record. You understand?"

"It's not that simple but I understand your concern about confidentiality. Did your attorney explain the nature of my role in your case?"

"He said something about a report. And, Honey, it better be a good letter, because I ain't going to jail for this. I can tell you that woman's husband didn't leave her because of anything I did to him. I didn't put any magic yuyoo in his coffee." Dora was upset. Her thundering voice could be heard from across the street.

"Dora, I can see you're angry. Why don't you tell me your side of the story?"

"My story, I can tell you one thing. When Rafael, that woman's husband, came to my Botánica, the guy was looking for some herbs. At first, he was not very honest about it. I could tell he was out for no good. Then he told me he was very unhappy and that he wanted to leave his wife, but he was worried she would take him to the cleaners for his money." Dora grabbed the medallion of La Virgen de la Caridad that hung from a thick gold chain around her neck. "La Virgencita knows my job is to help, not to hurt people. The orishas told me to be careful with this man. So I threw the *caracoles* [seashell divination] for him. He almost had a heart attack right there in front of me. Because the caracoles don't lie, and what we got was that Blanca, his wife, was having an affair with Rafael's best friend."

I was beginning to get the picture. Dora not only was the owner of the Botánica but she was a Santera.

"So to make the story short," Dora continued in her loud voice, "Rafael *se encabrono* [became angry]. His face was red as a tomato. He walked out of my Botánica as if he had been hit by thunder. A few days later, he came back and asked for my help. Again, we did the caracoles and this time the orishas were very direct with Rafael. They told him to transfer all his money into a different account. Blanca and Rafael's friend had it all planned to run out of the country with the *lana* [money]."

"Well, Dora, did Rafael think of confronting his wife or his friend?" I asked, and immediately regretted it.

"Chica, don't be a fool. In matters like that, you say nothing. You want to catch them, like we Cubans say, con las manos en la masa, right in the act. If you alert them, you make a bigger mess." Dora shook her head. I knew exactly what she was thinking and she said it. "You therapists go to school for nothing. This kind of business is not learned from the books. It's a human experience. And believe me I have lived long enough to tell you that those ideas you shrinks have about confronting don't work in such a case."

"I didn't mean to offend you," I said with some embarrassment.

"All I want is to be left alone. I've been in this country for more than twenty years and I'm not about to lose my Botánica. I've worked too hard to get here. For ten years, I worked two jobs to save money. Ha, Santa Barbara Bendita, Doctor." She meant, oh my holy Saint Barbara. "You saw me then, I was skinny like a *palillo* [toothpick] from lack of sleep and rest. Even on Sundays I was out on the streets, collecting cardboard boxes and aluminum cans that I took to the big recycling place for a few extra bucks."

"I'm sorry you had to work so hard."

"I didn't mind. I knew in my heart that if I didn't open that Botánica the orishas were going to be very upset with me. They kept coming into my house. At night, they didn't let me go to sleep with their heavy knocks on the walls."

"But, Dora, why are you afraid of losing your Botánica?"

"Well," said Dora, and for the first time, she looked at me with her big hazel eyes full of tears. "Rafael's wife accused me of practicing *brujería* [witchcraft]. She hired an attorney who wants to prove that I caused her emotional damage." Dora looked straight into my soul. "I am not a brujera!" Her gaze had the intensity of a volcanic eruption with hot lava spouting out from the depths of the earth.

"Dora, I never dealt with a case like yours but I don't think they can take away your Botánica."

"No, but she also claimed that I took Rafael's money and that I need to pay her back. Good old Rafael refuses to reveal the location of the money."

"Dora, this is all very confusing."

"Tell me about it. And now to complicate matters the evil lady manifested a bottle of some potion she said she found in the pocket of Rafael's jacket. She attached a label on it that says, 'Quita amor.'"

"Take love away?"

"It means she's trying to prove that I gave this potion to Rafael so he would stop loving her. She wants the courts to believe that I seduced Rafael and I manipulated him into giving me the money. Is that clear?"

"Yes and no. I don't see how any court in this country would buy that."

"Ay mi Dios!" Dora threw her arms in the air. I could tell she was growing impatient with me. "Listen. You're too intellectual and I don't have the time to teach you. Can we just leave it on a simple note? This case can go on forever and the cost of the attorney is making a big dent in my savings. I can't believe how expensive this business is turning out to be. I just want you to say on a letter that I'm not crazy and that I'm no liar."

As soon as I heard Dora's words, I realized how naïve the woman was about my job, though perhaps no more so than I was about her work at the Botánica. Therapy in a traditional sense was not the approach to follow in her case. I pretended to write some notes on my pad while I thought about the situation. During this brief interlude, I remembered the times when as a child I had witnessed my nanny Carmen perform her healing sessions in the back room of our house. Like Carmen, the world of Dora was anchored in a dimension of unseen spirits and helpers. How could I bring Dora back to her power? I could see that this ordeal with attorneys and the courts had taken her away from her sources of wisdom.

"Dora, I will write you the letter but...I don't believe that letter is going to put an end to all this."

"No? What do you mean?"

"Well, the legal side needs to be handled by your expensive attorney, but you need to figure out what to do to get this woman off your back. Do you understand?"

Dora was a smart woman. It didn't take her long to see my point. She frowned and reached over to touch my arm. I was a bit puzzled myself by the fact that Dora had not thought of using her powers. I looked into her eyes. I could detect the dance of her doubts inside her head. I wondered if Dora was the real thing, meaning a true Santera or whether she was just a businesswoman.

"You know," Dora said in a softer voice, "I just feel very scared. Fear is no good. It has taken my ashé. This whole business with the courts reminded me of the time when I was thrown in jail by Castro's militia men. I don't sleep well at night. I have all these nightmares of me locked behind bars. I see myself back in Cuba, inside the dark and cold cell, where I spent two years of my life."

Dora's face sank and tears ran down her cheeks, leaving clear lines of wet make-up on the surface of her dark skin. Dora, like many Cubans, veterans of war, or victims of trauma, suffered from post-traumatic stress disorder. There was no point in explaining this to her. It would mean nothing, but I could certainly talk to her in familiar terms. This loss of ashé was the language she understood. Ashé is energy and power. Everything is made of ashé. When one is in touch with ashé, one feels strong and confident to face problems and enemies. In Santeria, all the invocations and rituals are done for the procurement of ashé.

During the last part of our session, Dora shared with me the horrors of those two years she spent in a Cuban prison. She told me how she was beaten up by her jailers. One time she ended up with two broken ribs. Another time they dislocated her arm. Head concussions and a bleeding nose left Dora semi-conscious for hours.

"How did you end up in jail?" I asked.

"Hmm! Only mi virgencita knows how unjust my situation was. The reason they threw me in el bote was for practicing my religion. My mother, my sisters and I were celebrating the orisha Babalúe-ayé. We invited some relatives and friends over for the feast and traditional dancing. You know, Castro prohibited the practice of any religion. Well! You know, Doctora, in Cuba, no one ever really stopped their traditions. We simply hid in our house and did our thing in a quiet fashion. But this time, a traitor from the neighborhood alerted the militia and right in the middle of our bembé, we were surprised by the vicious dogs. Except for my mother, we were all taken to the Havana prison where we rotted for two years. We were ex-communicated so when my mother passed away I was not allowed to go to her funeral. Can you imagine this? I couldn't see my mother for the last time."

Dora broke into a quiet sob. Then with some pride, she wiped her face and composed herself. She did not want me to see her tears and I understood. Dora had a tough life and she was not a woman who would enjoy the victim label. She was a warrior and a survivor. In Cuba, she would be considered someone with *agallas* [courage]. But I knew that people who had experienced such traumatic situations could easily fall prey to old fears in the face of similar threats. The stressful environment inside a courtroom could evoke in Dora past feelings of powerlessness. And there was the Santera. She was in need of support and of realignment with the forces she believed to be the source of her strength.

"Dora," I said, "you're a Santera, right? You have helped many with their problems. What can you do for yourself?"

Dora looked at me with a spark of hope in her hazel eyes. She knew where I was going. With effort, she got up and walked to the window. Slowly, she pulled the blind up. Suddenly, the room filled with the light of the bright sun. Dora looked outside. Cars were speeding along the road up to the hill.

"Life in this country is fast. There is no time to think or feel. Look at those people. Where do they think they're going? They live in the fast lane. I miss Cuba. I long for the lazy afternoons of my hometown. It was hot! But those moments when I sat out on the porch, next to my mother and my sisters, were precious. We talked and we laughed for hours while we sipped cold lemonade. It was the real thing, not that junk you buy here in the stores. Our lemonade was always made from fresh lemons that we picked with our own hands."

For a moment I was tempted to tell Dora about my own childhood memories of the famous lemonade my mother used to make. I could almost taste the sweetness of the brown sugarcane mixed with the crispy sour juice of the lemons my mother gathered from the tree that grew in our backyard. I held back. As a therapist you're not supposed to share much of your own emotions with your clients. Instead, I re-focused on my work.

"Dora, do you work alone or do you have a family of Santeros?"

"I miss Cuba but I don't ever want to go back to the kind of poverty and oppression I left behind," Dora said, totally disregarding my question. "I think I know what to do. I need to take a little trip to downtown Los Angeles where mi familia is at. They can help me. Julio is an old Santero. He is my *padrino* [godfather]."

A week later when Dora returned for her next appointment, she was a different woman. There was a radiance in her eyes I hadn't seen before. I noticed her simple white cotton dress. A piece of cloth of the same material and color was wrapped around her head in a low turban. Dora sat across from me and told me she had gone to see her padrino.

"It has been an eventful week," she said with a smile. I knew not to ask her anything about her visit with the padrino. It was disrespectful to inquire about such a private and sacred connection. Having grown up in Cuba, I was always told by my nanny Carmen not to ask any questions about people's personal experiences, more so when it came to Santeria.

"My padrino told me to take a series of herbal baths for cleansing of negative vibrations. And you won't believe the revolution I have been through. It all started right after I took the first bath. That night, as I lay on my bed, all these negative deities showed up in my room. One of them was a feeble old man who told me he was Blanca's dead grandfather. You remember? Blanca is the wife of Rafael. Then another man, much younger, showed up and introduced himself as Blanca's uncle who had been hanged from a tree during the revolution. I tell you, Doctora, the comparza of bad spirits lasted for a while."

"What were these spirits doing there?" I asked with hesitation.

"They're part of Blanca's ancestral line. They were brought into my Botánica by Rafael. Of course, he doesn't know that. They're working through his wife, who is an evil woman. She has bad yuyoo!"

"Why would they want to hurt you?" I asked.

"Doctora! These spirits are restless and angry. They are thirsty vampires. You should be aware of that because lots of people come into your office every day and they bring their stuff into your place. They come into my Botánica, too. Don't think that because you don't see them, they're not here."

"Oh, I know. I'm aware of that," I said and I remembered the many sessions with clients who brought in their dead relatives and friends.

"Once they move into your place, they create illness and bad luck for you and that's what happened in my Botánica. They were there lingering in the corners, touching my herbs and my sacred objects." Dora paused to take a deep breath. She leaned forward and touched my hand. "I thank you for helping me." Dora looked me straight in the eyes. "They're all gone now! Everything is going to be okay."

I looked at Dora with gratitude. It was in moments like that, I was reminded of the fine line that exists between us and the world of the spirit. I thought about the many therapists who walk into their office every day, so vulnerable to the unseen dimension brought into the therapeutic encounter. The education and the training we receive in schools do not address in any way or shape the dangerous dynamics of the invisible web we enter when dealing with the complex psyches of our clients.

"What do you shrinks do for protection?" Dora asked as if she had read my thoughts.

"I was just thinking about that," I said. "You know, Dora, this type of phenomena is never talked about in our training. This world of spirits and deities is very much ignored in traditional psychology. It is foreign to the profession, and therefore prohibited."

"Hmm, Doctora, that's dangerous!"

"You bet it is."

"Well, if you ever need any help, you call me. I'll come and take care of bad energy for you. Although..." Dora paused and she looked around my office. "There're good spirits here.

You have helpers." She stopped and waited for me to say something.

"I'm glad to hear that," I replied.

"There is an old woman with short gray hair around. She sits by your left and there is another woman. Hmm, mi Dios. She's black like me. She's a good woman. Big heart."

Dora was the first client ever to see my Grandmother Patricia and my nanny Carmen. I could tell Dora was no longer in need of my help. She had regained her powers and she was now on her way to be the Santera she had lost in her entanglement with the courts and attorneys. The cleansing baths her padrino had prescribed helped Dora restore her connection to the ashé. My role as a therapist had been simple. Dora was a healer. She just needed to be reminded of her great gift.

TWELVE

Twin Souls

E DGAR, AS I'll call my client, was well educated and a successful business executive, properly dressed in a dark suit and a blue tie. At forty-five, he appeared much younger. He was tall and slender with well developed muscles. I could tell by his uptight posture that he was nervous. Not unusual, most people are quite anxious during the first few minutes of the initial session. As I waited for Edgar to talk, I noticed he was busy with his own process of examining me. I smiled to ease his tension.

Edgar began to describe his symptoms. For the past six months, he had experienced much anxiety, depression, loss of interest, and low motivation. Basically, he dragged himself to his job every morning. He felt tired but he couldn't go to sleep at night. Off and on for the past five years, Edgar was awakened by nightmares. Covered with sweat, he lay on his bed as he attempted to figure out these dreams.

"I'm not sure what to do. I toss and I turn on my bed. Sometimes I get no sleep at all."

Edgar was not preoccupied with his finances or his job. He had been divorced for more than five years. With no children, he was free to travel and play golf. But lately, he had not enjoyed his favorite sport, and the idea of taking a plane made him anxious.

165

It was now at a point where he had frequent panic attacks during business trips. Edgar was disturbed by not having control over his emotions.

I asked Edgar to tell me about his nightmares. At first, he was hesitant. Gradually, he loosened up and he shared a sequence of dreams. In every one of them, Edgar found himself back in the home where he spent most of his childhood.

In one dream, Edgar is a young boy and sees himself standing in the middle of a dark room in the back of the farmhouse. He can hear the loud cry of a baby but can't find where the infant is. Edgar knows something is wrong. He walks around in a desperate search that lasts for a long time until he finds a bundle in a corner of the room. It's the baby wrapped inside a white blanket. Happy, Edgar uncovers it. The creature has no eyes! From the empty sockets, blood gushes out. Terrified, Edgar drops the baby on the floor and runs, but soon he hears the cry again. He turns around and sees the eyeless little monster running after him. Edgar is awakened by the sound of his own loud scream.

By the time Edgar narrated his nightmare, his forehead was covered with sweat. He managed to loosen his tie. He took a deep breath. And as I waited for him to recover, a blue light flashed around Edgar's head. It flickered several times as if wanting to get my attention. Of course, my client was not consciously aware of the event and I was careful not to mention anything. Instead, I stayed tuned to any possible message from the gentle spirit. Right away I saw the luminous body of a newborn and I received the message: "I'm Edgar's twin brother." There was a flash across my office and the spirit baby was gone.

"Edgar, do you have siblings?" I asked.

"I have a sister who is three years older than me. She lives in Florida with her husband and two daughters."

"No brothers?"

"I had a twin brother who died a few hours after birth."

"What happened?"

"All I know is that he died. My parents never said much

about him. As a child, I had great curiosity about my brother but I was afraid to ask any questions. Once, I overheard a conversation, where my mother told a friend that she never quite recovered from such a loss. I guess I grew up sensing her deep pain. Often, I even thought that somehow it was my fault."

"That's a heavy burden for a young child."

"Most of my life I've felt the weight of my brother's death. From the time I was a young child, I was aware of feeling tremendous pressure to do real well. After all, my dead brother didn't get a chance and I did. It was as if every time I turned around I could see his shadow right next to mine. There were moments when I could see and feel his presence everywhere I went. Even these days, I can hear the whisper of his angry voice. And I know that's crazy, because newborns don't talk."

"What makes you think your brother is angry?"

"Because he died and I got to play with all the toys, go on vacation to the beach house with the family, have friends, ride the horses. I don't know! All those things he didn't get to experience—the world! Life!"

"What is his name?" I asked.

"It's funny that you would ask, my brother was not named."

"Was he buried somewhere?"

"I'm ashamed to say I don't know," Edgar said with sadness. "I was thinking about a recent nightmare. I'm back in my childhood home. I'm in my room playing with my army toys when a boy, around age five, jumps in through the window. He wants to play with me but I'm not sure I should let him because I'm thinking I don't know him. The boy gets angry and he proceeds to kick everything he finds in my room. I try to stop him but he is a lot stronger than me. He pins me down to the floor. I struggle to free myself but this boy is now getting taller and bigger. Finally, I give up. I'm breathless. But when I get to see his face again, he looks just like me. Surprised, I ask, who are you? He doesn't answer. I ask again. He says nothing but suddenly he is crying and his face is covered with big white maggots. I panic and feel like I'm ready to empty out my gut. I don't want to look at him but I feel sorry for the boy. I turn to him and my eyes meet with a terrifying fleshless face. And I hear a baby voice saying, 'I have no name.'"

Edgar's blue eyes filled with tears. He reached for the box of Kleenex. I noticed how his hands trembled as he held the soft tissue. Edgar was not the first client I had witnessed suffer for the loss of a twin sibling. Over the years of my practice, I had met several individuals who had lived their lives in search of a lost twin. Also, in most cases the dead twin has never been given a name or even a proper burial. I could see that both Edgar and his twin had not been able to complete their separation and the process of grieving. Across from Edgar, I imagined the experience of bonding and the closeness Edgar and his brother must have experienced inside their mother's womb. Then...the sudden shock of separation at birth and, later, the finality of death.

As I looked over Edgar's right shoulder, I noticed the presence of his baby brother. The blue aura of his energy, like long fingers, touched Edgar on his shoulder, I believe in an effort to communicate with him. I observed in silence as I waited for a reaction. Sometimes, even if people are not aware of the spirit world, they can feel its gentle touch. Sure enough, a few seconds later, Edgar reached out with his left arm and began to rub his left shoulder and neck.

"Is your shoulder bothering you?" I asked.

"Not really."

"Would you mind taking a couple of deep breaths as you pay attention to any sensations on your shoulder?"

"I feel a tingling from my shoulder down into my arms."

"Would you feel comfortable enough to close your eyes and see what images, feelings or thoughts come up when you focus on that area?"

He closed his eyes. "My shoulder and neck feel very hot. There is some pressure, as if a hand is resting on my shoulder. Wait...I'm having some flashback about a time during my childhood when I became very ill. I believe I was about six and I had a very high fever. I see my mother putting cold compresses on my forehead. I can tell she is worried about me. I can hear her talking to my father and saying, 'We need to bring his fever down. Please call the doctor and see what else we can do.' As I recall, my father left the room and my mother, exhausted from sleep deprivation, closed her eyes. In and out of consciousness, I wasn't sure if what I saw next was a dream, a hallucination or indeed was a real event. I saw a little boy who looked just like me, he walked into the room and he sat by the side of my bed. He told me, 'Come back, Edgar. You're supposed to stay alive and watch over Mom and Dad.' He placed his right hand over my forehead. His hand was cool and soothing."

Edgar opened his eyes. He had an expression of surprise. He jumped off the couch and he stood in the middle of the room. "My God, he was my brother! He was there that night and, you know, when my father came back with instructions from the doctor and my mother touched my forehead, the fever was gone. He healed me! It was the magic of his little hand!"

Edgar walked to the window that faced the waters of Lake Union. Outside, the gray skies almost appeared to be one with the lake. A few boats moored by the dock moved up and down with the changing currents. Edgar's eyes were fixed on the waters. Next to him was his spirit brother. He was still holding on to Edgar's shoulder.

I remained silent. I realized that for a man like Edgar, this whole experience was beyond comprehension. I could tell how hard his brain was working in an effort to make sense of his feelings and thoughts. Edgar had learned to rely on his intellect but not on his intuition and psychic abilities. My job as a therapist was to respect those boundaries and never to disclose any information outside that realm. I knew what his brother was there for, but I would wait for Edgar to discover that on his own at the appropriate time.

When Edgar came back for his next session the following week, he was excited to share with me information he had gathered about his brother. He had phoned his parents and he had asked all the questions he had been afraid to ask before. To his surprise, his parents gave him details of past events. As the story goes, Edgar's brother was never named. After the birth of the twins, the mother remained in a delicate condition. The father, overwhelmed by the loss and the responsibility of having to care for his wife, gave permission to his own brother to arrange the burial of the deceased child.

"Last night I had another dream," Edgar said and he smiled. "I know what my brother needs. He came into my dream and he told me that he wants to be named. He also wants a service."

"What type of service?" I asked.

"Well, we're Catholics and even though I haven't set foot in a church for years, I have a feeling that it should be some form of religious ceremony conducted by a priest."

"Would your parents be open to that?"

"I'm not sure, but I've decided to fly back east and take care of things personally."

Edgar appeared confident in his pursuit. He shared with me that for the first time in his life he felt lighter in spirit, as if a heavy weight had been lifted off his shoulders. Not only was he feeling hopeful about the future, but, overall, he felt more relaxed and less anxious. During this session, Edgar struggled with his own belief system about the spirit world. With great hesitancy, he accepted the idea of his brother's spirit being restless and unhappy. And yet, he was certain of the need to do something to appease his twin. Edgar knew that in doing this work he was not only helping his brother, he was freeing himself of the heavy burden of having to live for both of them.

The intricate web of connections he had with his brother became more clear when Edgar remembered how, oftentimes, as he drifted into sleep, he had the sensation of being inside a warm place, like a pool of water. In the darkness of what Edgar thought to be his mother's womb, he could feel his brother's body wrapped around his. Like dolphins, side by side, they could feel each other's heartbeat.

"I am not sure if this was part of a fantasy I created to comfort myself or a true memory of my life as an embryo. I don't know, but it doesn't matter!" Edgar said with sadness. "Sometimes, when I'm very anxious and unable to go sleep, I feel a heavy apprehension and see images of people dying. I wonder if that's the way I felt when I knew my brother was not going to make it. I must have known. We were so close.

"Do you know that, when I was a kid, I always had this feeling I was not sleeping alone on my bed? One night, when my mother was putting me to bed, I told her my secret, and until this day I remember the sadness in her eyes. I didn't believe what she said about imaginary friends. Even at my young age, I was sure it was not my imagination. I was not alone in my room at night."

"What do you mean?"

"My brother was there. He was my guardian angel."

Edgar went on to say that as he grew older, his brother's presence as a protector was clear to him. Edgar remembered how at the age of ten he almost drowned during a family camping trip. He and his cousin Alex had decided to go for a swim in the river. Suddenly, Edgar found himself caught in a strong current. He screamed for help as he felt his body being pulled down and deep into the foamy waters. Alex, two years younger, thought Edgar was playing at first, but as the distance between him and Edgar grew, he realized his cousin was in trouble and went for help.

Edgar was struggling to keep himself afloat, as the current dragged him into an even more dangerous area, where he was thrown against dead tree branches and logs caught in the fast flow of the river. He felt the pain as his skin scraped against the rocks at the bottom. Edgar's body was growing weak. Even though he kept fighting, he realized the river was stronger than he was. The river was winning.

"I was terrified. I was drowning! I remember how I had been pushed down and pulled up by the swirling body of the river. I must have fallen unconscious because all of a sudden the river turned into a water dragon. Its big arms carried me into its dark cave. I saw no hope for survival. The giant was about to devour me. Its large throat looked like a dungeon filled with deformed creatures with long limbs. I braced myself for the worst. Then, as I looked into the entrails of the dragon, I saw a young boy, my age. He reached out with his hand and he said, 'Come on. I'll help you out.'"

Edgar paused to catch his breath. I could tell he was back in the river. He was caught in the swirl of his own emotions. His eyes were filled with tears. I waited. This was an important moment for him. This incident at the river and the water dragon were metaphors for what he had experienced in the past few months. He had been prey to fear and panic attacks. Now Edgar had a chance to heal from his terror.

"At first, I didn't have the energy to reach out for his hand. The boy kept egging me on. 'Come, Ed. You can do it! Grab my hand.' And he moved a little closer to me. I was so tired. My muscles, stiff from the cold, were not responding. It was as if my body was disconnected from my brain. Several times, I tried to reach out and take the boy's hand, but the river dragged me away even farther. Defeated, I let go and I sank to the bottom of the river. I swallowed more water and my lungs hurt. Then I saw the boy next to me. He put his arm around my neck and he pulled me to the surface. When I finally regained consciousness, I rested on top of a large log that floated with the current, down the river. I looked around for the boy who had saved my life, but he was gone."

Edgar went back east and, as he had planned, his brother was named in a ceremony conducted by a Catholic priest at the gravesite. James was the chosen name. As the family gathered around for the ritual, both parents confessed their feelings of relief and they thanked Edgar for his courage to face the past. Edgar came back to my office with a renewed sense of hope.

"I have a question for you," he said. "Was my brother with me when I came to see you the first time?"

There was no simple answer. In my role as a therapist, I was not to contaminate my client's beliefs. I had often thought my work as a therapist was similar to that of a midwife. We guard the gates with careful intent and we prepare to do what is necessary to bring the new spirit out of the womb and into this world. We become Oyá, the Afro-Cuban deity of transformation. We go back and forth from the realms of death and life. We wear whichever mask fits the occasion. Sometimes we wear the black mask of death in disguise, as we help our clients peel off unhealthy patterns, behaviors, and relationships. Other times, we wear the multicolored birth mask where we assist in the receiving of new ideas, of insights, of healthy attitudes and connections.

The process of healing is about death, birth, and rebirth. Knowing that we are not alone in the dark underworld of our pain and suffering is a major part of the therapeutic encounter. As a therapist who navigates in the mysterious realms of my clients' psyches, it has been helpful for me to know that I am not doing this work by myself. There are many allies by my side. They are the co-pilots in the journey. Unexpectedly, they fly into my office. They help me mediate between the invisible and mysterious world of the spirit and a tangible reality. With these thoughts, I turned to Edgar and changed my expected answer into a question.

"What do you think, Edgar? Was your brother here that day?"

"If you had asked me that same question two weeks ago. I would definitely answer with a NO. Today, I believe he was. There is no doubt in my mind that he has been around for most of my life and that he will always be."

THIRTEEN

Doña Tita

APRIL BRINGS THE light of spring, with its tender rays of sun shining through the new leaves. For those whose lives are in the perpetual darkness of depression or devastating illness, this time of year is harsh. Heavy eyelids refuse to open up to let in the light. Spring is the season when my clients complain of not wanting to get out of bed. The daily struggle is, without a doubt, a torment that never ceases. Outside the window, the bright day is a painful contrast to the darkness of the soul. As a woman client describes: "I just don't want to get up. I pull the covers over my head and I pretend it is nighttime."

Doña Tita was one of those people. She was old and tired of living. After her husband Hector passed away, she lost interest in this world. The woman was thin and pale. At seventy-two, her face was wrinkled and her back was hunched.

As soon as Doña Tita walked into my office, one April morning, she let me know she was not there by choice. Cecilia, her daughter, who accompanied her, introduced herself and, without wasting time, told me how it had taken weeks to convince her mother to come to see me. In turn, Doña Tita looked at her daughter and told her she had agreed because she was tired of hearing her daily litany. I knew then that Doña Tita was not going to be an easy client. Still, I could sense her loneliness and

175

her need to talk to someone about her final days. One did not need to see auras to notice the grayness around her.

Cecilia retired to the lobby and I waited for Doña Tita to open a dialogue. Her eyes were small, with eyelids that half-covered her opaque pupils. The black dress she wore gave her face a ghostly appearance. Finally, the elder spoke with a raspy voice, as if she were coming out from a deep trance. "Doctor, this is a waste of your time. There is no life force left in me."

I searched her eyes for a tiny spark but I was met with an impenetrable wall. "You don't need to apologize," I said and leaned forward. "Time is relative. I just need to know how I can be of help to you."

"I have no desire to live." The tone of her voice was flat. "I am dying." Doña Tita told me about a recurring dream she had had for the last year. In that dream, she sat in front of a large movie screen and watched her whole life unfold from the second she was born up to her present age. Right at age seventy-two, she hears a loud click and the film stops.

"Have you talked to your children about the dream?" I asked.

"Only with my daughter Cecilia," Doña Tita said in the same monotone.

It was not the first time Doña Tita had had a premonition. A year before her husband Hector died, on a road trip to visit his sister in New Mexico, she'd had a dream that warned her about his death. On the second night of their vacation, she dreamed she was attending a funeral. At first it was not clear who the deceased was. There were lots of people. Some of them were family and friends. They were looking at Doña Tita and they made comments she couldn't understand, except she could tell they were talking about her. Then a woman with long black hair emerged from the crowd. She walked towards Doña Tita who recognized her as Alicia, Hector's mother. In the dream, Alicia was young. She took Doña Tita by the hand and guided her to the casket. Doña Tita tried to pull away. She didn't want to see. Alicia grabbed her by the shoulders and said, "You must take a last look at Hector!" In disbelief, Doña Tita peeked inside, and there was Hector. His pale skin had the texture of wax, the cold of death had hardened the soft expression of his features. The body inside the casket was not her Hector. It was an empty shell no longer housing the warm spirit of the man she'd loved.

In my office, Doña Tita paused to take a deep breath and to wipe the tears from her wrinkled cheeks. "When I woke up the next morning, I was relieved to see Hector peacefully sleeping next to me. I lay there on the bed and I watched him breathe. It was then that a crashing thought flashed across my mind. I knew Hector was not going to live very long."

The old woman's hand shook as she reached out for another tissue. While we were in silence, I took a sip of my coffee and waited for her to recover. From my therapist's chair, I witnessed how the fragile body of Doña Tita appeared to be shrinking, as if death had already begun to claim her flesh and spirit.

A month after their vacation, Hector went to the doctor for a routine exam. Three days later they received a phone call from his doctor, who wanted to see Hector back in his office the next day. Hector had a large tumor in his right lung.

"He never smoked in his life, but there he was dying from cancer." There was some anger in Doña Tita's voice.

Hector had not had any warning symptoms, but according to Doña Tita he was a quiet man who didn't like to complain. The day before he left for the hospital for his last chemotherapy treatment, Hector organized all his tools in the garage and filed notes and papers on his desk. Doña Tita was very upset with him for spending all his time on what she thought was a waste of his energy. Hector was stubborn, and when she complained, he told her to leave him alone and to go back inside the house. Upset, Doña Tita screamed at him, "If you keep up with this nonsense you're going to die before your time." Hector ignored her words and went back to his digging out papers from boxes and drawers. Even though he had hardly any life left in his body, Hector spent his last hours in the house inside the garage.

The next day, Hector got up early and prepared himself to

go to the hospital for his treatment. Usually, Doña Tita went with him, but that morning he asked her to stay home. Doña Tita protested, but he was firm on his decision to go alone.

"I'll always remember that morning," Doña Tita said to me. "Before he left, Hector looked at me and he said, 'Don't worry viejita, I will be back for lunch.' And he hugged me good-bye."

Hector never came home. Around eleven, Doña Tita received a call from her son Alejandro, who told her he was coming over to take her to the hospital. He had received a phone call from the doctor with the bad news. Hector was in a delicate condition. He had suffered a heart attack during the chemotherapy treatment. While Doña Tita waited for Alejandro, she couldn't stop herself from shaking and pacing around the house. During one of her visits to the kitchen, she noticed the clock on the wall had stopped right at eleven forty-five. She didn't think much of it and poured herself some coffee. A few minutes later when Doña Tita went to turn off the light in the bedroom, she saw the arms of that clock were frozen, too. Doña Tita walked into the room and she was greeted by a cold chill. She was surprised because all the windows were closed.

Doña Tita stood in the middle of the bedroom, feeling a heavy weight pressing on her chest. She could hardly breathe. Maybe she was having a heart attack. She panicked at the thought of dying all alone. "Hector! Hector!" she called out.

At that moment, the pressure went away, replaced by a sensation of calmness. She took a deep and long breath. Suddenly she was very relaxed. Doña Tita's gaze traveled around the room and rested on the side of the bed where Hector slept. He was right there. He lay on his back with a peaceful expression on his face. Then, the vivid image turned into a glow of blue light that bounced towards her. When it finally reached her, she experienced the warmest hug she had ever received.

"It was Hector hugging me," Doña Tita said with sadness. "I heard his voice, 'Tita, my beloved Tita, I love you.' The temperature in the room turned hot and the lamp in the corner turned on and off. It was then I knew Hector was gone."

When Alejandro arrived that day, Doña Tita was still standing in the middle of the bedroom. She kept waiting for Hector to come back one more time and tell her he loved her. She did not share the experience with her son. She knew he wouldn't believe her, but when he said, "Mother, let's go. We need to hurry up," Doña Tita turned to him and said, "There is no need to rush. Your father is gone."

To me, Doña Tita appeared lost in the web of her painful memories. I waited for her to continue but she was quiet and her eyes filled with tears. I could see the old lady's pain all around her heart. It had a murky green aura I'd seen in clients suffering from acute grief. In the case of Doña Tita, not only could I see her intense sorrow but I could also feel it in my own heart, like a sharp knife cutting through the chest wall, leaving a burning sensation on its way in. I'd known through the years that oftentimes when clients come into my office, their suffering is so heavy that as a therapist I need to protect myself from their pain.

In psychology classes, the word "transference" is well discussed, but we are never taught how to protect ourselves from the invisible thoughts, emotions, negative entities and spirits a client brings into our office. That is a different story. It is too esoteric! That realm of connection between the client and the therapist is never touched upon. Here, as I sat across from Doña Tita, I could feel the pull of her death wish, like an octopus, its long tentacles reaching for my heart.

Glancing again at Doña Tita's aura, I discovered a couple of brown spots in the area around her pelvis. First I thought of tumors attached to her ovaries, but as I tuned in more closely, the images became clear and the word guilt echoed inside my mind. Of course, I couldn't talk to Doña Tita about what I had seen, but I could find my way to the subject. Shamans have known from the beginning of time that in order for our work to do its magic, the therapist must wear different masks, as I've mentioned in previous chapters. She must be able to camouflage according to the landscape of her client's mind. She must be ready to speak the different languages of metaphors and symbols.

"You must feel very lonely without your life partner," I said.

"Lonely? It is deeper than that. Hector and I were together for fifty-three years. I met Hector when I was nineteen. We were inseparable. We truly enjoyed each other's company. That's why I feel so much pain and guilt about him dying alone on a hospital bed. I have been angry with myself for not having insisted on going with him to the treatment, that day he died. I have not been able to forgive myself."

"He wanted to go alone," I reminded her.

"Hector knew something was going to happen. He wanted to spare me the pain. He was that way. I should have known better than to let him go without me."

"Maybe he had his own reasons."

"Yes!" she said. For the first time her eyes sparked. "He was a chicken when it came to saying good-bye."

"Maybe he knew that with you there by his side it was going to be too difficult for him to leave."

"I know, but there is no excuse for that. I wanted to be there and hold his hand. I feel so bad about him dying alone. If only I knew! I can't sleep at night. I think and I think about that morning. I replay every minute of the hour we spent together before he left for the hospital. I search hard for any hints I have missed. It is haunting! I see Hector at the breakfast table. That morning he looked paler than the day before and he had dark circles under his eyes. I knew he was tired of the chemotherapy. It is brutal to go through such a treatment and the nausea and the diarrhea. Oh my God! It is so demoralizing. My poor Hector was like a little bird with broken wings. It hurt me so bad to see him so sick. I feel so guilty for not paying more attention to him but...I was scared. I was so afraid of even looking at him because it was like looking at the face of death."

Embarrassed by her own behavior, Doña Tita expressed her shame about how she had avoided Hector during the last few weeks of his life. She was angry with him for not having the energy to do the things they'd enjoyed together, such as gardening. She had turned impatient when he didn't eat his meals and when he couldn't sleep at night. There were days when she wished to go away from the house and from him. She didn't want to see Hector slowly wasting away. Doña Tita busied herself with her house projects and phone calls to friends and the children.

"Now I wish so much I had spent more time with him. I'm so mad at myself! The children don't understand that. Maybe they don't want to hear it because they feel the same way I do. Even when they come to visit, they don't stay very long."

"You know, Doña Tita, the feelings you're describing are not uncommon for people in your situation. For most people it is difficult to face the death of their loved ones."

"It doesn't really help to know others feel the same way I do. The truth is that I was not emotionally there for Hector. I didn't do my job right. To be honest, I knew he was dying, but I didn't want to admit it to myself. I kept saying that the chemotherapy was going to kill the tumor, that life was going to go back to normal like it was before. I didn't want to believe that Hector was leaving. I closed my eyes to the signs, and I shut down my heart so that it wouldn't hurt as much."

I asked if she ever dreamed of Hector.

"Not lately. He showed up in my dreams a couple of times when he first died. In one, he looked younger and he talked to me but I couldn't hear his words. In the other dream, he looked worried and sad."

Doña Tita pondered. I was careful to give her the space she needed to make her own decision. When it comes to my clients' spiritual values and beliefs, I always try not to contaminate them with mine. Even though I could see Hector had been hanging around Doña Tita, that was not information I needed to share with her. I would wait for her to tell me, if she chose to do so.

When Doña Tita returned the following week, she looked as depressed as she had the week before. The only difference I could notice in Doña Tita's aura was a cloud of anxiety around her solar plexus, or the abdominal area. After our routine of questions and answers, where she informed me about her lack of energy, sleeping difficulties and low appetite, I could tell Doña Tita was beginning to feel comfortable in my presence.

"Doctor Fernández, do you believe in spirits?" she asked bluntly.

"Why are you asking me that?"

"I have a feeling you do, but I'm not sure how you therapists see things."

"What really matters here is what you think, Doña Tita."

"Well, in that case, I wanted to tell you about something that has been happening since I saw you last."

Doña Tita took her time to make herself comfortable on the couch. She had not shared very much about her background, but by her accent I could tell she was a native of Argentina. Her Spanish was colored by the soft intonation of the "j" and "g" where words slip into one another as if she were singing. In spite of her depression, Doña Tita had an aura of simple elegance. She reminded me of a delicate porcelain doll.

Finally, Doña Tita found the courage to tell me that on the night of the day when she had been in my office, she was getting ready to go to bed when she heard a noise in the house. At first she thought it was her cat, but then she noticed Pedro sleeping by the foot of the bed. She heard a stamping sound coming from the living room. Afraid it could be a robber, she grabbed the phone to dial 9-1-1. She waited and a few seconds later she heard steps coming towards the bedroom. She braced herself, dialed 9, and before she had a chance to dial 1, the blue glow she'd seen the day Hector died appeared in the room. Then, it quickly disappeared down the hall leaving behind the distinct smell of Hector's cologne.

Doña Tita sat by the bed and waited for Hector, who didn't come back again until the next night. She was awakened by the weight of a body next to her on the bed. Afraid to open her eyes, she could feel a warm presence. She asked aloud, "Hector, are you there?" There was no answer except for a slight movement on Hector's side on the bed. Doña Tita went back to sleep, comforted by her husband's company.

"That night I did not have any problem falling asleep. The next morning I woke up with vivid images of a dream where Hector and I were together. He held my hand and he said, 'Tita, I don't want you to worry so much about me. You need to get on with your life. Enjoy the years you have left. I didn't want you by my side that day I died. You know me. I don't do well with good-byes.'"

Doña Tita shifted her position on the couch. For the first time, she looked relaxed and at peace. I understood that the dream had given Doña Tita the gift of forgiveness. In her eyes were tiny sparks of light. There was hope for Doña Tita. Maybe now she could move on with her life, knowing that her Hector had not entirely abandoned her.

"That dream is quite a gift," I said.

"Sure it is. I'm not sure if there is such a thing as life after death, but it is good to know that Hector is around. He's watching over me at night. I've always been scared of the dark. Knowing that he's there makes me feel safe."

I glanced at my watch. Our time for the day was over. I helped Doña Tita get up from the couch, and as we walked to the door, she stopped and turned to me. We were only a foot apart. At such close proximity, I could see the wrinkles around her lips. She looked older and tired but I could detect a renewed feeling of confidence in the way she held my gaze. Doña Tita lifted her thin and bony arm and placed her hand on my left shoulder. Then her eyes moved away and she took a long glance around my office.

"Doctor Fernández, you have a nice office."

"It certainly helps to be so close to the waters of Lake Union."

"Sure, but it's more than that. You have good spirits helping you to do your work. Who is the old woman with short gray hair?"

"You mean that picture on the wall?" I said, thinking Doña Tita was referring to the picture of Lila, a Native-American elder, a basket-weaver friend from the past.

"She is very wise, too," Doña Tita said. "I was talking about the beautiful old woman with strong hands. She stands by your left side when you're in the chair."

Surprised, I tried to compose myself. Doña Tita was one of the few clients to see one of my helpers from the spirit world. I hesitated to answer her question but then I decided it was only fair to validate her perceptions.

"That old woman is my Grandmother Patricia."

"She is a generous soul," Doña Tita said as she removed her hand from my shoulder. "Doctor Fernández, please thank your grandmother. Tell her to keep an eye on my Hector."

Doña Tita did not wait for an answer. She shook my hand and walked towards the reception area where her daughter Cecilia was waiting. It was not until that moment I realized we had not set a date for Doña Tita's next appointment.

"Doña Tita," I called.

The old woman turned to me and, as if she had read my mind, said, "No need for another appointment. Please don't be offended, but I believe that Hector and I can take it from here. I'll give you a call if my depression comes back."

I stood in the middle of my office, somewhat mystified. Doña Tita's kind eyes stayed with me for a while. I felt blessed by the opportunity to be in a place where the worlds meet at one point and we are made aware of the infinite web that exists between the spirit world and us.

From the corner of my eye, I saw the spirit of Don Tomas standing near my grandmother and my nanny Carmen. Next to Don Tomas was giant Jaguar, peacefully resting on the carpet. He licked his fur with an air of total relaxation and confidence. Jaguar was the guardian of the underworld, the one that keeps us connected to the ancestors, to those who have gone before us, for they are the source of our vitality. They are the roots of the great Tree of Life.

FOURTEEN

There Is a River

The nurses' station at the cancer treatment center was like a busy colony of ants. The white uniformed men and women rushed in and out, totally absorbed in their duties. My efforts to get someone's attention were ignored as though I were invisible. As she hurried into the hall, a nurse almost bumped me to the ground. The folder she carried in her hand flew open, wafted into the air, and pages of medical records scattered all over the floor. I dropped to my knees and began to gather papers. The nurse followed me and soon we were crawling on the shiny tiled surface. Our eyes met briefly as we stood back up. She didn't apologize. Instead, she asked me who I was. I told her I was a therapist and I was there to see a patient who had undergone a bone marrow transplant.

"Doctor Fernández, I'm so glad you're here." Her green eyes appeared to brighten. "Elisa and her family have been waiting for you." She checked her watch. "Gee, right now she is getting her platelets transfusion. Come with me. You can meet the parents."

The strong smell of antiseptics and body fluids nauseated me. The air was saturated with the stench of illness. Even though the bed was empty, I could detect the contours of the body that had rested on it prior to my arrival. By the side of the

185

bed, on top of a metal table, were a glass of water and an empty paper cup. Right above, on the wall, pinned to a board were three pictures of a young woman.

"They must have gone down to the cafeteria," the nurse said.

The nurse showed me to a chair by the window. She handed me a mask to wear, asked me to wash my hands and walked out of the room. From the photographs on the wall, I could see how the illness had taken possession of Elisa's body. The first picture showed a young Elisa with long brunette hair. Her big brown eyes, like two bright stars, stood out from the dark olive skin. In the second picture, a thinner and paler Elisa smiled to the camera. By now her hair was gone and a wig of short hair, in the same color, had replaced the healthy mane. There was a pronounced expression of tiredness in her eyes. In the third picture, Elisa was bald and her face was swollen with a grimace of pain.

I stood in front of the photos, unable to move away. Elisa was only fifteen but in her short life she had endured the challenges of many lives. This was her second bone marrow transplant. The first one had taken place in Spain, after which Elisa enjoyed good health for three years, then leukemia claimed her body again. Filled with despair and under the advice of doctors, Elisa's parents sold everything they owned, including their home, to come to the United States. They had high hopes to save their daughter with a second transplant, at the most reputable facility in the world, which is in Seattle.

The Gonzalez family, as I will call them, moved into housing provided by the hospital, a small apartment where they would reside for the next five months of their lives. In addition to Elisa, the Gonzalezes brought with them their twelve-year-old son Mauricio and Catalina, who was Mrs. Gonzalez's only sister and thirty-two years old. Immediately, they faced the difficulties of a new culture and a different language, not to mention the grief and loneliness without the support of their extended family and friends.

Soon after their arrival, Elisa was admitted to the bone marrow transplant unit where she underwent several days of chemotherapy and radiation therapy. This regime had the dual purpose of destroying both bone marrow and cancerous cells, to make room for the new bone marrow.

As soon as the preparation phase was completed, healthy bone marrow was harvested from Mauricio. This procedure, which involves "little risk," was done while Mauricio was under anesthesia. A needle was inserted into the cavity of the rear hip bone, where a large quantity of bone marrow is located. The thick red liquid was extracted with a needle and syringe. A few hours later, this bone marrow was infused into Elisa intravenously.

The day of the transplant is known as Day 0. This is the time when the medical staff carefully monitors the success or failure of the transplant. Usually three to four weeks after a successful transplant, the first sign of engraftment appears with a noticeable increase in the patient's white blood cell count.

Sadly, in the case of Elisa, the transplanted marrow cells did not take hold in her body. By the time the social worker contacted me, the family had been at the hospital for four months. Elisa had developed chronic graft-versus-host disease after the third month of the transplant. This is when immune cells in the transplanted marrow attack the patient's body. As result, patients develop life-threatening complications.

The nurse, whom I'll call Kathy, returned to the room where I'd been waiting, accompanied by three adults and one child. She introduced them to me. Mr. Gonzalez, tall and slender, was the first one to talk. He was quick to let me know how exhausted they were from so many sleepless nights and gruesome days by the side of their daughter's bed. In the last few days, things had taken a turn for the worse, and now they had no hope of ever taking Elisa back to Spain. Mrs. Gonzales broke down and cried, while Mauricio placed his arm around his mother's waist and pressed his body closer to her. Catalina, the aunt, moved right behind Mauricio.

"I'm so sorry," I said but I knew that nothing I could say would take away their pain.

"Elisa fought very hard but..." Mr. Gonzales said and burst into a soft sob.

"She hasn't given up," Catalina said. "Elisa is a fighter!" she continued as if trying to give herself some hope.

"Yes. She is a fighter, but she is tired," Mrs. Gonzalez said and wiped off her tears with the back of her hand.

We were interrupted by Kathy, the nurse, who announced that Elisa was being brought back. She reminded us to put on our masks. We moved around the room and found places to sit. A few seconds later, a male nurse wheeled Elisa into the room. Immediately, the Gonzalezes went to the side of their daughter and helped the nurse transfer her to the bed.

"She needs to rest," the nurse said on his way out of the room.

From my position in a corner of the room, away from the group, I couldn't see Elisa. The family had formed a barrier between them and the outside world. I was a stranger invading the privacy of these precious moments. I lowered my eyes out of respect for their pain.

All of a sudden, I had a strange sensation in the pit of my stomach. I was nauseated and confused. My legs felt weak. I sat back on my chair, afraid I was going to faint. What was I doing there? What made the social worker think I could be of help to this family? Oblivious to my thoughts, the Gonzalezes were busy tending to Elisa. Thinking that perhaps it was best for me to return the next day, I got up from my chair, only to be pushed right back on it by some invisible hand.

"You chicken! Are you afraid of facing me?" I heard the voice of a woman coming from behind. Surprised, I turned to see who she was. "Ha, ha! Don't waste your time! You can't see me."

I waited a few seconds and tried to get up again. Once more I was thrown back on my chair. What was it? Who are you and what do you want from me? I thought to myself. But I didn't receive any answer. Glued to my chair, I observed how the Gonzalez family, unaware of my situation, was busy with Elisa. A cold breeze brushed my right shoulder. It was freezing! I turned to the only window in the room. It was firmly shut. The voice came back. "You need to help Elisa. She's afraid. Help her to see the river. There is a river that runs into heaven."

"What river?" I asked. I didn't hear the voice again.

Kathy came back into the room and asked the family to accompany her. A conference with the doctor was about to start. All the Gonzalezes, except for Mauricio, left. Mauricio pulled up a chair and sat by the bed. This was my chance. I got up and walked towards Elisa. My heart shrank at the sight. Elisa was unrecognizable. Her bald head was big. Her swollen face was covered by a rash, dark patches and blisters. Overall, her skin was yellow. I could hear the wheezing of her lungs as she took very short breaths.

I sat opposite Mauricio. Elisa rested with her eyes closed. I hesitated, not wanting to disturb her, but I realized that with the family gone this was the best time to talk to her.

"Elisa, my name is Flor. I'm a psychotherapist. Your social worker asked to come and see you. She thought you might need someone outside your family to talk to."

Slowly, Elisa opened her eyes. A semi-transparent film covered her dark brown pupils. She squinted a few times and then her lips parted in a futile attempt to smile. It was then I noticed more blisters inside her mouth. How painful! Poor girl! How could this be? Looking at Elisa was like looking at the face of death. There was no resemblance to the young woman in the first picture. She had been disfigured by a horrible illness. With her immune system destroyed, she was left at the mercy of viruses and fungal infections that were rapidly claiming her entire being. Elisa was like a disarmed soldier in the middle of a battlefield. She had no defenses left to fight the enemy.

"It hurts," she said with effort.

"I'm sorry. If you want, I can come back tomorrow."

"No, no, you stay." Elisa turned to Mauricio and told him to go and play outside.

"Esta bien," Mauricio said with a clear Castilian accent. The boy looked pale. I tried to imagine his sacrifice. He had been living inside the hospital for months. No school, no friends. And on top of all that, he had to witness the gradual process of his only sister dying. He left us alone there.

"Poor Mauricio, he has suffered a lot." Elisa paused to catch her breath. "I'm tired. I feel very tired. I don't think I can do this any longer but I'm afraid."

"What are you afraid of?" I asked.

Elisa replied she was afraid of death. She shared a dream she had had a few days before where she saw herself climbing a tall mountain. It was very painful because all her bones and muscles ached. She managed to climb half-way to the top and then she fell and rolled to the bottom. She lay there, with her arms and her legs broken. She couldn't move. She screamed for help but no one could hear her. She was all alone.

Feelings of helplessness are common among bone marrow transplant patients. As soon as Elisa moved into the hospital, she found herself totally dependent on strangers for survival. Elisa was by herself unable to take care of basic daily functions, such as washing and using the toilet. It was embarrassing to be constantly exposed to the medical staff. She was undressed, poked with needles, treated for rashes and blisters that covered her entire body, her private areas.

Elisa told me about a second dream where she was going on a trip. She was confused in this dream because she didn't have any luggage and she was concerned about not having any clothes to wear. A woman, unknown to her, told her not to worry because she was going to be well cared for on her arrival to her destination. Elisa was scared to travel by herself, and her family was not allowed to go with her. In the dream she was taken inside a pink bus. Her parents and Mauricio were outside. With their arms extended, they reached out to her, but a lady dressed in black would not let them in. Elisa woke up screaming.

She was comforted by her mother, who rested on a chair by the side of the bed.

"I didn't share the dream with my mother. I didn't want to scare her," Elisa concluded. She was wheezing very hard.

I realized Elisa was very fatigued and that she needed to rest, so I told her I would return the next day to continue our conversation. On my way out, I met Kathy who was returning to the nurses' station from her rounds. I took this opportunity to ask about Elisa's condition. She invited me to come in and we sat behind the counter in front of a computer. Kathy placed her hands on her knees and lifted her shoulders. Then she shook her head and blew a puff of air out of her mouth.

"Doctor Fernández, Elisa has a few days...maybe a few hours. Her condition has worsened. The infection is not responding to strong antibiotics."

Kathy informed me of a new complication they were trying to fight—Veno-occlusive disease, where the flow of blood through the liver becomes obstructed. The symptoms of VOD are jaundice, an enlarged liver, pain in the upper right abdomen, fluid in the abdomen. On top of all that, Elisa had developed renal insufficiency. Her kidneys were failing and the doctors didn't think dialysis was appropriate in her case.

"She is in a lot of pain," Kathy said. "At this point our goal is to make her comfortable. There is nothing else we can do."

"How is her family doing?" I asked.

"They keep waiting for a miracle," Kathy said and turned her face in the direction of Elisa's room.

According to Kathy, the Gonzalezes were relentless. They stayed by their daughter's side night and day. Mr. Gonzalez read every single medical report. He was well informed about the pros and cons of the different medical procedures. Mrs. Gonzalez was different; she did not want to know much about the process for fear of losing her faith. Instead, she spent hours praying with her rosary. Once a day, she visited the hospital chapel and lit candles to the Virgin Mary. Catalina would pray, too, but she was a heavy smoker and forced to take frequent trips outside the hospital. There, by the entrance door, she would soothe her anxiety by taking deep and long puffs from her cigarettes.

The next day, I returned to the hospital in the afternoon. I found Elisa in the company of her mother. The rest of the family had gone to the cafeteria to have lunch. Mrs. Gonzalez's face lit up when she saw me. Still, she looked pale and had dark circles around her eyes. I figured she was in her late thirties but she had aged rapidly from all her suffering and had the appearance of a fifty-year-old woman.

"Elisa is sleeping," she whispered. "She had a   restless night."

I reached for a chair but Mrs. Gonzalez got up and signaled me to go outside. She asked if she could talk to me in private. I followed her down the hall to a small room with a table and two chairs. We were alone. Mrs. Gonzalez put her rosary inside the pocket of her blue skirt. I waited for her to talk but instead she broke down in tears.

"Mrs. Gonzalez, I'm so sorry." I reached over and held her hand.

"Call me Beatriz." She dried her tears with a Kleenex she pulled out of her pocket. "I know my Elisa is dying. I'm no fool but it's hard for me to let her go. Last night when she was in so much pain, I kept asking for a miracle. Oh Jesus, dear Jesus, don't take my baby." She paused and looked at me with a pleading expression on her face. "Can you help me, doctor? I need to let her go. My Elisa is suffering so much."

I thought for a moment. What words could I possibly say to comfort her? My mind went blank. I looked into Beatriz's eyes, dark pools of sadness, infinite black tunnels that took me to the other side of life. It was a strange experience. I was transported back to the day of Elisa's birth. I saw the radiance of Beatriz's face when she looked at her baby daughter the very first time. What a gift Elisa had been to her mother! From the beginning, Elisa had always been a peaceful and happy child who made everyone laugh. Her short existence in this world had brought much joy to all those around her.

"Beatriz," I said. "Think about the day when Elisa was born."

A sudden radiance emanated from her being. She looked younger. Beatriz went on with her narration of the birth of her daughter. Through her words, I realized that death and birth were similar processes. I had asked Beatriz to go back and to remember that place of deep surrendering that she must have experienced as a mother—the feeling of a life force rushing through the birth canal and the final burst of it into the world. I thought of Oyá, ferrying souls from the land of the dead into this world and vice-versa.

"Isn't that amazing?" Beatriz said. "I feel like I have been carrying Elisa in a different kind of womb. This womb is invisible but it feels as heavy and watery as when I was pregnant with her. I know that the time is coming and that I can't stop her from leaving. She's going. She's going! And I'm causing her pain by closing my legs."

I moved to her side of the table and held Beatriz in my arms as she wept for her daughter. She had remembered what she needed in order to relinquish her baby to the hands of Oyá. Now it was just a matter of waiting for both Elisa to free herself and for Oyá to arrive with her ferryboat.

Two days later, in the evening, I was driving home from my office. Right before the entrance to I-5 south, while I waited for the green light, I heard the voice I had heard in the hospital. It was loud and clear. "Go to the hospital." I did not dare question such an authority, the one who had pushed me back onto the chair when I had tried to leave Elisa's room. I believed this entity to be very capable of driving me off the road if I refused her command.

I drove to the hospital, feeling a sense of urgency. I knew Elisa was dying. When I arrived at Elisa's room, the Gonzalez family greeted me with their somber and grief-stricken faces. Elisa lay on her bed, her pale and swollen face covered with purple and red patches. She was unrecognizable. The grip of death was palpable and visible. The air had the stench of rotten squash, which my nurse clients had described when talking about the smell of death. It was asphyxiating and it burned inside my lungs.

Elisa opened her eyes and mumbled words I couldn't understand. Beatriz moved away from the bed and the rest of the family followed. It was Mauricio who said to me: "Lisi wants to talk to you." Lisi was the name Mauricio used affectionately to call his sister. Before I moved close to Elisa, I pulled my mask over my mouth. It had become an instinctual habit. I heard Elisa mutter, "Noo maask." She coughed and a thin string of blood ran down from one of her nostrils. Elisa swallowed and cleared her throat. I reached over and cleaned her nose with a Kleenex.

"Thanks," Elisa said. Her voice was almost inaudible, a soft whisper. "I'm scared." Two tears, like silver threads, ran down her cheeks. "I'm afraid. It's very dark." She paused. Her breathing was labored and shallow.

I moved closer to Elisa and held her hand in mine. It was cold and sweaty and bloated, like the rest of her body. I looked at her and her eyes met mine. Her brown irises were opaque, as if the curtain of death was closing over them.

"Elisa," I said. "You have my permission to go." It felt strange to say those words. A feeling of peace filled my whole being.

"I don't know how," Elisa murmured back.

And I heard the familiar voice say: "The river. Take her to the river." Except this time, I felt the warm touch of a hand on my right shoulder, and as I turned, I saw the glimpse of a shadow next to me. I closed my eyes and I saw the vivid image of a large river. It reminded me of the Amazon, with murky brown waters swollen by the seasonal rains. Many years ago, on my journey down the Amazon I had experienced the calming and peaceful energies of the great water snake as we floated on her elongated body among the giant trees of the forest.

"Elisa," I said, feeling the vibrancy of these images in my own body. "Elisa, there is a place I want to take you. There is a river. Imagine this river of emerald green waters. It runs down through a thick forest of tall and wide old trees. We are standing on the shore. Can you see it?" Elisa responded with a nod of her head. "The natives of this place believe that there is a spirit canoe that comes and takes us to the other side, to the island of spirits."

Elisa pressed my hand and her body shook. She opened her eyes, "I'm afraid of the water. I see the canoe...but I can't reach it."

"Okay. Let's do it together. I'm a good swimmer. I'll carry you on my back to the canoe."

"Wait!" I heard the voice behind me say. "Wait! You can take her to the canoe but not any farther. Do you hear me?"

"Yes! Why?"

"Because if you do, you won't be able to return."

I understood and followed her directions. Again, I guided Elisa to the bank of the river. She held tight to my hand as we took small steps into the refreshing body of the river.

"This feels good," Elisa said. "My body feels light as a feather."

I saw Elisa slightly open her lips in a tiny grin of joy. I took it as a sign that she was no longer afraid. It was time for me to carry Elisa to the canoe. And just as I was preparing to do so, the image of a pink dolphin flashed in my mind. The beautiful creature swam in circles around Elisa.

"Dolphin!" Elisa muttered. "There is a dolphin. It is splashing water on me. She wants my attention."

The dolphin had come to take Elisa to the canoe. It was time.

"Elisa. This is..." My voice broke down and I felt a thick lump in my throat.

Elisa opened her eyes and looked at me. "Remember the pink bus in my dream? This is like that." She paused to rest. "The dolphin wants me to hold on to her fin. If I do, it will take me to the canoe. The lady dressed in black is standing behind you. She told me she would push the canoe down the river. That lady doesn't want you or my family near the canoe. That's why dolphin is here."

Hmm! I thought to myself. That's Oyá. She's here. What a trickster!

"Your job is done," I heard the voice behind me say. "It is now up to Elisa to grab that dolphin's fin. Sometimes it takes a little practice. Go home."

Elisa looked worn out and the Gonzalezes were about to return any moment now. I knew it was time for me to go. Still in a daze, I left the hospital and drove home. That night as I prepared for bed, the image of Elisa flashed in front of me. She looked exactly like the young woman I'd seen in the picture by her bed. Elisa looked happy. Her long hair was blown on her face by the wind. Her laughter had the sound of crystals, and hundreds of tiny sparks were glowing from her dark brown eyes.

I didn't need to call the hospital. I knew Elisa had crossed the wall of her fears, and now, inside the canoe, she was journeying to the land of the spirits. Oyá carried her. The next morning when I retrieved my voice mail I had a message from Beatriz. She was letting me know Elisa had passed on in her sleep the night before. The family planned to take Elisa back home to Spain.

A month later, I received an envelope from Spain. The Gonzalez family sent me a thank you letter and a tiny medallion of Saint Theresa that had belonged to Elisa. As I held it in my hand, I remembered that Saint Theresa was the disguised name given to Oyá by the African slaves. I laughed and pressed the medallion to my heart. Life has many mysteries. I was thankful for the blessings Elisa brought with her death into my life.

FIFTEEN

The Ghost House

WITH A CUP OF steaming coffee, I sat at my desk and dialed the number to access my voice mail. Checking my messages was a comforting routine that helped me prepare for my day at the office. As I listened, I looked out to the calm waters of Lake Union. The large glass wall that faced east was the only boundary between Lady Union and me. I named the lake Lady Union because its sweet cadence of changing tides and undercurrents reminded me of the orisha Oshún, the Afro-Cuban deity of the rivers.

Every morning, Lady Union greets me with the swaying of her hips. Her sensuous dance is so contagious that the moored boats join her with their rocking motion. A few seconds later, gentle waves begin to slap against the concrete wall of the building. In my mind's eyes, I see the goddess Oshún, dressed in gold and yellow. Her arms and ankles are adorned with bracelets of the same colors. She is so beautiful! We Cubans call her Mama Cachita. She brings into life her kind and loving touch, which teaches us that love is the secret to all healing.

Of all the messages I scribbled down on my pad, the one that caught my attention was from a woman named Frances, co-founder of the Richard Hugo House, a literary center in Seattle. This is a haven where writers and readers can attend

197

classes, readings and retreats. In addition, they have full access to the facility, to write, do research and make connections with the literary community.

Frances was not interested in making an appointment for therapy, but rather she wanted to talk about some wandering ghosts that lived at the house. Moved by curiosity, I called her right away. Frances was excited to hear from me. She said the subject made her uncomfortable, but a friend had suggested she give me a call. Frances was concerned about the presence of ghosts at the house. In the last few weeks, these scary entities had been spotted by residents, workers and volunteers.

Frances wanted to know if I could do some sort of cleansing. She informed me that during the 1900s, the Richard Hugo House had been a mortuary. The house was sold and was used by different groups, most recently a theater company that ran out of financial resources. Frances and her husband Gary believed that before they could move on to creating what they envisioned as an artistic and literary sanctuary, they needed to clear out these ghosts.

She explained that several people had seen shadows moving across different parts of the house. Some of these spirits were playing tricks with a construction man who was remodeling some of the basement rooms. Frances's major concern, however, was the apparition of a young girl. It appeared in her daughter's bedroom at night, right before bedtime. Frances and her family resided in the upstairs part of the Hugo House.

Before I gave my answer, I consulted with myself: was I prepared to clear spirits from an old haunted house? Did I have the skills and the knowledge? I pondered for a few days in search of an answer. It came in the form of a dream where Don Tomas, my teacher, came and spoke to me. In this dream I was back in the Yucatan, and the old shaman had a rattle in his hand. He asked me to close my eyes and to listen to the sounds as he shook the object all around the top of my head. I was transported to the site of an old cave. Don Tomas led me inside where I found the skeleton of what appeared to be a big cat, maybe that of a dead jaguar. Don Tomas pointed at the bones and asked me to choose one. I chose one of the ribs.

"Take a look," Don Tomas said. "Bones are the very source of life, both human and animal. Ancestors live inside bones."

Don Tomas asked me to lie on the ground next to the cat's skeleton. I did, and instantly, I saw how the flesh of my body melted off my bones. In terror, I tried to get up and run. Don Tomas laughed at first, then he began to sing in Náhuatl. Even though I didn't understand the ancient language, I knew the shaman was singing about my re-entering the womb of life, and about the renewal and restoration of my soul.

"Bones can't be destroyed," Don Tomas sang in clear Spanish. Then he stood right next to me and put his hands in the air above me. "I bring back injured parts of your soul," he prayed. With these words, my skeleton regained its flesh.

I woke up from my dream not quite knowing what to do with these images. It was not until later that day that I became aware of their meaning. The old shaman was letting me know that I was ready to visit the underworld of the Hugo House. My power animal, the Jaguar, would help with the spiritual restoration of the restless graveyard and make peace with these ghosts from the past.

I called Frances and we agreed on a date for the cleansing. While talking to her, I became aware of the importance of community in this healing. We decided that Frances would invite other members of and workers at the Richard Hugo House to participate in the ritual.

On a cold and sunny afternoon in December of 1998, I drove to the Richard Hugo House. The 1902 Victorian mansion of at least 16,000 square feet was nestled in a quiet neighborhood, across from a reservoir and a park. The high-pitched roof of the three-story house painted with gray colors, tall wood columns and wide porch were inviting. A well-kept garden bordered the walkway to the entrance. The main door had been left open and I could hear voices and laughter coming from inside. I began to feel eerie. With some hesitation, I stepped into a reception area where I was greeted by a cold gust of air that made me shiver.

I took this greeting as a message from the resident spirits of the house. They were not happy with my visit. I acknowledged their concerns and quickly went on into the adjacent area, a café with a small cabaret stage. To my surprise, at least forty people sat at the tables drinking coffee and chatting. The atmosphere was friendly. A woman with dark and long hair introduced herself to me as Frances and invited me to join them. Among the participants were a Jesuit priest, a psychic, local artists and writers, and members and friends of the literary home, which included a group of homeless youngsters.

After my informal introduction to the group, we moved into a spacious but dark room next to the café. It felt cold and had a musty odor. By now the mood of the crowd had changed and I could feel tension in anticipation of the unpredictable. Ours was an unknown journey into the realm of mystery.

As I looked around, ghostly appearances clung to the corners. It was an ethereal world of luminous beings dressed in garments that dated back to the 1900's. A young woman captured my attention with her large peek-a-boo hat. She was busy flirting with a handsome and unaware volunteer of the Richard Hugo House.

In preparation for the cleansing, I asked the group to form a circle around a large table that had been set as an altar with candles, flowers and sage. I was well aware of the restlessness of the entities at the house. Some of them were disturbed and angry. I could feel their fear in my own body. My skin was already tingling from so much of this ghost energy around me. They were hungry for attention and wanted their own voices to be heard. Trapped inside this ghostly existence, they had waited for years to be free.

Opening the door to their world was a dangerous endeavor. It was important to ask for permission, as well as for protection from our guides. So as we lit the black and white candles on our altar, I invoked prayers to call in our power animals and spirit helpers, as Don Tomas had taught me.

"You be careful," I heard the voice of the old healer. "You do not let ghost get a hold of your soul. You keep your distance and you let Jaguar guide you."

I understood. I had done this work in the safety of my office but now I was about to enter a place that was unknown to me. The Richard Hugo House was home to these entities. More than a house, this place had memories of their physical, emotional and spiritual suffering. Therefore, as I went into their territory, it was important to maintain a certain level of detachment and of alertness.

"Call Jaguar if you find yourself lost in the underworld. He will bring you back." It was Don Tomas again with another piece of advice.

With this in mind, we began the process of cleansing. The main level of the building was free of ghosts, with the exception of the ghost of an old man we met by the fireplace. He informed me that he was the keeper of the books. He wanted to be reassured that this area in the house would be designated as the library. The group agreed to his request. The other trouble spot was a bathroom where we encountered a resistant old lady who wouldn't leave because she didn't have anyplace to go. We granted her permission to stay there so long as she did not disturb others.

Then, we moved to the basement, to a section of the house where in the past the bodies of the dead had been embalmed. Here, the temperature dropped a few degrees. It was cold and humid and there was a stench of antiseptics and of decomposing flesh. Even though the walls were clean, I could see stains of blood and other body fluids. Naked and stiff bodies of purplish complexion had rested on top of metal tables and waited for the final make-up ritual.

I had a sudden feeling of déjà vu. A cold gust of air enveloped my entire body and I was transported to an ancient temple. Inside, a sacred ritual was taking place. The body of a dead man was being dressed in his finest clothes, then wrapped in a cotton blanket and carried by family and friends to an altar.

There, a priestess blessed the body. She poured a potion made of herbs from a crystal chalice into the lips of the dead. This magic formula would help and protect the man's spirit in his journey to the other world. Gifts and offerings were made. People sang songs, wept, and mourned the dead.

Back at the Richard Hugo House, I acknowledged that as a culture, we have forgotten the sacred rituals of death. My vision of the temple came as a reminder of the importance of proper and respectful ways to treat the dead. Whether a loved one, an aspect of the self or a part of our lives, the releasing must be done with compassion and with all the ceremony required to honor the "dead one's" essence, gifts, and contributions.

As if in synch with my thoughts, a man in the group spoke about the vision he had received. "The ghosts want an altar built in this part of the house. They want to restore sacredness. They are angry with the workers of the funeral home for handling their bodies with so much disrespect."

We promised the group of restless souls to build the altar and they agreed not to bother the residents of the house anymore. Our procession moved into a larger room in the basement. Here, I felt the sensation of many wet and cold fingers reaching out to us, touching our warm bodies. They were hungry for the life force that emanated from us. I could feel the fear in the group, some participants became quiet and held onto their candles for their lives. A woman next to me began to shake and drops of sweat covered her face.

"Are you okay?" I asked.

"I don't know," she said with a broken voice. "I feel very cold and hot at the same time."

"You're taking energy that doesn't belong to you," I said and ordered her to shake her hands and legs. "Harder," I said. "Let it go!"

The woman turned pale. The rest of the group joined in and began to shake their bodies and stomp on the floors. The temperature in the room rose. Another woman spoke and said she had been told by a spirit to go and open the large and wide door facing east. As we did, a beam of sun entered the room and created a demarcation between light and dark. Someone suggested that we bless that line between the worlds of life and death.

The energy in the room was like thunder and lightning spreading across dimensions. We were at a point of no return in our cleansing ritual. We had moved into a place where we were no longer conscious of the divisions. We had transcended our ordinary existence and traveled across time. We were dancing with the ghosts of Hugo House. We could hear, feel and talk to these spirits that for so long had been neglected. The black box of their confinement had been opened. These souls were free to express their pain.

The forty members of the cleansing brigade were busy shaking their rattles, beating their drums, and smudging the corners with the smoke from the burning sage and incense. They pounded the floors and screamed messages to the ghosts. A young man, one of the homeless kids, moved closer to me. He told me he was feeling excruciating pain in his left leg. I asked him to relax and to listen. The young man grabbed his leg and dropped to the floor. With his body all contorted, he spoke with a voice that sounded much older than his actual age. Neal, as I'll call him, was serving as a medium for one of the resident ghosts: a man whose left leg had been severed in a motorcycle accident. He had bled to death. Except he did not know he was dead.

I asked the group to create a circle around Neal. I spoke to the ghost. I said, "It is okay now, you are dead. It is time for you to leave." To my surprise, Neal's face changed and took on an expression of terror. His bulging eyes fixed on mine. A cold chill ran down my spine. I felt the grip of strong hands grabbing my legs. I struggled to keep my balance. My mind was turning fuzzy. I was dizzy! The room began to spin fast and I found myself caught in a swirl. It was a dark funnel, like a tornado sweeping me into a pitch-black space. "Jaguar! Jaguar!" I called in a panic. At first, all I saw was the big and glowing golden eyes moving towards me. Gradually, the large cat made himself visible. Then, Jaguar opened his strong and sharp jaws and, in an instant, devoured me.

"No, no, I'm not dead!" Neal screamed.

"Yes, you are. You must go now. Go!" I yelled and tried to free myself from the ghost's grip.

"Go, go!" the group shouted.

Finally, Neal's body relaxed on the floor and the ghost let go of my legs. Relieved, we moved on to the next challenge. We were now in the inner guts of the Richard Hugo House, the part that was being remodeled. Our candles flickered. The air was saturated with humidity and it reeked of old rotted wood and damp soil. Our senses were sharp and ready to detect signals from the spirit world.

All of a sudden, the group turned and faced the entrance of a small room. I could see the ghostly figure of a woman. As if pulled by a magnetic force, I walked toward her. Now I was able to see her long blonde hair. She was in her mid-thirties and dressed in black.

"Who are you?" I asked. Other participants followed.

"Elizabeth," I heard the ghost say, loud and clear. There was blood running down from her wrists into the palms of her hands. "Please, help me," she implored. "I made a mistake. I was desperate! I didn't know how to stop my husband from leaving me. I don't want to die."

"It is too late. You're dead," I said.

"Noo!" Her scream echoed in my ears.

Elizabeth kicked the wall and pulled her hair. She began to shred her dress to pieces. A woman I'll call Martha joined Elizabeth in her tantrum. For the first few seconds, the rest of the group appeared intimidated by the display of rage. Martha did not rip her clothes but she yelled loud enough to hurt our ears.

"I hate you!" Elizabeth shouted and pointed at one of the men who stood next to me. "I wish you would rot in hell! You and your lovely mistress!"

I realized the man was not aware of what was happening.

Elizabeth raged on. "I hate you!" I could feel the group getting anxious. By now Martha had calmed down and was sobbing quietly. Another woman comforted her.

Then a man I'll call Carl turned to me. "I have a sharp pain in my shoulder. It feels like a knife. What should I do?"

I told Carl about Elizabeth and asked if he was willing to talk to her. Taking my request very seriously, Carl walked inside the room and stretched his hands out in search of her.

"You feel cold," Carl said. "You're shivering. Let me hold you in my arms." Carl closed his arms in a tight hug and began to rock his body with a gentle motion. "Elizabeth, I'm sorry you hurt yourself. You're a beautiful woman!" Carl's voice was soft as if he were whispering a love poem in his lover's ear.

The tenderness of Carl moved the rest of the men to take action. Together they spoke lovingly to Elizabeth. They were joined by the women who shared their words of compassion and of self-love. I stood back and treasured the precious moment. There was no doubt in my mind that the goddess Oshún was there among us, dancing with us and embracing us with her healing love.

We said good-bye to Elizabeth and moved to the upper floor of the house where Frances and Gary resided with their four-year-old daughter. We went right to the room where Frances's daughter slept. Only a few seconds in there and my throat felt tight. I could hardly swallow, and feelings of sadness filled my chest. My eyes traveled to a box of toys in a corner. I noticed a bright glow of light and heard the laughter of a young girl. As I walked towards her, the gentle radiance assumed the form of a girl about five years old with long blonde curls. I was taken with her innocent expression. She was beautiful and did not appear to be frightened by my closeness. I kneeled down and asked who she was.

"My name is Cindy."

"What are you doing here?"

"I'm waiting for my mommy to come home." She shyly started to play with one of her curls.

"Who is your mommy?"

"Alice. Her name is Alice. Do you know where she is?"

"No," I said.

It was then that I saw the shadow of a woman by the door. Tall and slender, she was like an older version of Cindy.

"I'm Alice," the woman said. "My daughter is confused. She was a little girl when she died. She drowned in the swimming pool of our home. That happened more than twenty years ago. We brought her body to this funeral home. Somehow she refuses to come with me. She thinks this is her home. I died ten years after her death. I couldn't bear the suffering of having lost her. I died from grief."

Alice told me that Cindy thought Frances's daughter was her little sister. They played together all the time. At night, they stayed up and giggled while Frances and Gary slept in the other room. During the day, Cindy wandered around Hugo House where some of the volunteers had seen her ghost. She liked to play tricks on them. They got scared. Alice begged me to help her with her daughter. She wanted me to convince Cindy that she was dead and that it was time for her to leave Hugo House.

I wasn't sure how I could talk to a young girl about being dead. Then, I thought maybe I could take Cindy back to that moment when she left her body.

"Cindy," I said aloud, "do you remember the swimming pool?"

Her expression changed to one of terror. "I don't like swimming pools. I'm scared to go in the water. Something happened to me in the pool."

"Yes. What was it?"

Cindy started to cry. In between sobs, she told me how her cousin Mark had asked her to jump in the pool with him. She didn't want to do it but he had promised her candy if she did. They both jumped in the water. Cindy didn't know how to swim and Mark who was only a year older than her couldn't pull her out. Finally Mark got out and went for help but it was too late.

I asked Cindy what was it like not to be able to breathe under water. She stopped crying. She told me that at first it was hard. She felt like her lungs were going to burst like a balloon. Her lungs hurt. But then, everything turned bright and she was no longer in the water, but she could see her body at the bottom of the pool.

"I was a little bird flying above the pool," Cindy said with some sadness.

I told Cindy that now she was a little bird and that she needed to fly high to the sky and find her mommy who was waiting for her. I explained the Hugo House was not her home and that it was time for her to leave. She asked if she could stay a bit longer and say good-bye to her friend. I said, "Of course, but after that you must leave."

After hours of intense work, the healing ceremony came to an end. We were exhausted from the arduous task of reaching into another world. Many of the ghosts of the Richard Hugo House were sent away. Finally, their restless souls had been put to rest. Some other benign spirits were allowed to stay under the condition that they would help with the building of the literary community. Our journey into the world of the dead had been successful. The negotiation between the old and the new energies inhabiting the house had been completed.

I realized the importance of the message that Don Tomas had given me through my dream. Bones are a symbol of the indestructible fabric of the human spirit. As I learned in my physics class many years ago, matter cannot be destroyed. It only changes its form. Bones are the structure not only of our bodies. Bones carry within them an infinite web of connections to those who have been here before us. When the spirit leaves the body, bones stay to remind us of that soul.

Like bones, places like Richard Hugo House become the homes for lost and transient spirits. The confused entities find refuge in the dark corners and high ceilings. With time, their personal tragedies, feelings and personalities become part of the décor. Once we learn to see with the eyes of our own souls, their presence is no longer invisible. To the newly fine-tuned ear, their whispers change into clear voices. Soon, we realize that we are never alone!

SIXTEEN

Yemayá

THE VOICE WAS CLEAR and loud. It whispered in my ear: "There is light and there is love." I woke up from my dream entranced by images: a beautiful lady of cinnamon skin and dark brown eyes held me in her arms. Her long black hair emitted a scent that permeated my senses. She smelled of salt and seaweed from the depths of the Caribbean. She had the calmness of the clear, turquoise waters at morning, when the tide is low and the seagulls circle the shore.

With my eyes closed, I lay in bed and replayed my dream. Yemayá, the deity of the oceans, had visited me during the night and brought the dreaded message that my aunt Linda was going to die. Yemayá came to reassure me of her light and love for all of us creatures of the earth. In the dream, Yemayá held my aunt Linda in her arms and sang her lullabies. Then Yemayá said, "She is my child and she is suffering. It is time for her to come home."

For the past three years, my aunt Linda had struggled with cancer. She was losing the fight. Bit by bit, the illness had annihilated her body—first her colon, then her liver, now her lungs. Her strong faith and her hope for a miracle had kept her going against all odds. Even when the doctors had given up, Aunt Linda continued with her prayers and daily meditations,

209

and her spirit became more radiant than ever.

My Aunt Linda was not alone; she had friends who prayed for her and she had my cousin Tomas, a doctor who also was a believer in the powers of Saint Lazarus, also known as the orisha Babalú-Ayé, the Afro-Cuban deity, who can heal from all illnesses, including cancer. Aunt Linda blindly trusted Dr. Tomas Barrios's advice and made no single decision about her health without consulting him first. Cuban all the way to his bones, Tomas not only examined every single medical report, but he also consulted Saint Lazarus and made him offers of candles and rum. With fervor, Tomas made deals with his favorite orisha and begged him to heal Aunt Linda.

Still in a stupor, I got up from the bed and walked to the window. I expected to see the ocean; instead, a centenary tree greeted me. Its large branches reached to the sky, and I imagined its roots, like strong arms, grabbing the entrails of the earth. That tree reminded me of my grandmothers and all the strong women of my family. Like that tree, they held their babies and nurtured them. They carried the maternal essence of Yemayá and her unconditional love.

My Aunt Linda was like the tree outside the window: her spirit had large branches that reached out to all those who came into her life. She was a child of Yemayá with a giant aura that exuded the warmth and softness of the ocean. In 1962, she left Cuba and went to reside in New Jersey, but she never abandoned those left behind. She worked hard, and most of the money that she earned went back to the family in Cuba. Up until the last week of her life, Aunt Linda made sure that her sisters and brothers in Cuba had their heart pills and other medical necessities. In 1982, when the Mariel Cubans began to arrive here, my aunt took into her own home one of what Castro's government called "undesirable elements." She housed and fed a young man, whose relatives had turned him away upon his arrival to the United States, because of his homosexual orientation. To my Aunt Linda, all people are God's children and therefore her kindness had no conditions.

As an active member of her church, she was a leader who inspired others with her dedication to human causes. As a social worker, Aunt Linda helped many. She was well loved by the Cuban community in New Jersey. Retired at age 65, she never stopped her philanthropic work. And at 69, her life was ending. She was withering from her cancer. She had fought a good battle. Like a brave warrior, she had endured three years of experimental chemotherapy and invasive procedures. I never heard her protest or complain. Her positive attitude and her unbreakable faith were like the wings of the angels that would carry her through these difficult times.

In spite of her weekly reassurances to me, when she said she was doing well, I could sense in her voice the weakening of her life force. She kept saying, "Don't worry about coming to visit. Wait until the summer so we can go places." But knowing time was running short, I bought an airline ticket and flew to New Jersey for a four-day visit.

I had not seen my Aunt Linda in five years. The image I had of her was that of a robust woman with rosy cheeks. On the ride from Newark Airport to her house, I prepared myself for an encounter with a woman debilitated after so many rounds of chemotherapy and radiation.

The Haitían taxi driver dropped me off right in front of the house. Franco, my uncle, came down to greet me. Franco, who usually gave the impression of a much younger person, ready to joke and laugh, looked older and tired. He was at least thirty pounds heavier and had lost most of his hair. As soon as we hugged, he broke down in tears and told me, "Prepárate para lo peor." He meant "Be prepared for the worst." Franco's Spanish had a strong Italian accent that often made his speech dramatic. We went up the steps to the entrance. My heart beat fast. When the door opened, I had to hold on to the railing in order not to fall down. The woman standing in front of me had little resemblance to the woman I had known. Aunt Linda had lost weight. Her face was sunken and had dark circles around the eyes. The thin hair that grew around the frontal and occipital areas of her head was like baby fuzz. The skin of her face and the whites of her eyes were yellow.

I struggled to conceal my feelings. Aunt Linda opened her thin arms and welcomed me. She was fragile! I wrapped my arms around her, careful not to hurt her. She had a catheter below one of her clavicles and a plastic pump that had been inserted right above her liver. From what I knew, the chemotherapy pump no longer had a function, but the doctors didn't want to "poke" anymore into her body. Aunt Linda was now on a new drug called Xeloda, a type of chemotherapy that she could take in capsule-form and which made her both vomit and swell like a balloon.

We sat in the living room where she rested on her recliner. I could tell that she was tired. I noticed her swollen abdomen. I held her hand. My sensitive aunt could tell I was about to break down in tears.

"You don't look so bad," I lied. Aunt Linda didn't answer. "What is the swelling?" I asked.

"My liver," she said and closed her eyes.

I asked how the new chemotherapy was working.

"It's not. My body is too tired. The doctor discontinued it again."

Later that evening, Franco told me my aunt had had a blood transfusion the day before. They'd spent eight hours in the hospital but my aunt wanted to return home for my arrival. What a woman! I thought, and the image of my grandmother Petra flashed in my mind. Aunt Linda definitely had the strong will of her mother.

Memories of the old matriarch fighting for her life after a debilitating stroke came back to me. At first, Grandmother Petra couldn't move a finger but after months of struggle, she was able to walk again and to go back to her kitchen and her embroidery. The doctors couldn't believe it. Grandmother Petra was like a stubborn mare and she gave us a lesson of mind over body.

The morning after my arrival, I sat across from my aunt at the breakfast table. Oh virgencita, have mercy! I said to myself, when I noticed the jaundiced coloration of Aunt's Linda skin. I poured some Cuban coffee for her café con leche. Franco tried to lecture her about coffee and her liver. Aunt Linda's reply was firm and clear. "Franco, my darling, I have no liver." And she took a sip from the steaming beverage.

I watched her savor her coffee. Aunt Linda was right, coffee could not be any worse then the toxic chemotherapy. Her poor liver was fried. It was painful to admit how impotent science still is when it comes to fighting an enemy such as cancer. In spite of all the technology, chemotherapy was nothing but another killer. It was just a matter of choosing how to die.

That night I tossed and turned in bed, upset about my aunt. I was angry with the doctors who had given her false hopes. She was a guinea pig for some new experimental drug. Yes, it did work for a while, until her body developed an immunity to the chemical. Then cancer cells took revenge on her fragile body. Seeing my aunt was like looking at the face of death. She looked like a concentration camp survivor. The only part of her that remained intact was her spirit. I could see the bright sparks flickering inside with defiance and courage.

I sat in bed and rubbed my eyes in a futile attempt to shake away my disturbing thoughts and go to sleep. All of a sudden the temperature in the room rose. I was very hot. Drops of sweat ran down my face and back. I pulled the covers to the side and got up to open the window. Outside, the air was cold and smelled of roses. Strange, because it was not a time of year when roses would be blooming. The fragrance intensified and a cool gust brushed my face. It was then I sensed a presence near me. I turned to look and saw the image of a young girl with light brown hair. She was dressed in white.

"Hi," she said shyly.

"Who are you?" I asked.

"I'm an angel," she replied. "You know Linda sleeps here?"

"No. I didn't know that."

"She does and I visit her every night. She's not doing well. She's afraid of the dark. Her mother sent me to watch over her."

"Her mother? How do you know...?"

"Yes, Mamá Petra and Papá José. They're waiting for her. They know."

"What do they know?"

The little girl did not answer. She left the room and I was alone with my thoughts for the rest of the night. In the evening of the next day, I had a chance to talk to my Aunt Linda. Uncle Franco had gone to visit a friend. I didn't need to bring up the subject. My aunt asked me if I had slept well in the back room. I told her about the young visitor. She was not surprised.

"She's my angel." Aunt Linda closed her eyes and two tears ran down her cheeks. "She is not the only one. Mamá and Papá have been around, too." She paused to take a deep breath. "You know what that means, don't you?" I knew, but I was not sure I wanted to answer her question. We stayed in silence for a few seconds. This was the moment of truth-telling, which I'd thought of many times during my flight from Seattle. Finally, Aunt Linda was the one to speak. "I know my time is coming."

Aunt Linda didn't say much more. She reclined on her big chair and I offered to do some acupressure on her feet to alleviate her pain. As I worked on her liver, stomach, and colon points, she went to sleep. Our communication took place in silence. She was telling me how tired she was and that she didn't want to fight anymore, but she was afraid.

"Tía, let go and relax."

Aunt Linda did not answer but I could feel her letting go. I saw how her aura floated above her body. Like a dedicated athlete preparing for the Olympic games, Aunt Linda was practicing how to let go of her body. Her spiritual muscle was getting stronger and she was gaining confidence in her ability to travel farther away from her physical temple. I worked deeper on the pressure points until the pain began to melt under my fingers. Finally, my aunt was relaxed and I could feel the opening of the energy channels pulsating with life.

My hands were hot from the energy work. My mind traveled

to Santa Barbara, California, where I had gone to test the new mystical experience of flotation. It was one of those New Age ideas, popular in the early eighties. A group of friends and I went for a session inside flotation tanks. My excitement about the experiment lasted until the moment when I was instructed to go inside the tank.

To me, the flotation vessel looked more like a coffin than a tank. Before leaving us, the attendant explained how the best results are obtained when the door of the tank is firmly shut. All of a sudden, I felt claustrophobic. I could feel the proximity of a panic attack. With hesitation, I undressed and entered the warm saline solution inside the tank. I lay on my back, allowing my body to float. So far so good, but the idea of closing the door made me terribly anxious. I took a few deep breaths and finally convinced myself to reach out and close the lid. My intention was to leave a little crack open, so it wouldn't be entirely dark, but the lid slammed down and I was in total darkness. My heart pounded furiously against the walls of my chest. I was certain that I was about to end my days inside this New Age vessel.

In the tank, I prayed to all my favorite saints while my heart continued racing. After a few minutes of my body floating on the saline solution, I could feel the tension in my shoulders and low back. I was hurting. The more I focused on the pain, the heavier I felt. In the darkness, my notion of space and time changed. It seemed to me as if I had been there for hours. Not only was this experience excruciatingly painful physically but, emotionally, I was aware of how fear was suffocating me. Like a boa constrictor, it was wrapped all around me, squeezing every bone and muscle. The more fearful I was, the tighter the grip of this snake around my throat. It was a struggle for me to stay inside the tank. I had to fight my impulse to open the door and leave the chamber of torture.

At some point in my inner fight, I must have surrendered, because the fear melted away and I could no longer feel my body or its pain. With the dissolution of the physical boundaries came deep relaxation and feelings of oneness with the saline solution.

I was back inside my mother's womb. At the same time, my spirit—now free from the body—was able to wander outside the tank and explore the surroundings. I equated my experience inside the flotation tank with the process of dying and of death itself—one where the total relaxation of the body frees the spirit to fly away.

The sound of the front door brought me back to the room with my aunt. She looked as if she had slept deeply. Uncle Franco came in and I signaled for him not to make any noise.

Three weeks later, the morning of my aunt's burial, I was sitting in my kitchen, drinking my coffee, when I saw from the corner of my eyes a big flash of light. It was my aunt who had come to say her final good bye. I was relieved she was no longer in pain. I could hear her laughter.

A week after her death, I had a dream. I was in the company of my friend Beverly Galyean who had passed away many years before. In the dream, Beverly looked young and healthy. We were at her home in Long Beach, except the view looked more like the Olympic Mountains enveloped by the mist of the morning. Beverly put her arm around my shoulders and pointed at a distant island across from us. She said, "That's my home and the home of your aunt. That's the island where we go."

I woke up from my dream feeling the grief of my losses. Both women had been role models for me. They had taught me about the power of prayer and meditation. Their strong faith in the human ability to heal led them to test their beliefs. They had suffered in their battles with experimental treatments. Beverly exhausted many alternative healing modalities, from Native-American sweat lodges to crystal healing. My aunt Linda took a more conventional path of chemotherapy and radiation treatment. The oncologist gave her a year to live but she lasted three. I believe that it was her strong commitment to prayer and meditation that kept her alive.

At the end, both Beverly and my aunt Linda died from liver cancer. Beverly died in 1982 and my aunt in 2002, twenty years apart. In both cases, I was left to sort through my doubts and my own fears about death and life after death. Once more, the spirit world came to my rescue. Beverly appeared in my dream with the reassuring message that my aunt had made it to her new home, on the island of our ancestors.

Two weeks later, my Aunt Linda herself came to visit me in my dreams. We were walking on a beach. I knew she was there next to me but I couldn't see her face. The ocean was calm and people were bathing and swimming. My aunt pointed to the ocean and said, "Remember Yemayá? She is the great mother, the giver of life. She is with me and she will be with you." We kept walking in silence. At one point, I decided to go for a swim but as I approached the water, I found myself standing high on a cliff and the ocean turned dark and turbulent. The people in the water began to glow as if they were fluorescent beings. I heard my aunt say, "They are not from the earth. They're spirits bathing in the womb of Yemayá."

Giant waves began to crash against the shore. I realized it was time for us to go before we could be swept away. I began to run, but my aunt did not move. She said, "You go now." Without questioning her command, I ran as fast as I could and found a stone tunnel going from the beach to another place. I crawled into it and ended up in a parking lot. I could see my aunt on the other side, by the ocean. We were separated by an invisible membrane, delicate as the web of a spider, yet strong and impenetrable as the stones of the tunnel.

I woke up from my dream crying. I wanted to stay with my aunt but I knew it was not my time to be with her again. For now we could visit each other by moving across the transparent wall that separated our worlds. I was assured that beautiful and loving Yemayá was with us. She was there holding my aunt inside her watery womb. Yemayá, the eternal mother, would nurture Aunt Linda and carry her to a new home. And from there, Aunt Linda could continue weaving the invisible threads of connection between her and us. I was comforted to know that any time I needed her she would be there by the ocean, right where the waves kiss the shore.

SEVENTEEN

La Brava

I'M HERE BECAUSE I want to be a woman again. I have no desire to live. Life is flat and colorless. Every morning, I struggle to open my eyes. I don't want to wake up. If it weren't for my children, I would have taken the whole bottle of Xanax...and ended my misery."

Those were the words of Julia, my new client, a woman in her mid-forties and a hysterectomy survivor. For years, Julia had fought doctors who wanted to surgically remove her female organs. Large and fast-growing fibroids had invaded Julia's insides causing severe bleeding and pain. Four years earlier, she lost her battle and had a hysterectomy. Even though her physical recovery was quick, Julia was left to struggle with feelings of depression and emptiness.

"I'm dying slowly, like a log that rots under the elements. I have no energy to do anything. I sit or I lie in bed and stare at the ceiling for hours. Sometimes, I have conversations with God and I curse Him. I don't even feel bad about it. I just want Him to give me an answer. I want to know why in the hell I'm still here in this world. It doesn't make any sense at all. I want out!"

According to Julia, life was a monotonous routine. Formerly a successful public defender that enjoyed every minute of her job, since the surgery, she had no interest in her profession or

219

in her life at home with her husband and two children. Alfredo, her husband, complained about the lack of intimacy in their relationship.

"Did you enjoy sex before the surgery?" I asked her.

"Sex?" Julia's eyes turned darker. She shifted her position on the couch so that she could look out at Lake Union. "You have a nice office." Julia took a deep breath. "Sex is painful. That hysterectomy dried out my vagina. Even with lots of lubricants, I can still feel the excruciating pain and the piercing from my husband's penis. Even when he tries to be gentle, it doesn't work!" Julia paused for a second, then shook her head. "It was never fun to begin with. I was raised by Catholic parents, and my mother did an excellent job of hammering all her puritanical thoughts into my head."

Julia ran her fingers through her long black hair. She dropped her head back and pushed her shoulders up against her neck. Her face was pale. She wore no make-up to cover the premature lines around her eyes and mouth. Her whole being exuded a fatigue that went deep into her soul.

"My mother believed all men were perverts." Julia's voice sounded tired and distant. "The day I had my first period she told me, 'Don't get pregnant before you marry because I'll kick you out of the house.'"

Julia was date-raped by her first boyfriend. At first, Julia had no idea of what was happening to her body: her breasts were swollen and her belly grew fast. Initially, Julia was in denial, but her mother, who closely monitored her daughter's menses, promptly noticed the absence of sanitary napkins inside the wastebasket.

One afternoon, when Julia returned from school, her mother was waiting for her, all dressed and ready to march down to the office of the family doctor. Julia has not been able to forget the face of her mother when the elderly male physician announced the truth. Filled with rage, the mother began to slap Julia's face, right there in the doctor's office. She was so out of control that a nurse had to help restrain her.

"I haven't been able to forgive my mother for that," Julia said with a harsh tone. "She's been dead for five years and I can find no mercy in my heart for her actions. She forced me to give my baby away."

I asked how old she was then.

"I was only seventeen."

Her flat affect melted away and her eyes glared with defiance. There was rage in her voice. "My mother and the doctor made all the arrangements for the adoption." Her fists were clenched. "I gave birth to a boy." She pounded her thighs. "My boy was taken away and given to his adoptive parents."

Julia stood up and walked to the glass wall that separated my office from the lake. She pressed her forehead against the pane. In spite of her rage, she looked fragile, and smaller than her five feet, four inches.

"I hate myself!" Julia cried. "I should have fought my mother and not let her take my baby away."

"You were only seventeen," I reminded her.

"I deserve that hysterectomy! It was God's punishment for my weakness. I will not be at peace until I find my boy. I must apologize to him."

Julia went back to the couch and shrunk into a fetal position. She looked like a five year old. Her hazel eyes were like deep pools of water reflecting the darkness of her pain. Her moon-shape face lost its roundness, and the angular jaws stiffened as she clenched her teeth. In a protective gesture, she crossed her arms over her chest, and she sobbed.

"I've always been a nice girl," Julia said and dried her tears. "I was never allowed to express any emotion. Nice girls smile and don't show any anger. Well, I was really angry with my mother, but I knew it was best to hide it. I kept it inside and it burned like hot coals. I pushed it down, together with all my other emotions. For many years, I wished my mother dead, and when she finally died of a heart attack, oh God! I believe I caused her to die."

At forty-five, Julia still held the belief that she had killed her mother. She had a recurring nightmare where her mother would appear in her room and accuse Julia of causing her so much suffering. In the dream, the mother calls Julia a prostitute and a sexual pervert. She yells at Julia, "You will go to hell for dishonoring the name of our family." Julia wakes up screaming at her mother to go away and leave her alone.

"My mother is evil. She killed me! She destroyed in me the passion for life. Even though she's dead, her voice is inside my head. I feel haunted by her presence in my home, and everywhere I go, I can feel her dark spirit lingering around me. The night before the hysterectomy, I dreamed of my mother cutting my body with a big butcher's knife. In the dream, I was a young woman, maybe seventeen. I was in my room, except the décor was different. The walls were painted bright red and yellow. Instead of a carpet, the floors were covered with soft and moist green moss. I was naked and my body was decorated with a mixture of mud and red pigments. Unexpectedly, my mother walked into the room with the big knife. I remember the sharp blade shining in the light. My mother was outraged. She was screaming and yelling, 'You wild and sick creature. You're not my daughter!'"

Covering her face, Julia sobbed and cursed her mother. Her eyes were those of a wounded animal. Sparks of fire were shooting out from the depths of her broken spirit. The intensity of her gaze made me shiver. I did not recognize her. It was as if some unknown force had taken possession of her body. I waited for Julia to snap out of it, but instead Julia continued glaring at me with fury.

For the first time in many years of practice as a psychotherapist, I was afraid. I did not know of what exactly, but the atmosphere had turned dark and heavy. I could feel the presence of a frightening entity. Julia did not look like Julia. Her eyes were the eyes of rage.

"Julia. Julia, come back here!" I said.

Julia did not answer. She was like a dormant volcano waiting for the right time to spit out its hot lava. Her face became contorted, her body tensed, her muscles constricted. Veins in her arms and neck were engorged with blood. A loud scream, like rolling thunder, came out of her throat. "I hate you!"

Julia stood up from the couch and came towards me with her fists in the air. She was ready to hit me.

Quickly, I jumped out of the chair and was able to grab her arms before she could touch me. "Julia. I am not your mother!"

Julia continued struggling to free herself. I held her tight while I spoke in a soft and reassuring manner. The temperature in my office was rising fast. My body was shaking and my shirt was soaked with sweat. Julia was lost in her own world of pain and anger, unable to respond to my commands. I doubted she could even hear my voice. It was then I decided to call my grandmother Patricia for help. She was not one to come on request, but more when she wanted. A few seconds went by without any response. I was growing anxious, then I felt the warm touch of her hand on my shoulder. I relaxed.

"Hmm!" I heard Grandmother say and I could almost see her frown. "This is big trouble. Look at her belly. You got your hands full with this lady. She has la negrura that her grandmother gave to her mother and that her mother passed onto her."

"I see the darkness around her belly," I said quietly to my grandmother.

"That's la negra de los mares." Grandmother meant the black woman of the ocean. She came and stood right next to Julia. "La negra is pregnant with rage." Grandmother placed her hands on Julia's abdomen. Julia body's jerked back and her arms dropped in my hands. I helped her back to the couch.

Grandmother went to sit next to Julia. "See? It is dark in her womb. Julia's grandmother was a woman of many secrets. She never told anyone about the child she had abandoned at a stranger's door. That child never made it. He died of pneumonia a few days after he was born. Well, la negra doesn't forgive such a crime. When she's made angry, she turns her machete against anyone who harms her children."

"Who is this black woman?" I asked.

"In Cuba, we call her La Brava or 'the fierce one' because she is a warrior. You know she is a guerrera with her machete and her knife. La Brava has very little patience and she can be very violent. She is an aspect of Yemayá. You know Yemayá is all love and compassion, she is the great mama. But she has this other side that is fierce and that can cut heads with her machete and rip the flesh with her cuchillo. Believe me, she can be brutal with her knife. Well, you see my child, women oftentimes turn their machete against themselves. They do that when they push La Brava into jail. They chain her to the bottom of their own wombs, and then, you see, women end up with all sorts of female problems."

Oblivious to the conversation I was having with my grandmother, Julia stared at me. Her pupils were fixed, her body stiff, as if she suffered from catatonia. Grandmother Patricia frowned. With her right hand, she tapped Julia on the belly. As if Julia had been struck by lightning, she leaped from the couch and threw herself on the floor. She was convulsing, flapping her arms and legs.

"La Brava está furiosa," Grandmother Patricia said.

"Julia, Julia, come back!" I shouted. I was afraid Julia was going to hurt herself.

"No!" Grandmother yelled. "Leave her alone." And she gave me the same look she used to give me when as a child I did something wrong, a clear and firm message to stop immediately. "La Brava doesn't like weak people. You've got to face her and look deep into her eyes."

I sat back in my chair and watched Grandmother place her hand over Julia's forehead. Julia relaxed, straightened her body and let her arms rest on her lap. With her index finger, Grandmother poked deep into Julia, at a point right below the navel. As if Julia had been blasted by pain, she wrapped her arms around her abdomen and bent over. She pushed her shoulders up and dropped her head onto the carpet. Julia's eyes were closed, anguish reflected on her face.

After a few seconds, Grandmother released the pressure,

but continued with a circular motion of her finger over the same area. She circled to the left. By the seventh rotation, Julia let out a loud scream that resonated throughout the room. I was sure everyone else outside my office heard the primal cry. It was like the roar of a large bear.

The scream was followed by laughter. The energy around Julia's pelvis turned dark and thick like molasses. It was impenetrable to my eyes. Chills went down my spine. With both hands Grandmother began to scoop the pelvis, as she pronounced La Brava free.

"Libérate," I heard Grandmother said and Julia began to weep.

"Julia, are you okay?" I asked.

"I'm remembering the hysterectomy." Julia's voice sounded as if it came from far away. "I see myself back in the operating room. I see my body on the table surrounded by machines and the medical team. My belly has been cut open and the doctor is busy cutting and removing parts. He has no feeling for what he's doing. To him this is just one more surgery. He's not even there! He's thinking about the new car he promised his wife for the wedding anniversary. Then, he turns to one of the nurses and asks her about her favorite car. Oh, I can't believe this! He removes one of my ovaries while he talks about his next sailing trip to the Bahamas."

Grandmother was still there by Julia's side. She was scooping out the stuff from her belly. I watched her hands do the work, with so much tenderness and care, so different from that of the surgeon. Grandmother was so present in the process that I almost forgot that hers was not a physical presence but the spirit of Patricia.

"This is not surgery," I heard Grandmother say. "This is the casting away of the unseen negrura this poor woman holds in her belly. Too many bad memories were stored in her belly. You go ahead and make her talk. I'm almost done."

Julia went from talking about the surgery to talking about her experiences in the delivery room. She remembered how, as she was pushing, the helping nurse kept humiliating her. "See, this is what you get. Next time you think of having sex, you'll remember this pain." The old doctor was enjoying his power over her and wasted no time in saying things such as "Women like you should have their ovaries removed."

"Maybe that old doctor cursed me with his words," Julia reflected.

It was at that moment I realized my grandmother was no longer in the room. She had gone. Instead, I saw another presence standing next to Julia. This was the fierce-looking negra, La Brava herself. She was looking straight into my eyes.

The appearance of La Brava in my office was intimidating. She was a dark, mulatto woman with long and wild woolly black hair. Her amber and big almond-shaped eyes had a savage expression. Large silver rings hung from her ear lobes. La Brava was dressed in a dark blue and coral dress, a giant snake coiled around her strong shoulders and arms. As my grandmother mentioned, La Brava had a knife and machete fastened to her waist.

The presence of La Brava was brief. With her feet firmly rooted on the ground, she danced around Julia with a slow and undulating motion of her hips. Then, pulling her machete out, she swayed the sharp blade in the air with fierceness. La Brava circled the space around Julia, cutting and clearing stuff away from her aura. When she was done, La Brava stared at me with piercing eyes, lifted her machete and pressed its pointed tip against my chest. I heard her say, "I heal by severing the fears and doubts that live in your heart."

In a flash, La Brava disappeared. I was left wondering if Julia had any idea of what had taken place. She was talking about the sensations she had experienced as her baby was descending out of the birth canal. I looked at my watch. We were out of time, and this was a perfect place to end our session.

The following week, when Julia returned to my office, she still looked depressed. Dark circles under her eyes were a sign of many sleepless nights. Julia sat on the couch, her legs crossed.

She took a sip from the steaming cup of coffee she had brought. "I hope you don't mind that I'm drinking coffee in your office," Julia said. Her voice sounded tired. "I could hardly wait to talk to you today. I have been having some strange dreams."

I took a sip from my coffee and waited for Julia. In spite of her tired appearance, her aura was brighter, with an abundance of green and yellow colors, especially around her lower body. To me, that was indicative of changes in her emotional world.

She said: "I had one dream that seemed very important. It was very vivid! I was in the middle of a forest. I had gotten lost and couldn't find my way out of the place. It was getting dark and I was beginning to panic. All of a sudden, a black woman appeared in front of me. She looked like a wild creature with long and black bushy hair. She was tall and her strong shoulders were wide and her arms were as muscular as those of a gladiator. She was dressed in a leopard skin. Hanging from her waist was a large knife. She said, 'Follow me,' and taking her weapon, she began to open a trail through the underbrush. Next, we were out of the forest and in my mother's house. My mother and the doctor who had delivered my boy were there. 'Don't let her see the boy,' I heard my mother say to the doctor. Quickly, he threw a white flannel blanket over the infant he held in his arms. The wild woman stepped forward and grabbed the baby from the doctor. She handed the baby to me and said, 'Look at him.' With fear, I held my child in my arms. I could feel the warmth and softness of his tiny body. The baby cried and...I uncovered his face. He was beautiful with his rosy cheeks and long eyelashes. I held him close to my chest and I felt his heart beating next to mine."

According to Julia, the feelings of holding her baby in her arms stayed with her. She could close her eyes and, with no effort, transport herself to that moment in the dream. She had spent endless hours re-running these images in her mind. It was comforting to her. It provided her with the opportunity to bond with her baby and to feel the oneness she had experienced when he was inside her womb.

"I know deep inside that someday I'll see my boy. My husband doesn't believe me, but I know my son is going to find me." For the first time, Julia sounded strong and alive. Then she changed the subject to tell me about another strange event.

Julia had gone to the hardware store with her husband. During the visit, Julia separated from Alfredo and went to the gardening tools section. She couldn't remember what she was looking for, but she ended up standing in front of a shiny machete.

"I couldn't get my eyes away from the large machete. I stood there glued to the floor, mesmerized by its elongated and sharp blade. I wrapped my hand and fingers around the handle. Wow! It was powerful. I felt like the black woman in my dream. I could see myself opening my way through the forest. I was energized by the whistling sound of the blade as it cut through the air, the sharp snapping of branches and the smell of the freshly chopped tree bark.

"Then I had some thoughts that were really dark. I saw the old doctor who delivered my baby and the doctor who performed my hysterectomy in front of me. I lifted the machete and with incredible force I cut off their heads."

Julia was brought back to reality by another customer who walked by and saw her with the machete lifted in the air. A man came from behind and held her arm. "Lady, are you out of your mind? Put that machete down!" Julia did not let go. She simply turned around and looked fiercely into the stranger's eyes and said, "Let go of my arm or else..." Without saying a word, the scared man let go and quickly walked away.

Julia bought the machete and took it home with her. During the trip back to her house, Alfredo kept asking her what she was going to do with it. Tired of his questioning, Julia said she would keep it underneath her bed just in case anybody tried to steal her life again.

Alfredo raised his eyebrow, shook his head and was quiet for the rest of the ride.

In my office, Julia laughed and swung her arm in the air as if she were holding the machete. "I swear that machete is mighty powerful!"

"What are you going to do with it?" I asked,

"I don't know yet, but I'm keeping it in my room to look at and to remind me of the wild woman in my dream. She is a warrior goddess. She is that part of me that knows how to fight and how to cut off heads if needed, for protection."

"My grandmother called her La Brava or 'The Fierce One,'" I said.

By the time Julia left my office, she was convinced that good things were about to happen in her life. A week later, when she returned to my office, she brought the machete with her. She had it well wrapped inside buckskin, and placed beside her on the couch.

"I'm not crazy," she said and waited for my reaction.

Julia was dressed in a beautiful red skirt and short-sleeved white blouse, which accentuated her Italian olive skin. She wore her shoulder-length hair down. Black and shiny, it reflected the light from the sun that filtered through the glass window. Julia was a different woman. She was no longer depressed. Her aura had the radiance of good health and life.

"Do you mind?" she asked and proceeded to untie the skin around the machete in a way that appeared ceremonial, the movement of hands slow and elegant, as if she were uncovering a precious gem. When she finished, the exposed machete looked more like the sword of a warrior. The handle had been adorned with several strings of multi-colored beads and two large feathers and one large clear crystal.

"Amazing!" I said.

According to Julia, the night after our last session, she had woken up from a dream where she heard the voice of the wild black woman telling her to go and get her machete. It was around one o'clock in the morning. She got out of bed, being careful not to wake up Alfredo. She took the machete and went in her office.

"I couldn't believe it! I sat there, holding the machete in my hands. I lost track of time. I'm not sure if I fell asleep and had another dream, or if I was awake. But...I saw sparks coming off the blade," Julia paused to check my reaction.

"You're not crazy. Go ahead," I reassured her.

With some hesitation, Julia shared with me how the blade of the machete was enveloped by flames and the handle was so hot she could no longer hold it in her hand. The spirit of the machete appeared in the room in the form of a dancing flame. It spoke to her. It said, "Julia, I'm here to help you but if you don't use me, I will turn my power against you and hurt you. I will cut you to pieces. I'll destroy you!"

Alfredo found Julia on the floor of her office, sleeping right next to the precious machete. That same morning, while they were having breakfast, Julia informed Alfredo of her new plan. She was going back to work full-time. She was going to be an advocate for and defender of the rights of teenage mothers and their babies.

When Julia left my office, she walked away with a renewed sense of hope. I closed the door behind her and went back to my desk, feeling the warm touch of my grandmother's hand on my shoulder and the familiar tingling of her energy on my neck.

"She has no more negrura," I heard Grandmother say, "La Brava took care of it."

I rubbed the back of my neck and shook my head. I understood her message. She wanted to remind me of the humble nature of our work. We are vessels of the spirit world. Our job is to stay clear and open to their messages. We are dancers always moving in-between dimensions. Inside the modern ambiance of our offices, lives the world of Oyá with her invisible winds of transformation.

The Mask of Oyá is not just a myth, but is alive in every step of the healing journey. It allows us therapists to hide behind it and to work our way into the underworld of the mind in search of a lost soul or a fragment of it. Like Oyá, the therapist must swirl through narrow labyrinths and sweep the dusty corners of the psyche. That's the place where I found La Brava. She was waiting there, hidden under the dirt of Julia's painful past. And when La Brava was brought to light, her true and vibrant colors gave way to a new Julia charged with fire and life.

EIGHTEEN

Masquerade

A S A CHILD, my favorite time of the year was the month of February, when Cubans celebrated and paraded around the streets for days wearing costumes and masks. The carnival allowed us to free ourselves from the daily routine and confining structures. Spirits soared as the rhythms of drums set the tone for the *comparsas* [dance parades]. There was an aura of mystery mixed with excitement as people transformed their daily garments into elaborate disfraces that concealed their identities. Just as the mask of Oyá free the goddess to go in between the realms of the dead and the living. This act of concealing was also liberating! It allowed people to experience and experiment with duality. Men transformed into women and vice-versa. The prohibited became acceptable and fun. What had been in shadow within the culture emerged from the depths with bright lights and colors and magical sounds. During carnival, the entire country became a big masquerade!

The arts of masking and performance, known as masquerade, are as ancient as our world. From the beginning of time, human beings have been telling and acting stories of their lives and dreams. Through the masquerade, they contact and interact with both ancestors and supernatural beings, who in turn become the agents in rites of passage: rituals of births, death, marriage, fertility and so on.

As a therapist living in a modern society, I am aware of the huge lack of rituals. The experience of carnival is primal and cathartic. It brings people together in a frenzy that allows for a full expression of the personal and collective self. In this earthy celebration, the boundaries of society expand to embrace the full spectrum of emotions, without exception. And as the carnival comes to an end, the boundaries contract to bring order to the chaos. There is a complete sense of renewal and restoration, of transcendence and transformation.

In the absence of rituals, psychotherapy becomes one of the few means for an individual to explore the boundless energy of the psyche. The average client who comes to see me is in search of "meaning" and of some form of spiritual awakening. Depression and anxiety are major affects. Despite the accumulation of material wealth, there is a deep hunger for something not found in shopping malls and big homes! Clients come to look for "it" in the privacy of my office. They come in hopes that the process will lead them to happier lives and into enjoyable relationships.

Having practiced psychotherapy for more than twenty years, I hope I have learned to remain humble in my efforts to help those who come to me. My job is similar to that of a conductor of an orchestra. In my case, I oversee how the different parts of self interact and struggle for integration and balance. I mediate between the realms of helping spirits and the physical world. My office becomes a place where the healing masquerade of each individual is performed. The therapist's role is simply to don a "mask" that conceals the "healer."

Therapists have their own tricks and techniques that vary depending on training and school of thought. In essence, these are merely props, just like the altars, feathers, and other tools of my grandmother and Don Tomas. The "healing" happens within the invisible masquerade of the psyche as it dances and performs the multiple faces of the self. The therapist's mask protects the healer, just as the mask of Oyá protects the spirit from death. The healer is free to navigate in the elusive world of the unconscious in search for lost fragments of the soul.

As I learned from Don Tomas, the underworld is a dangerous labyrinth inhabited by a client's inner demons. Could I get trapped in the sticky web of unresolved issues and pain? In graduate school, we are taught about counter-transference and trained not to falling into an abyss of projections. Early in my career, I learned this is not enough. Subterranean tunnels of the mind are better addressed by curanderos, santeros and shamans, who are more alert to the possibility of getting attacked by invisible evil winds. Their awareness and recognition of other realms such as ancestors, the dead, the orishas, and Tonals empower them to navigate in between worlds a lot more safely.

Every morning as I enter my office, I am aware of an instinctual transformation. As I open the door, "the therapist's mask" is activated. The healer crawls behind the protection of my own ancestors and spirit helpers. We prepare to meet the clients who have their own parade of unseen dancers. And as this occurs, I feel the same excitement I felt as a child when I waited for the mysterious reappearance of the carnival. I'm safe, knowing that I am not alone in the journey.

From ancient times, masks have played an important role in different traditions and cultures. Masks have the power to transform those who wear them as well as those who interact with them. Across cultures, we find a common element among many tribes and the use of mask as a transformational tool. Here on the Northwest coast, tribes have masks that depict humans and creatures.

In Hopi land, Kachinas visit the villages every year beginning in February, after descending from their home on top of the San Francisco Mountains near Flagstaff, Arizona. Both male and female Kachinas are personified by costumed men wearing elaborate masks with headdresses. The Kachina represents spirits of nature and the ancestors. By wearing the mask, the Hopi believe that they actually transform into the spirit of the Kachina as they dance during the ceremony. It is through this interplay that Kachinas teach the Hopi about farming, hunting and healing.

In West Africa, the Gelede and the Egungun dances of the Yoruba are performed to ensure the renewal and affirmation of the spiritual and ancestral worlds. In these ceremonies, the ancestors return as masquerade performers.

The annual Gelede festival honors the creative and dangerous powers of women elders, female ancestors and goddesses. According to Chris Rainier, a photographer and co-director of the Society's Ethnosphere Project, the Gelede mask acts out daily life, the conflicts and misdeeds of humans. All the events of the past year—theft, love affairs, corruption—are brought to light. The head performer, "Efe," a female character, acts out her performance with sarcastic remarks and reprimands that serve to lighten intricate village tensions.

In the Egungun dances, the masks represent societal and cultural stereotypes. They are brightly painted. The bodies of the dancers are covered with multiple layers of cloth, so the identity of the dancer is completely concealed. The dancer becomes more like a disembodied spirit of the ancestor that his dance seeks to honor. According to The Centre for Social Anthropology and Computing at the University of Kent at Canterbury, the word "Egungun" means "power concealed." The power and purpose of the custom only come together in the presence of the spirit-ancestor. The elaborate textures and color between cloth layers are necessary in order to have the masker experience a "transformation."

Across cultures, masquerade seems to embrace the feminine principle of mystery and secrecy. The masquerade is like a womb itself. It envelops the new life and carries it to term in complete concealment. Then, the dance of contractions begins with the final triumph of the delivery. Masquerade is about the creative process, where raw essence becomes manifest. In therapy, masquerade is about the birthing of a new part of the self. It never comes without pain!

Oyá is the original masquerader. She is the owner of the

cloth. She is the witch with the magical powers of the invisible and the elusive. Oyá is the keeper of the ancestral cloth, the matrix of the universe, and DNA with its genetic encoding of humanity and its evolution. In this concept, patterns are repeated and re-enacted. Every thread is a form of ancient and new wisdom. Stories are told and danced, bringing forth meaning and healing to the personal and collective. Our link to the cloth connects us to the place of our origin, to the beginning of life.

As a therapist, my power as a healer is concealed by the invisible mask of Oyá. Therefore, I am able to navigate the mysterious dimensions of the soul in search of that magical substance that would bring revelation and change to my clients. My work embraces the concept of masquerade. The healer part is always concealed from the keen eye of my clients. Like the masquerade dancers, I perform daily contortions, not of my body but of my mind and spirit.

In my own healing journey, my Grandmother Patricia became the personification of the deity Oyá. She embodied the essence of the wind that blew, disrupting my stagnation and my resistance to change. Don Tomas borrowed from his own traditional arsenal the energy of the Tonals to teach me about connection and power. The jungle became a metaphor of the feminine principle. As the home of Oyá and of the Tonals spirits, the jungle forced me to encounter the essence of the wild in myself.

As my Grandmother Patricia told me, without my deerskin I would be lost in the forest of the world. The claiming of my deerskin is a lifelong process that will take me to many unknown places. Some will be dark and terrifying and filled with unpredictable challenges. As long as I hold on to my deerskin, I will be reassured and never alone.

The deerskin is very symbolic of the instinctual, animal part of us. It is a symbol of the feminine mysteries of transformation and renewal. It is my connection to the spirits of the jungle. As Don Tomas taught me, Tonals are wise teachers and guides.

Without a constant exchange of knowledge between them and us, the growth and evolution of our planet are hindered. We become alienated from nature and from each other.

In my work, I am constantly weaving the connections between the body and the brain. We live in a world where the intellectual is overused at the expense of the physical. That deerskin allows me to stay connected to the body. Oyá's home is the forest that resides in the old part of our brains, the limbic system. She resides in the turbulent dimension of our basics needs, fears and survival. Oyá lives in the swamp of our psyche.

Oyá as an archetype represents those aspects of the psyche we are afraid to face. Her fierceness and destructiveness are parts of nature we disregard. She is a warrior goddess who is not welcomed into the circles of society. Oyá has been repressed and chained to the bottom of our womb by the patriarchal mind. Not allowed to exist, she creates havoc in the forms of depression, anxiety and body ailments.

For many of my female clients, Oyá is the sword that, turned against the self, cuts the flesh in hysterectomies and cancer. She becomes la negrura that my Grandmother warns me about in La Brava. Restoring a connection to Oyá in these women brings much balance and healing into their lives. Women are not taught to be hunters. They are not given the tools to survive in the world jungle. They don't know how to use the machete of Oyá to sever and to kill what needs to be destroyed in order for them to move forward. Therefore, they often stay in situations and relationships that are abusive and confining. Their creative energy becomes stagnant in depression and physical ailments.

Ironically, as I enter the final phase of this book, the call of Oyá comes to unveil that which must be brought in to balance. Oyá, as my nanny Carmen and Grandmother Patricia taught me, comes and sweeps. She cleans, she purifies. When I was a child living in Cuba, my nanny Carmen used to get up as soon as the sun came up. She would pick up her broom and sweep the entire house from back to front. I knew better than to bother her. She was doing serious work. "Nina, when I am sweeping...Oyá is with me. She is making sure the house is clean. Not just free of dirt but also of any *energía mala* [bad energy]. You want to sweep all that mugre out of the house, so that you can make room for all the *cosas buenas* [good things] coming our way."

The night before Hurricane Katrina hit New Orleans, my sweet nanny came to remind me of the importance of honoring one's commitment to the spirits. A clean house attracts good energy. There are daily rituals one must follow to continue deepening the connection to the spirits. It is no different than the relationships we have with family and friends.

I had a dream. I could see Carmen's beautiful face. Her big and dark brown eyes looked at me with such warmth! Then, she turned around and grabbed the long broom, and with long strokes she started to sweep the street in front of my house— except that the neighborhood was different. The architecture was colonial, so unlike Seattle. All of a sudden, it became very hot and humid! Thick drops of sweat ran down my face, burning my eyes. I was melting inside my clothes.

Out of nowhere came a strong wind, and Carmen turned her face back to me. Her hair was wild with uncombed, long dreadlocks. She wore a bulky crimson-colored dress of many layers of fabric. A giant spiral of dust and leaves formed around her and then spiraled down the street. Carmen herself was spinning. She was fierce!

"Carmen, Carmen!"

She does not respond. She is twirling on her feet. She is singing a song in some foreign language. All I hear are the words "Oyá , Oyá....is coming."

I woke up from the dream feeling disoriented. The images were as vivid as in the dream. Even with my eyes open, I could see Carmen and feel the force of the wind against my body. I knew Carmen came to alert me but...of what? The stormy nature of Oyá worried me, not to mention her role as transporter of souls back and forth between worlds. Was she coming for me or for any other member of the family?

Not fully awake, I walked to the kitchen and made myself a cup of strong coffee.

As if guided by Carmen's hand, I went to the TV room and turned on the news. I was immediately bombarded with pictures of Hurricane Katrina and her devastating impact on New Orleans. Is that what Carmen was trying to communicate to me? "Oyá, Oyá is coming." Well, she did, and she swirled and swept without mercy. Her fury destroyed the entire city. She filled the streets with the murky waters tainted with fecal and decaying matter, deadly bacteria and poisonous waste.

As I drove to work, I kept asking aloud: "Why Oyá? Why those poor people?" Of course, there was no answer at the moment, but as the days passed, I realized the complexity of the situation. More than anything, Katrina destroyed the invisible fortress around my office. All of a sudden, the world outside was leaking inside my space. Almost every single client who came to see me brought the pain and suffering of the hurricane victims with them.

And I said: "Oyá, she came and she unveiled the dark side of our country, the shadowy aspects we have chosen to ignore and disregard. Yes, Oyá, you came and you peeled off the mask of denial. You blatantly revealed the smoked mirrors of the American soul.

Oyá, Oyá , she came and knocked at my door, reminding me of the world outside my office. Oyá, Katrina brought to me the awareness of that connection between the personal and the collective; that storms, physical and emotional, clean the air and dispel pollution. Storms change structures and reveal the weak and vulnerable aspect of the self and the world at all levels: physical, emotional and spiritual.

As structures crumble, so do old stereotypes and patterns of thinking and behaving. They must die for the new ones to emerge. We cannot disregard Oyá's power and wisdom. Oyá with her strong winds is a major recycler, removing old, outdated ways of relating to ourselves and the world when they no longer serve the best interest of evolution. Both my

Grandmother Patricia, Carmen and Don Tomas taught me about the importance of maintaining deep communion with the spirit world and with our ancestors in order to bring forth the healing forces of the universe.

In watching the destruction of Katrina, I heard the guttural sound of her voice forcing us to become humble. As my Grandmother said, "Oyá teaches us about humbleness and death." The tale of Changó and Oyá is one to remember. Changó was unable to control or tame Oyá as he did his other wives. Not patriarchal, Changó was wise, he acknowledged the powers of Oyá, and instead of killing her he kneeled down and offered her favorite food.

In all the United States, New Orleans is the city that most likely houses the energies of Oyá. The above-ground tombs in the cemeteries have been referred to as "cities of the dead." Oyá is the owner of the cemeteries. Her presence there is undeniable! The crosses and statues on the tomb tops bring the visitor into touch with a world of shadows and mystery. There is an impending sense of danger along the narrow paths and tombs. Tour agencies warn the tourist of concealed hazards and advise you not to go alone.

New Orleans has been home to the paranormal—with its history of spiritualism, Voodoo, ghosts, and even vampires. It is without doubt the place that houses the dark and elusive nature of Oyá. Katrina swirled, bringing to consciousness the truth of a nation that in spite of all claims of being good and caring, failed its own people by abandoning them to the terrifying masquerade.

The ancestors of New Orleans rose with the waters to teach us about the conflicts of our communities. Even though we claim to live in a global village, the class and racial issues that co-exist beneath the surface were brought out in the complexities of this unexpected tragedy. The faces of the people of New Orleans became a masquerade of poverty and suffering for the world to see. As we watched the images on television, we were pulled in, we became part of this parade and its terror. Our ancestors spoke clearly about the weakness of our system, of our government, of the inequality that exists. It was all brought to light by the goddess of the winds.

In the ever-changing world of the Yoruba people, one thing that remains consistent is a close connection with their ancestors. The ancestral spirits of the Yoruba are sought out for protection and guidance and are believed to possess the ability to punish those who have forgotten their family ties.

Not only have we forgotten the ties to the family but to our ancestors and to our communities as well. The ancestors of New Orleans rose to remind us that we do have a responsibility to other members of the global clan. Ultimately, we have to take care of our planet. We must stop creating conditions that fuel the fury of our goddess of the storms. Oyá, with her contractions and expansions, brings an awareness of our actions and reactions. In this concept of life, one can't disregard the contamination and pollution of our world which is also Oyá's habitat. Global warming has the danger of creating more furious and destructive appearances by the deity of hurricanes. She will come back to remind us of the need for balance, not just on a personal level but collectively as well.

Wise Don Tomas said to me: "The old ones are worried about this world. Man with so much greed in his heart, is destroying the land. When all jaguars are gone, the world will be left at the mercy of the evil winds." Indeed, the people of New Orleans were abandoned for days. Are all the jaguars gone? Is it time for us to focus our attention on the restoration of all our connections?

My nanny Carmen taught me about Oloddumare as the owner of all destinies and of creation. She told me, "Oloddumare is ashé, the blood of all life." She warned me: "Your ashé is given to you by your ancestors, and it is your job to give good ashé to those who will come after you."

This concept of responsibility towards those before you, around you and after you is the essence of masquerade. It is a principle that ensures the continuation of life on this planet.

Each one of us is a thin but strong thread in the great fabric of life. As Native Americans teach us that life is a circle where we are all connected, the Orishas, the Tonals are ancient archetypes of the self. They are mirrors that reflect these elemental forces and forms of intelligence. The deeper our connection to them, the greater our understanding of life and death. Our voices become the voices of our ancestors. From the old, we begin to weave the new patterns of healing. As my Spiritual Madrina, Rosa Parilla, said, "Oyá is the owner of the breath. She is the first and our last breath in life. The whisper of Oyá brings *esperanza* [hope] and change."

F LOR FERNÁNDEZ BARRIOS was born in Cuba. She emigrated to the United States in 1970 when she was fourteen years old. She graduated in 1985 from International College with a Doctorate degree in Transpersonal Psychology. She is currently in private practice as psychotherapist in Seattle. In addition to her practice, she is a nationally recognized workshop leader on multicultural issues and spirituality.

Her book *Blessed by Thunder* was published in 1999. Her writing has also appeared in *Raven Chronicles*, and she was one of the featured writers in *Seattle Arts* magazine celebrating women of color. Her work has been anthologized in several collections, including *Storming Heaven's Gate: An Anthology of Spiritual Writing by Women, Intimate Nature: The Bond Between Women and Animals, The Fabric of the Future: Women Visionaries Illuminate the Path to Tomorrow, Face to Face: Women Writers on Faith, Mysticism,* and *Awakening, I Wanna Be Sedated: 30 Writers on Parenting Teenagers.*

CPSIA information can be obtained
at www.ICGtesting.com
Printed in the USA
FSOW02n0849191216
28743FS